seafood
sensation

Carol Selva Rajah

TIMES EDITIONS

seafood sensation

The publisher wishes to thank **Aktif Lifestyle, Malaysia** for the loan and use of their crockery and tableware, **Maxly Resources Sdn Bhd** for the loan and use of their barbecue grills, and **Abel and Gomathy Arumugam** for generously opening their home for the photography session.

Chef	:	Carol Selva Rajah
Chef's Assistant	:	Yvette Lee
Managing Editor	:	Jamilah Mohd Hassan
Editor of the English Edition	:	Lydia Leong
Art Direction/Designer	:	Lynn Chin Nyuk Ling
Photographer	:	Jenhor Siow
Project Co-ordinator	:	Christine Chong
Production Co-ordinator	:	Nor Sidah Haron

First published as The Best of Asian Seafood © 1993 Times Editions Pte Ltd

© 2004 Marshall Cavendish International (Asia) Private Limited

Published by Times Editions – Marshall Cavendish
An imprint of Marshall Cavendish International (Asia) Private Limited
A member of the Times Publishing Limited
Times Centre, 1 New Industrial Road, Singapore 536196
Tel: (65) 6213 9288   Fax: (65) 6285 4871
E-mail: te@tpl.com.sg
Online Bookstore: http://www.timesone.com.sg/te

Malaysian Office:
Federal Publications Sdn Berhad (General & Reference Publishing) (3024-D)
Times Subang, Lot 46, Persiaran Teknologi Subang
Subang Hi-Tech Industrial Park, Batu Tiga, 40000 Shah Alam
Selangor Darul Ehsan, Malaysia
Tel: (603) 5635 2191   Fax: (603) 5635 2706
E-mail: cchong@tpg.com.my

National Library Board Singapore Cataloguing in Publication Data

Selva Rajah, Carol.
Seafood sensation / Carol Selva Rajah. - Singapore : Times Editions, c2004.
p. cm.
First published as: The best of Asian seafood. c1993.
ISBN : 981-232-545-X

1. Cookery (Seafood) 2. Cookery, Asian. I. Title.

TX747
641.692 — dc21   SLS2003018902

Printed in Singapore by Times Printers Pte Ltd

Contents

Introduction

> **"**This sukhothai is good
> In the water there is fish
> In the fields there is rice
> The faces of the people shine
> Bright with happiness.**"**
>
> *Inscription on a stone in 13th-century*
> *Sukhothai, ancient capital of Siam.*

Asia is an extensive continent peopled with as many different races, religions, cultural and ethnic types as there are food styles. Many factors determine the cuisine, making it what it is today.

The influence of China and India on the whole of Asia cannot be overemphasised. There were Chinese and Indian travellers taking the Buddha's teachings across land routes in Southeast Asia from the 1st century. In the reign of Emperor Chien Lung, Burma and Vietnam were Chinese vassal states; by the 11th century, the Indianisation of parts of the continent meant that Indian influences and cultural practices were in effect. In the 14th century, Arab traders introduced Islam and Arabic food styles. The impact of colonisation on Asia was an important modifying factor in Portuguese, Dutch, French and British colonies.

Water also determined what directions the cuisine would take. A third of Asia consists of islands and peninsulas; the remaining two-thirds is crossed by mighty rivers like the Ganges, Yellow, Yangtze and Mekong. Water is a familiar medium. Asians have been as used to water as they have been to seafood, especially in Southeast Asia, where paddies are flooded and fish abound in the 'wet'.

Asian cuisine is obviously not one cuisine, but many cuisines, embracing many styles. Japanese, Vietnamese, Thai and Korean food reflect Chinese flavours: the immigrant peoples of Singapore, Malaysia and Indonesia brought with them not only methods of stir-frying, wok and curry cooking (in *karhi* or curved vessels), but vegetables, spices and sauces from their countries of origin.

There is, however, one constant. Fish and seafood are consumed in Asian countries more than any other type of protein, especially in Japan, Korea, China and Southeast Asia. Throughout, seafood recipes, techniques and tools—such as the earthenware pot in Indonesia, India, Malaysia and Cambodia, for example—are centuries-old and still in use, occasionally adapted for use in modern kitchens.

To understand the area better, it is necessary to divide Asia into three traditional food regions: South Asia, encapsulating India, Pakistan, Bangladesh and Sri Lanka; East Asia, including China, Japan, Korea, Taiwan and Hong Kong; and Southeast Asia in between with Thailand, Myanmar, Vietnam, Cambodia, Laos, Malaysia, Singapore, Indonesia and, with a cuisine somewhat separate, the Philippines.

Traditionally, the people of South Asia have a strong dependence on dairy products introduced by early Aryan pastoralists. This, combined with a range of spices such as coriander, cumin, fenugreek and chilli in their cooking, has produced a cuisine that is distinctive and recognisable.

In East Asia, the soy bean and its derivatives, mainly soy sauce, bean curd and salted soy beans, have been used traditionally for many centuries as sources of protein, while dairy products have never been used as sources of food generally, possibly because the peoples of East Asia may have had an intolerance for milk lactose contained in dairy products.

The countries of Southeast Asia, sandwiched between these two culinary giants, have the most incredible blend of foods and styles of cooking. To the five major flavours the Chinese speak of—the pungent, the sweet, the sour, the salty and the bitter—are added the hot spices of India and the aromatic and colourful saffrons of the Arab world. The Arabs also introduced the cooking of fruit with meat and fish. On the islands of Southeast Asia were found the sweet herbs, the lemon grass-citronellas, galangal-ginger rhizomes, cloves and nutmeg and pepper. And the introduction of the chilli-pepper to India from tropical America in the 16th century completed the spice scene. In the south there were the rich and *lemak* (rich and oily) flavours of the ubiquitous coconut found growing all over the islands and tropical areas of Asia, which enriched the food and tempered the hot spices of curries.

It is no mean feat to speak of the cuisines on a continent spread-eagled across a quarter of the earth's surface and peopled by numerous ethnic groups who uphold as many schools of food preparation. There is however one thing that these countries have in common—access to water, either to the sea or to rivers or inland lakes—and therefore a great range of sea- or freshwater food.

Asian markets are exciting places. Here life stirs at midnight as trawlers begin to unload their slippery and silvery catches in the dim light. The variety of seafood brought in on a normal morning can be staggering. Fish flap and swish while high-powered jets of water spray and clean them. The screech of dragged crates sets nerves on edge as auction time draws near and bidders gather. Fish markets in Hong Kong, Bangkok and Singapore are organised and business-like. In other countries, less so, while in rural areas, a few concrete slabs make do as market tables. On a rural beach in India the scene is picturesque as fisherfolk heave nets to the accompaniment of age-old chants, and the market is set up on a strip of dry land close by.

Asians are comfortable and not at all squeamish with fish. Housewives in rural Asia prefer to buy a fresh fish and watch it being cleaned. In some cases they may even prefer to scale, gut and cut it into fillets themselves to ensure pristine freshness. Food is prepared with gusto: crabs are dunked in boiling water, lobsters pierced, mullets stunned and prawns bathed in wine where they swim in bacchanalian frenzy, while fish are filleted and squid de-inked with ease.

There is a huge variety of fish in Asian markets. Nothing is spurned, from the octopus, giant squid and large shark to the tiny needle-like krill that are gathered to make piquant salads, *sambals* and fish sauces; from the rock lobsters of Thailand to the crayfish and crabs of South Korea; the blue swimmers of Kerala to the tiny *talangka* of the Philippines which are prized for their orange caviar-like roe; the fresh *udang gala* or blue freshwater prawn with one feeler to the myriad spotted, striped and brindled fish. Clams, pipis, cockles, mussels, scallops, oysters, winkles...some are eaten raw, some sucked through the shell, others prised open and still some more slurped with sauces. Fish are dried, mashed, salted, pounded, powdered, stuffed, dried into crackers, dried in the sand, pickled, curried, steamed, made into sauce or soup, stir-fried, baked or grilled in foil, banana leaf, yam leaf or shell. What a bounty!

In general terms, the darker-fleshed fish are deep-sea fish with a greater amount of oils in their flesh. These fish are best grilled or curried, while the white-fleshed fish have less oil in them and are consequently drier if cooked longer. These are best steamed or stir-fried, as are prawns (shrimps), squids and crabs. Mackerel does not steam well but sautés well as do bream and red mullet ; seabass and turbot are delicious steamed and pike poached. Fish-based soups and bouillons are popular, especially in Myanmar, Thailand, and Cambodia. All over Southeast Asia the fish sauces and fish pastes rich in vitamin B are used daily. The *yin* and the *yang* do not refer only to things Chinese: all Asians believe that some foods heat the body and inflame passions while other foods cool the body and calm the person. Food can regulate a person's life or make him a walking disaster.

There are many traditions connected with food and fish. In China, the sound of the character meaning fish, *yu*, is synonymous with *yue*, meaning prosperity and abundance. During Chinese New Year's Eve celebrations, serving a fish dish is part of the tradition to ensure that the following year is prosperous. Twin fish swimming together are symbols of conjugal bliss in China. In Hong Kong, where the fisherfolk have developed a healthy respect for the fickle waters of the typhoon-ridden South China Sea, they are also superstitious about fishing, and preparing and eating fish. It is their belief that when a whole fish is served at the table, it should never be turned over and that the flesh on the underside should be reached with a deftly handed pair of chopsticks in between the bones. Fisherfolk believe that every time a fish is turned over, a boat will overturn at sea. In Melaka, the *Festa San Pedro* (Feast of St Peter, the patron saint of fishermen) is celebrated by Malaysian-Portuguese in a festival of singing and dancing that culminates in the blessing of the boats for another year of safe and productive fishing. In Asia, no mermaids are carved on the prows of boats but stylised eyes are painted in garish colours on either side of the prows to guide and protect the fisherfolk from the dangers of the deep.

Asians take their food and entertaining seriously. Great attention is paid to what fish is in season, what will cook in the best manner—whether sautéed, steamed, grilled or fried—and which crunchy whitebait goes well with a whisky or sundowner. Food in Asia has always been a means of communicating with others. Food has a language of its own and can convey messages of friendship or concern from the giver to the receiver. Communication through food is central to Asian life: it punctuates the rite of passage from the time of birth to the rituals of death. Whenever people meet to socialise in Asian society, food is included, and fish and seafood are major ingredients in this process.

Indonesia, Malaysia & Singapore

The Fabled Spice Islands

> " Here lies Columbus' unattained goal—
> the fabled Spice Islands, Buru, Ceram,
> The Celebes—where Sinbad the sailor found
> peppers, cloves, cinnamon, pearl divers
> and cannibal kings. "
>
> *Joseph Conrad, LORD JIM*

The Indonesian islands, Malaysia and Singapore are fortunate enough to be on a shallow continental shelf of warm subtropical waters and temperatures that vary between 17°C and 26°C. Because of their proximity to the equator, they have a humid climate that supports the cultivation of many exciting tropical fruits, a double cropping of rice and a seemingly inexhaustible supply of the most extensive seafood found in the tropics.

The lush vegetation and abundant seafood encouraged creativity—the people were able to conjure up a meal of fried whitebait, lemon grass and vegetables or make a tasty *sambal* with some fish, a few leafy backyard herbs and coconut milk. Improvisation was nurtured—there were no strict formulae, since one cooked what or how much was available. The simplicity of the meals made Asians sensitive to flavours—the bitter, the succulent, the aromatic and the sour. The simplicity and naturalness of their lifestyles taught them to waste nothing—neither vegetable stalk nor coconut husk nor fish head. They salted and dried food in the sun. This, then, was the native cuisine, one born out of the land- and the seascape, as well as through the means and lifestyles of people in agricultural societies.

Long before the arrival of Sir Stamford Raffles, the much traversed Straits had already experienced many waves of immigration and trade: the Siamese from the north, the Indians and Arabs from the west and the Chinese from the east. It was the gleam of gold that first attracted these traders. Pepper and spices from the spice archipelago exchanged places with silks and porcelain from China on stately ships that were either becalmed or sped on their way by obliging monsoons. Later, Portuguese, Dutch and then British traders brought further cultural influences to bear.

Singapore, Malaysia and, to a lesser extent, Indonesia are plural societies today. Their cultural heritage is based on the separate traditions which constitute their societies. Because of their geographical and historical positions, these countries have maintained a close relationship with India, China and Britain for many centuries, and today large numbers of people with Indian, Chinese, English and Dutch heritage are part of their permanent populations.

The main foreign influences on the cuisine of the region were those of India and China, but all arrivals contributed a new spice, cooking method, preferred ingredient, festive dish or religious taboo to the common culinary heritage. Traders and sojourners alike brought with them all manner of spices and herbs, and the various techniques of using them.

Some important foods introduced were the Chinese soy bean and soy products, light and dark vinegar, the art of cooking with Chinese and herbal wines, the taste of aromatic gingers and red Sichuan peppers, and all manners of medicinal herbs and spices that the East could hope for. This food, together with what was borrowed from the indigenous Malays, was developed and refined into a unique cuisine. It was a gastronomic explosion of tastes blended, to become one of the most exciting food styles in the world today.

The best example of this fusion of styles is the food cooked by the Peranakans (Babas and Nonyas), descendants of the Chinese who lived in the Straits Settlement towns of Penang, Melaka and Singapore. Ordinary dishes take on embellishments and reach a newer sophistication: if fish is fried, it has to be served with a *sambal*; if it is steamed, then the sauce is soured and the herbs used as decoration; pork is pickled, braised, coloured and roasted; the plain Chinese pancake wrapper became a deep-fried spring roll; and batter was fried into 'top-hats' called *pie tee*. Even noodles are sautéed with red spicy sauces, put into gravies as *laksa* and *soto*, or soured with tamarind and bleached with coconut sauces.

'Eating,' says Naomichi Ishige, a Japanese anthropologist, 'is the act of ingesting the environment.' It is also ingesting culture, since among the most discernable traces of foreign cultures are their food.

As trade has grown in the islands and the peninsula, so has the tradition of hospitality. It is not uncommon to be invited to a meal with a family on one's first meeting, where the guest can sample a home-cooked meal—the result of hours of work grinding spices and blending herbs to transform ordinary fare into a feast. These gregarious people enjoy company at meals. It is quite common to see a family, pyjama-clad children in tow, stopping for a snack at a late night stall or one of the *pasar malams* (night markets). Birthdays, engagements, office promotions, weddings and funerals are all grand affairs. Etiquette dictates the number invited—which may be up to 500 to celebrate the birth of a baby or the birthday of a patriarch, under temporary tents of tarpaulin.

The cuisine has become multicultural in character and homogeneous in its daily practice: a Singaporean, a Malaysian or an Indonesian family could on any given day sit down to a meal composed of Chinese soup, Malay curry, Westernised salad and Indianised vegetables, washed down with an Arabic sharbat or Chinese tea. In this region, to taste food is to taste the cultural synthesis of the society.

Kari Lemak Udang Galah (Rich Curried Lobster)

This dish is what Malaysians would describe as being *lemak*, so rich that it leaves an aftertaste on the tongue. Serve with rice and a lightly chilled Chablis wine for an elaborate dinner.

Ingredients

Lobster tail meat with shell	500 g
Garlic	5 cloves, peeled
Red shallots	10 or 2 medium brown onions, peeled
Lemon grass *(serai)*	2 stalks, chopped
Ginger *(halia)*	2-cm knob, peeled
Cooking oil	1 Tbsp
Fish curry powder	2 Tbsp
Chilli powder	2 tsp
Fish stock	250 ml
Cinnamon stick (kayu manis)	2-cm length
Coconut milk	450 ml
Salt	to taste
Ground black pepper	1 tsp
Onions	2, large, peeled
Butter or margarine	30 g
Prawns (shrimps)	250 g, shelled
Mayonnaise	1 Tbsp
Coconut cream	125 ml
Lime juice	extracted from 1 lime

Garnish

Red shallots	4, peeled, thinly sliced and crisp-fried

Method

- Cut meat from lobster tail into large chunks and reserve shell.

- Dip lobster shell in boiling water to clean it and also allow it to change to a red colour which is more attractive for serving. Set aside.

- Blend (process) 4 cloves garlic and shallots or onions into a paste with lemon grass and ginger.

- Heat oil in a wok and stir-fry paste until aromatic. Add curry and chilli powder and stir quickly. Do not cook too long as it will become bitter.

- Add fish stock and cinnamon stick and stir to mix well with curry paste.

- Add coconut milk and stir slowly. Simmer until curry is cooked and volume is reduced by half. Add salt and pepper and remove from heat.

- Slice large onions and remaining garlic finely. Heat butter in another wok and sauté sliced onions and garlic until golden.

- Add lobster meat, prawns and mayonnaise. Mix gently.

- Add curry sauce, coconut cream and lime juice. Stir, taking care not to break lobster pieces. Remove from heat.

- Pile curry mixture into prepared lobster shell. Serve hot sprinkled with fried shallots.

Laksa

Malaysia and Singapore cannot lay sole claim to *laksa*. All Southeast Asian countries have a version of the soupy noodle dish: the Burmese have *mohinga*; the Thais have *mee siam*; and the Indonesians have *soto ayam* or *soto ikan*.

Laksa evolved as a result of the cultural blend of Chinese noodles and the Melanesian penchant to curry. The Sunda Straits teem with fish and nowhere in the islands of Southeast Asia is the sea more than 160 km away. *Laksa*, a seafood curry ladled onto noodles, was merely a dish put together from all these factors.

Most families have traditional recipes and most enthusiasts have their favourite blend of ingredients. There are three main schools of *laksa*: the northern or Penang *laksa*, tart and sour, heavily dependent on tamarind and aligned to Thai tastes; the *laksa lemak* from Melaka, generally with a creamy, thick curried coconut sauce; and the south Malay or Johore *laksa*, my own favourite, a blend of fish, prawns (shrimps), tamarind and coconut milk.

Johore Laksa (Prawn and Fish Laksa from Johore)

Ingredients

Lemon grass *(serai)*	3 stalks
Galangal *(lengkuas)*	3-cm knob, peeled
Ginger *(halia)*	3-cm knob, peeled
Dried prawn (shrimp) paste *(belacan)*	3-cm square, roasted
School prawns (shrimps)	500 g
Wolf herring *(ikan parang)* or mackerel	1 kg
Cooking oil	2 Tbsp
Fish curry powder	2 Tbsp
Chilli powder	1 Tbsp
Asam gelugor	8 slices
Coconut milk	1¼ litres
Coconut cream	250 ml
Salt	to taste
Ground white pepper	to taste
Sugar	to taste
Spaghetti or *laksa* noodles	500 g

Garnish

Red shallots	4, peeled and thinly sliced
Cucumber	1, cut and shredded
Vietnamese mint leaves *(daun kesum)*	250 g, shredded
Lemon grass *(serai)*	1 stalk, sliced into thin rounds
Bean sprouts	300 g, tailed

Topping

Chilli sauce	2 Tbsp
Onions	2, peeled, sliced and crisp-fried
Kalamansi limes	6, cut into quarters

Method

- Blend (process) lemon grass, galangal and ginger into a fine paste. Crumble roasted prawn paste into spice paste and set aside.
- Shell prawns and boil shells with 125 ml water to make stock.
- Boil fish and prawns separately in 325 ml water each until flesh flakes off easily, then remove from heat. Strain and reserve all stock. Flake fish and blend (grind) with prawns in a food processor. Set meat paste aside.
- Heat oil in a sauce and fry spice paste until aromatic. Turn heat down slightly and add meat paste. Stir-fry for a while.
- Add curry and chilli powder and *asam gelugor* with 250 ml of reserved stock and prawn-shell stock. Mix well.
- Add coconut milk and allow sauce to simmer for about 20 minutes. Test until flavour is satisfactory: the sauce must be flavoursome but not too thick. Add 250 ml stock if it is too thick.
- Add coconut cream slowly and stir well, adding salt, pepper and sugar if needed. Keep sauce just under boiling point and do not boil.
- Blanch and drain noodles. Divide equally into 8 serving bowls. Top with garnishes.
- Turn sauce off heat and ladle onto noodles. Top with chilli sauce, crispy fried onions and lime.

Microwave Shortcuts

- Shrimp paste can be pre-roasted in the microwave for 1 minute on HIGH.
- Fish and prawns can be cooked in the microwave before blending for 8 minutes on HIGH.
- The sauce can be warmed using the microwave oven.

The other recipes in this book feed 4–6 people, but as this is a festival laksa, quantities given are guest-sized and will feed 8 comfortably.

Penang Laksa (Laksa in a Sour Sauce)

Ingredients

Whole wolf herring *(ikan parang)*	600 g, cleaned
Dried prawn (shrimp) paste *(belacan)*	3-cm square, dry-roasted
Dried chillies	7 or more
Lemon grass *(serai)*	2 stalks
Red shallots	20, small, peeled
Ground turmeric *(kunyit)*	1/2 tsp
Vietnamese mint *(daun kesum)*	4 stalks
Tamarind paste *(asam jawa)*	2 Tbsp, mixed with 125 ml water and strained
Asam gelugor	10 slices, soaked in water
Black prawn (shrimp) paste *(haeko)*	2 Tbsp
Salt	to taste
Fresh rice noodles, *laksa* noodles or thin spaghetti	500 g

Garnish

Cucumber	1, cut and shredded
Ripe pineapple	1/2, cut into chunks
Red chillies	6, seeded, if preferred and sliced
Red shallots	10, peeled, thinly sliced and crisp-fried
Vietnamese mint leaves *(daun kesum)*	4 stalks

Method

- In a pot, add sufficient water to cover fish (about 450 ml) and bring to the boil for 10 minutes. Cool and debone fish. Discard head, bones and skin. Reserve stock.

- Grind roasted prawn paste together with dried chillies, lemon grass and shallots. Mix with turmeric powder.

- Strip Vietnamese mint leaves from stalks and shred.

- Place 1.5 litres water in another pot. Add ground spices and mint leaves and bring to the boil, stirring well.

- Add fish meat. Stir well and allow soup to simmer, adding 450 ml fish stock, tamarind liquid, *asam gelugor* and 1 Tbsp black prawn paste. Allow *laksa* gravy to simmer for at least 15 minutes to reduce. Add salt before removing gravy from heat.

- Meanwhile, place garnishes in separate bowls, together with remaining black prawn paste.

- Scald noodles in boiling water and strain. Place into individual bowls and ladle in hot gravy. Serve with prepared garnishes.

Laksa Lemak (Laksa with Coconut Milk)

Ingredients

White-fleshed fish	500 g, cleaned
Prawns (shrimps)	500 g
Lemon grass (serai)	4 stalks
Galangal (lengkuas)	5-cm knob, peeled
Dried chillies	20, seeded, if preferred and soaked to soften
Red shallots	6–8 or 2 medium brown onions, peeled
Turmeric (kunyit)	1-cm knob, peeled or 1/2 tsp ground turmeric
Candlenuts (buah keras)	6
Dried prawn (shrimp) paste (belacan)	3-cm square, dry-roasted
Cooking oil	2 Tbsp
Coconut milk	1 litre
Ground white pepper	to taste
Salt	to taste
Coconut cream	250 ml
Vietnamese mint leaves (daun kesum)	75 g, shredded
Noodles, rice sticks or wheat noodles	500 g, blanched and strained

Garnish

Firm bean curd squares	2, pan-fried and cut into strips
Hard-boiled eggs	6, shelled and cut into quarters lengthwise
Bean sprouts	400 g, tailed
Fish balls	12, each cut in half
Mint leaves	50 g, shredded
Kalamansi limes	2, cut into quarters

Method

- Steam fish and prawns in a dish over hot water for 20 minutes. Reserve liquid from steamed seafood.

- Debone fish and flake meat. Shell prawns. Boil fish bones, skin and prawn shells in reserved liquid plus 250 ml water to make fish stock.

- Blend (process) lemon grass, galangal, softened chillies, shallots, turmeric and candlenuts until fine. Crumble in roasted prawn paste and blend again.

- Heat oil in a deep wok. Stir-fry blended spices until aromatic and oil separates from paste.

- Pour in 250 ml fish stock, coconut milk, fish and prawns and stir. Bring to the boil and lower to a simmer for 15 minutes. Add pepper and salt to taste.

- When gravy smells aromatic, add coconut cream and stir constantly until gravy reaches boiling point. Turn off heat at once or the gravy could curdle.

- Sprinkle mint leaves into gravy and ladle into large bowl.

- Place scalded noodles into another large bowl.

- To serve, place bowl of noodles in centre, surrounded by bowl of gravy and garnishes in individual bowls. Allow guests to ladle noodles, laksa gravy and garnishes of their choice into their bowls themselves.

Udang Masak Kicap (Prawns in Soy Sauce)

Indian Muslim cuisine is a unique blend of Malay and Indian culture. In this recipe we see prawns (shrimps) curried with Indian spices (chilli, cumin) and Malay herbs (lemon grass).

Ingredients

King prawns (shrimps)	1 kg
Red shallots	6 or 2 medium brown onions, peeled
Garlic	5 cloves, peeled
Cooking oil	125 ml
Cumin (jintan putih) seeds	½ Tbsp
Ground turmeric (kunyit)	1 tsp
Chilli powder	½ Tbsp
Curry leaves	1 sprig
Dark soy sauce	1 Tbsp
Salt	to taste
Tamarind paste (asam jawa)	1 Tbsp, mixed with 250 ml water, strained
Sugar	to taste

Garnish

Coriander (cilantro) leaves	4 sprigs, chopped
Brown onions	2, large, peeled and sliced

Method

- Trim heads and legs off prawns, leaving shells and tails intact. Make a cut through shells to devein prawns. This will also allow the thick gravy to penetrate.

- Blend (process) shallots or onions and garlic into a paste. If onions were used, squeeze juice from blended paste and reserve.

- Heat oil in a wok and stir-fry whole cumin seeds a little.

- Add blended paste, ground turmeric, chilli powder and curry leaves. Stir well. Increase heat and add prawns. Stir quickly to mix ingredients and cook prawns. Add dark soy sauce and salt to taste. When it starts to boil, add tamarind liquid, reserved juice (optional) and sugar to taste. Stir and simmer to reduce liquid and allow prawns to absorb gravy.

- Remove from heat and garnish with chopped coriander and sliced raw onions.

Cumi Masak Menado (Squid Cooked Menado Style)

Ingredients

Squid (cumi)	1 kg
White vinegar	1 Tbsp
Red shallots	10 or 3 medium brown onions, peeled
Garlic	3 cloves, peeled
Ginger (halia)	2-cm knob, peeled
Candlenuts (buah keras)	5
Cooking oil	250 ml
Tomatoes	250 g, chopped
Small red and green chillies	125 g, seeded, if preferred and sliced
Salt	to taste
Bay leaves (daun salam)	4
Spring onions (scallions)	5, roughly broken

Method

- Prepare squid by removing tentacles, washing and removing ink sacs and peeling purple skins from tubes. Slice tube area into thin rings about 2-cm wide. Alternatively, cut open tubes and score surface lightly with criss-cross cuts. Wash squid in a mixture of the white vinegar diluted with 500 ml water. Rinse, then strain immediately.

- Peel and blend (process) shallots, garlic, ginger and candlenuts. Heat oil in a pan and sauté ground ingredients until cooked.

- Add squid, tomatoes and sliced chillies. Stir quickly as squid toughens when overcooked.

- Add salt to taste, then bay leaves and spring onions. Toss and remove quickly.

- Serve hot with rice and a dash of lime juice.

Dried Fish Sambal (A Malayanised Sri Lankan Recipe)

Ingredients

Dried fish	200 g
Red shallots	4 or 1 medium brown onion, peeled
Salt	
Green chillies	2, seeded, if preferred and finely sliced
Lime juice	extracted from 2 limes or 50 ml vinegar
Sugar	to taste

Method

- Slice fish into strips and roast or grill until fish is golden and smells roasted. Break into small pieces. Set aside.

- Peel, wash and thinly slice shallots, then soak in 125 ml water and 1/2 tsp salt. Drain and squeeze well.

- Toss dried fish pieces with sliced onions, green chillies, lime juice or vinegar, sugar and salt to taste.

Rendang Ikan (Fish Cooked in Rendang Sauce)

Rendang is prepared using rich spices and toasted coconut. It is steeped in coconut milk and slowly simmered over a gentle flame. Since fish cooks fast, the sauce should be made first and then added to the fish.

Ingredients

Spanish mackerel (*ikan tenggiri*), cod, sea bass, snapper or threadfin (*ikan kurau*)	500 g, cut into pieces
Lime juice	extracted from 1 lime
Sugar	1/2 tsp
Salt	1/2 tsp
Red shallots	5–6 or 2 medium brown onions, peeled
Garlic	3 cloves, peeled
Red chillies	6, seeded, if preferred
Lemon grass (*serai*)	1 stalk
Galangal (*lengkuas*)	3-cm knob, peeled
Ginger (*halia*)	2-cm knob, peeled
Dried prawn (shrimp) paste (*belacan*)	2-cm square
Kaffir lime leaves (*limau purut*)	2
Turmeric (*kunyit*)	2-cm knob, peeled or 1/2 tsp ground turmeric
Fish curry powder	1 Tbsp
Cooking oil	2 Tbsp
Coconut cream	125 ml
Grated coconut	2 Tbsp, dry-roasted
Tamarind paste (*asam jawa*)	1 Tbsp, mixed with 3 Tbsp water, strained
Coconut milk	250 ml

Method

- Marinate fish pieces in lime juice, sugar and salt for 30 minutes.

- Blend (process) shallots, garlic, chillies, lemon grass, galangal, ginger, shrimp paste, kaffir lime leaves and turmeric into a paste. Mix in curry powder.

- Heat oil in a wok. And sauté mixed paste until aromatic. Add coconut cream a little at a time, until ingredients are cooked and oil separates.

- Add some dry-roasted grated coconut, reserving some for garnish, stir and cook a little longer.

- Place marinated fish in wok and surround with paste on a low heat. Add strained tamarind liquid and coconut milk and cook on low until liquid reduces and fish smells aromatic.

- Simmer until fish is cooked. Do not stir as fish pieces could break up. Carefully transfer fish to a serving plate. Garnish with a sprinkling of dry-roasted grated coconut.

Ikan Masak Nenas (Fish and Pineapple Curry)

Ingredients

Large prawns (shrimps)	600 g or 500 g mackerel fish heads
Red shallots	8 or 2 large brown onions, peeled
Garlic	2 cloves, peeled
Galangal (lengkuas)	3-cm knob, peeled
Lemon grass (serai)	1 stalk
Candlenuts (buah keras)	3
Red chillies	6
Dried prawn (shrimp) paste (belacan)	2-cm square, roasted, optional
Cooking oil	2 Tbsp
Tamarind paste (asam jawa)	1 Tbsp, mixed with 250 ml water, strained
Asam gelugor	3 slices or 2 Tbsp vinegar
Sugar	1 tsp
Salt	to taste
Ripe pineapple	1/2, peeled and cut into 3-cm chunks
Kaffir lime leaves (limau purut)	3 or fresh lemon leaves, shredded

Method

- If using prawns, clean and devein. Remove heads, but leave shells and tails intact. If using fish heads, clean well and chop in half with cleaver.

- Blend (process) shallots, garlic, galangal, lemon grass, candlenuts and chillies into a paste. If using dried prawn paste, crumble it into spice paste. Set aside.

- Heat oil and sauté spice paste. Cook until aromatic.

- Add tamarind liquid, 300 ml water, asam gelugor, sugar and salt. Allow to boil gently until liquid is thick and slightly reduced.

- Add pineapple chunks and cook for 5 minutes. Add prawns or fish heads. Cook for another 5 minutes, then add lime leaves. Remove from heat.

- Serve hot with rice and vegetable dishes.

Ikan Pepes (Fish Wrapped in Banana Leaves)

Banana leaves add a subtle aroma and flavour to this dish.

Ingredients

Whole snapper or mackerel	500 g
Tamarind paste (asam jawa)	2 tsp
Sugar	1 tsp
Salt	to taste
Red shallots	10 or 3 large brown onions, peeled
Garlic	5 cloves, peeled
Red chillies	6
Ginger (halia)	2-cm knob, peeled
Turmeric (kunyit)	2-cm knob, peeled
Lemon grass (serai)	2 stalks
Coconut cream	250 ml
Kaffir lime leaves (limau purut)	3, shredded
Banana leaf	1, scalded to soften

Garnish

Mint or basil (kemangi) leaves

Carrot slices

Method

- Clean, scale and gut fish, making incisions in its body so that the marinade can penetrate.

- Mix tamarind paste with 250 ml water, straining off dregs. Add sugar and salt and stir well. Pour over fish and allow to marinate for 30 minutes.

- Blend (process) shallots, garlic, chillies, ginger, turmeric and lemon grass. Mix with coconut cream and shredded kaffir lime leaves.

- Place banana leaf on a flat working surface and lay fish in the centre. Brush paste all over and inside fish.

- Fold banana leaf over into a package and secure the open ends with staples or cocktail sticks. Place on a heatproof (flameproof) glass dish and steam for 30 minutes.

- Alternatively, cook this dish in the microwave oven. Remove eyes of fish before cooking or the membranes will burst. Wrap marinated fish in plastic wrap or banana leaf, leaving an air vent so steam can escape. Secure package with string or cocktail sticks, but do not staple.

- Place parcel on microwave-safe plate and cook for 7 minutes on HIGH. Turn parcel over, taking care to rearrange the wrap to prevent the spices from leaking and cook for another 3 minutes on HIGH.

- Place cooked fish parcel on a dish and unwrap. Arrange garnish on top before serving.

Sate Udang (Satay Prawns)

Ingredients

Green king prawns (shrimps)	1 kg
Cooking oil	1 Tbsp
Garlic	2 cloves, peeled and chopped
Dried prawn (shrimp) paste (belacan)	1 tsp, dry-roasted
Lemon grass (serai)	1 stalk, bruised
Peanuts (groundnuts)	2 Tbsp, roasted and coarsely blended
Chilli powder	1/4 tsp or more if you prefer
Lime juice	1 Tbsp
Coconut cream	6 Tbsp
Salt	to taste

Method

- Shell and devein prawns, then thread bamboo skewers along the length of prawns, from head to tail so that they lie straight.

- Heat oil in a wok, and sauté garlic and prawn paste, crumbling the shrimp paste as you stir.

- Add lemon grass, peanuts, chilli powder, lime juice and coconut cream. Stir well until aromatic. Remove from heat and add salt to taste.

- Use half of this sauce as a paste and the other half as a dipping sauce.

- Brush paste on both sides of skewered prawns and barbecue on hot coals or under an electric or gas grill. Keep basting prawns until they change colour and are cooked.

- Serve with dipping sauce.

Sambal Ikan Terubok (Fish Roe Sambal)

Ingredients

Fish roe (telor ikan terubok)	150 g
Ground turmeric (kunyit)	1/2 tsp
Red shallots	10 or 3 medium brown onions
Salt	1/2 tsp
Cooking oil	125 ml
Green chillies	3, seeded, if preferred and chopped
Vinegar	2 Tbsp
Lime juice	extracted from 2 limes
Worcestershire sauce	1 Tbsp

Method

- Brush fish roe with turmeric powder.

- Peel and slice shallots or onions finely, then wash in 125 ml water and 1/2 tsp salt. Squeeze dry.

- Heat oil and fry fish roe until golden. Watch for splatters.

- Drain and crumble fish roe, then toss with shallots, chillies, vinegar, lime juice and Worcestershire sauce.

Selada Mee Rebus (Noodles in a Thick Sauce)

This dish combines fat, yellow Chinese wheat-noodles *(mee)* with a spicy and full-bodied Indian sauce, rich in prawns (shrimps) and peanuts (groundnuts) and thickened with a typically Melanesian standby, the sweet potato.

Ingredients

Prawns (shrimps)	500 g, shelled and deveined, reserve heads and shells
Dried prawns (shrimps)	2 Tbsp, optional
Red shallots	10 or 2½ medium brown onions, peeled
Chilli powder	½ tsp
Dried prawn (shrimp) paste *(belacan)*	2-cm square, dry-roasted
Vinegar	75 ml or 3 sour starfruit *(belimbing)*
Cooking oil	1 Tbsp
Crunchy peanut butter	3 Tbsp
Sugar	3 Tbsp
Salt	to taste
Ground white pepper	to taste
Fresh wheat or thick yellow egg noodles *(mee)*	1 kg
Sweet potatoes	3, large, boiled, peeled and mashed

Garnish

Bean sprouts	450 g
Onions	3, peeled, thinly sliced and crisp-fried
Hardboiled eggs	5, shelled and cut into wedges
Kalamansi limes	3, small, cut in half

Method

- Boil prawn shells and heads in 1 litre water for 10 minutes. Strain stock and discard shells. Add fresh and dried prawns, if using, to stock and bring to the boil. Lift prawns out immediately so that they do not toughen. Blend (process) to a mushy paste.

- Peel and blend shallots, chilli powder and prawn paste, using vinegar or sour starfruit to facilitate blending.

- Heat oil in a large pan, then fry blended ingredients until aromatic.

- Add stock, peanut butter, sugar, 2 litres water, salt and pepper. Bring to the boil, then simmer for 15 minutes. You may have to mash the peanut butter with a fork to mix well.

- Meanwhile, scald noodles and bean sprouts separately for a few seconds. Strain.

- Thicken gravy with mashed sweet potatoes, stir well and adjust for taste.

- To serve, place portions of freshly scalded and strained noodles into individual bowls. Ladle hot gravy over and garnish with bean sprouts, fried onions, hardboiled eggs and lime halves.

Otak Otak (Spicy Fish Parcels)

Otak otak is an aromatic dish of fish and herbs blended into a smooth paste with sweet spices and coconut milk. The paste is sealed in small banana leaf sheets and roasted over a charcoal fire.

Ingredients

Fillet of any firm-fleshed fish	500 g
Coconut cream	125 ml
Salt	1 tsp
Red shallots	8 or 4 medium brown onions, peeled
Lemon grass *(serai)*	3 stalks, peeled
Galangal *(lengkuas)*	3-cm knob, peeled
Dried chillies	6, seeded, if preferred
Ground turmeric *(kunyit)*	½ tsp
Candlenuts *(buah keras)*	5
Ground coriander *(ketumbar)*	1 Tbsp
Ground cumin *(jintan putih)*	1 Tbsp
Vietnamese mint leaves *(daun kesum)*	25 g, shredded
Kaffir lime leaves *(limau purut)*	2, shredded
Cornflour (cornstarch)	1 Tbsp
Egg	1, beaten
Banana leaves	8, cut into 20-cm squares, scalded bamboo skewers

Method

- Holding a spoon at 90° to the fish, drag flesh out of fillets. Discard skin.

- Chop fish roughly and blend (process) with 3 Tbsp coconut cream to a fine texture. Add salt. Set aside.

- Blend (process) shallots, lemon grass, galangal, chillies and turmeric into a paste. Add to fish paste and continue blending.

- Add candlenuts, ground coriander, ground cumin, Vietnamese mint and blend until well mixed. Remove and place in a bowl. Add remaining coconut cream, kaffir lime leaves, cornflour and beaten egg. Mix well.

- Place 2 Tbsp mixture onto each leaf and fold it flat lengthwise. Seal open ends with bamboo skewers.

- Cook under the grill for 20 minutes, turning as leaves brown. *Otak otak* should be cooked slowly to allow the flavour of the spices and banana leaf to be absorbed into the fish paste.

- *Otak otak* can also be cooked in the microwave for 2 minutes on HIGH, two at a time, but the texture will be different.

Ikan dengan Udang Tumis

(Fried Fish Sautéed in Dried Prawn Sauce)

In some ways, Nonya food is a synthesis and further refinement of the best of Malaysian cooking. This fish is fried with sauce, vegetables and dried prawns and has a truly exotic taste.

Ingredients

Fillet of any firm-fleshed fish (cobia, perch, snapper or mackerel)	600 g
Red shallots	12–15 or 3–4 medium brown onions, peeled
Garlic	2 cloves, peeled
Dried prawns (shrimps)	25 g, soaked for 1–2 hours to soften
Cooking oil	125 ml
Chilli powder	1 tsp
Sweet dark sauce (kicap manis)	1 Tbsp
Salt	to taste
Lime juice	extracted from 1 lime

Marinade

Tamarind paste (asam jawa)	1/2 Tbsp, mixed with 50 ml water, strained
Garlic	1 clove, peeled and pounded
Ginger (halia) juice	extracted from 2-cm knob
Ground turmeric (kunyit)	1/2 tsp

Garnish

Mint leaves	25 g

Method

- Prepare marinade. Mix tamarind liquid with pounded garlic, ginger juice and ground turmeric.

- Cube fish into 3-cm squares and soak in marinade for 2–3 hours.

- Meanwhile, blend (process) shallots and garlic together. Set aside.

- Drain prawns and break up roughly.

- Heat oil in a wok until it smokes. Fry a few cubes of fish at a time until golden. (As the marinade is liquid, the fish will splatter. You may cover the wok initially and then remove the cover as the fish cooks.) Drain the fish pieces and remove all except 1 Tbsp oil from wok.

- Sauté blended shallots and garlic and chilli powder in this oil until brown.

- Add prawns and stir until cooked. Add sweet dark sauce, salt and finally fish. Heat through, remove from heat and add lime juice.

- Serve hot, garnished with mint.

Sambals (Sauces)

Sambals are the highlight of a structured Malaysian or Indonesian meal, adding spice and colour to rice. *Sambals* are sauces that go with meat, fish, fruit or vegetables, of a consistency such that the diner can eat with his fingers, pinching a bit of meat here or a bit of sauce there. Make the *sambals* given here in tandem with curries, vegetables and rice, or store them in jars for future use or as gifts to friends and family.

Sambal Udang Lemak (Prawn and Coconut Sambal)

Ingredients

Red shallots	10 or 3 medium brown onions, peeled
Cooking oil	2 Tbsp
Lemon grass *(serai)*	2-cm length from root, sliced
Dried prawns (shrimps)	2 Tbsp, pounded
Grated coconut	150 g
Red chillies	2, seeded, if preferred and sliced
Salt	to taste

Method

- Peel shallots or onions and slice finely. Heat oil in a wok and sauté shallots or onions until brown.

- Add lemon grass and pounded prawns. Fry until prawns smell aromatic and are cooked.

- Add grated coconut and sliced chillies. Mix well and add salt to taste. Lower heat to simmer.

- Stir-fry to roast coconut slowly in its own oil until aromatic.

- Serve with rice and vegetables.

Belacan Ikan Atau Belacan Udang Goreng

(Fish or Prawns in Belacan and Chilli)

This Nonya dish originates from Penang.

Ingredients

Snapper	500–750 g or 500 g prawns
Red chillies	3, seeded, if preferred
Garlic	3 cloves, peeled
Ground turmeric *(kunyit)*	2 tsp
Dried prawn (shrimp) paste *(belacan)*	3-cm square, dry-roasted
Sweet dark sauce *(kicap manis)*	1 Tbsp
Salt	1 tsp
Cooking oil	450 ml

Garnish

Four-angled beans or snow peas	6, blanched in hot water
Sambal belacan	

Method

- Scale, gut and clean snapper. Score both sides of fish with diagonal lines. If using prawns, shell and devein.

- Blend (process) chillies, garlic, ground turmeric and dried prawn paste together. Brush sweet dark sauce and salt inside and outside fish or over prawns. Rub blended paste all over fish or prawns. Leave to marinate for 30 minutes in the refrigerator.

- Heat oil in a wok until it smokes. Lower fish or 5–6 prawns at a time into oil and fry until brown and crispy. Drain.

- Serve with four-angled beans or snow peas and *sambal belacan*.

Sambal Kerang (Cockles Sambal)

Cockles can be cooked using any prawn (shrimp) or cuttlefish *sambal* as a base. This unusual Indonesian recipe utilises cockles and krill.

Ingredients

Cockles	500 g
Krill *(gerago)* or whitebait	50 g
Red shallots	5, peeled and coarsely chopped
Green chillies	2, finely sliced
Lemon grass *(serai)*	1 stalk, bruised and sliced
Unripe papaya (pawpaw)	250 g, shredded or cut into chunks
Salt	1½ tsp

Method

- Scrub cockles in their shells until clean. Leave in a bucket of slightly salted water. Store in a dark place for 3–4 hours to leach some of the sand. Wash once more.

- Bring 450 ml water to the boil in a pan. Add krill, cockles in shells, shallots, chillies, lemon grass and papaya.

- Add salt. Cook for 5 minutes or until cockles open.

- Serve cockles in a dish accompanied with chilli-vinegar sauce, *sambal belacan* or bottled chilli garlic sauce.

Ikan Asam (Tamarind Fish)

The thick pulp of tamarind pods has traditionally been a prime ingredient in Malaysian curries. Today tamarind is available in a variety of forms: as blocks of strained and cleaned pulp; as thick reconstituted liquid tamarind; or as a rich paste that gradually dissolves into a stirred curry.

Ingredients

Mackerel	400 g or 2–3 hardtail trevally *(cencaru)* or yellow stripe trevally *(selar kuning)*
Cooking oil	2 Tbsp
Dried prawn (shrimp) paste *(belacan)*	3-cm square, roasted, mixed with 125 ml water
Tamarind paste *(asam jawa)*	2 Tbsp, mixed with 250 ml water, strained
Sugar	to taste
Salt	to taste
Mint leaves	25 g, chopped

Paste A

Lemon grass *(serai)*	3 stalks, sliced and crushed
Red shallots	5 or 1 medium brown onion, peeled
Red chillies	3, seeded, if preferred

Paste B

Dried prawns (shrimps)	2 tsp, pounded
Candlenuts *(buah keras)*	5
Red shallots	3 or 1 medium brown onion, peeled
Chilli powder	1 tsp

Method

- Scale, gut and clean fish but leave whole. Pat dry.

- Make Paste A. Blend (process) lemon grass with shallots and chillies.

- Make Paste B. Blend pounded prawns with candlenuts and shallots. Mix in chilli powder.

- Heat oil and stir-fry Paste A until aromatic. You may need extra oil. Add Paste B, stir well to mix. Pour in shrimp paste liquid and tamarind juice. Stir well and allow to cook. If liquid reduces too much, add 125 ml water and stir well. It should cook well or the mixture could smell too raw. Reduce heat and cook for 10 more minutes.

- Add fish and bring to the boil, then simmer for about 5 minutes until fish is cooked. Add sugar and salt to taste. Stir carefully to avoid breaking up fish.

- Add mint leaves to gravy and remove from heat to serve.

Gulai Udang Merah (Red Prawn Sambal)

This red-cooked prawn (shrimp) *sambal* is supposed to be fiery, but you can easily reduce the 'heat' by using fewer chillies and adding a bit of tomato purée or paprika instead.

Ingredients

Large prawns (shrimps)	1 kg
Red shallots	10 or 3 medium brown onions, peeled
Garlic	4 cloves, peeled
Ginger *(halia)*	2-cm knob, peeled
Red chilli paste	1 Tbsp or thick *sambal oelek*
Coconut cream	450 ml
Galangal *(lengkuas)*	1-cm knob, peeled and bruised
Lemon grass *(serai)*	1 stalk, finely slice lower portion
Turmeric *(kunyit)* or basil *(kemangi)* leaf	1, finely sliced
Kaffir lime leaves *(limau purut)*	2, finely sliced
Tomatoes	2, cut into quarters
Salt	to taste

Method

- Remove prawn heads and cut off feelers but retain shells and tails. Cut through top of shells to devein through shells. Wash and drain prawns. Set aside.

- Blend (process) shallots, garlic and ginger. Add chilli paste or thick *sambal oelek*. This is the *bumbu* or ground spice mixture.

- In a pan, bring coconut cream, ground spice mixture, galangal and lemon grass to the boil. Stir to prevent coconut cream from curdling. Turn heat down once mixture boils.

- Add shredded turmeric and kaffir lime leaves. Then add prawns and simmer for a few minutes until prawns are pink and cooked.

- Allow sauce to reduce a little as prawns will add liquid to the gravy as they cook. Add quartered tomatoes and salt to taste. Remove after a final stir.

Dried Fish Sambal (A Malayanised Thai Recipe)

Prepare dried fish by frying fish cubes or whole tiny dried fish. Add the following dressing.

Ingredients

Red chillies	2, chopped
Lime juice	125 ml
Fish sauce	1 Tbsp
Sugar	1 tsp
Salt	1/2 tsp
Coriander (cilantro) leaves	

Method

- Toss ingredients together with fried fish.

Sambal Ikan Bilis (Dried Anchovies or Whitebait in Sambal)

This *sambal* is versatile and can be applied not only to *ikan bilis* but to other fish and to prawns (shrimps). I make up a batch of three or four times the sauce recipe and freeze it as it is an invaluable stand-by for unexpected company.

Ingredients

Brown onions	2, large, peeled and halved
Garlic	6 cloves, peeled
Tender galangal *(lengkuas)*	3-cm knob, peeled
Lemon grass *(serai)*	2 stalks
Young ginger *(halia)*	3-cm knob, peeled
Red chillies	10, seeded, if preferred
Cooking oil	250 ml
Ground dried prawns (shrimps)*	3 Tbsp
Tamarind paste *(asam jawa)*	2 Tbsp, mixed with 3 Tbsp water, strained
Tomato sauce	2 Tbsp
Lemon juice	1 Tbsp
Sugar	2 Tbsp or to taste
Salt	to taste
Coconut cream	2 Tbsp
Anchovies *(ikan bilis)*	500 g, heads and intestinal tracts removed

Method

- Plunge brown onions in boiling water for a few seconds to remove bitterness. Drain at once. Blend onions, garlic, galangal, lemon grass, ginger and chillies together into a fine paste.

- Heat half the oil in a wok until it smokes. Add blended paste and stir continuously over medium heat for about 5 minutes until aromatic.

- Add ground dried prawns, tamarind juice and tomato sauce while stirring. Cook for 5–10 minutes. You may need to add 50 ml water for added bulk, or dribble some oil around the edges of the wok to prevent sambal from sticking to the wok. Stir in lemon juice. Keep scraping dregs off bottom of wok and stir well.

- Add sugar and salt to taste. Stir and cook until thick. Just before serving, add coconut cream and remove from heat. Set sauce aside.

- Using a clean wok, heat remaining oil until it smokes. Fry anchovies, a handful at a time. Remove as they turn golden brown and drain on absorbent paper.

- Keep anchovies warm and separate from sauce. Just before serving, combine them in a dish and spoon thick sauce over. Serve while crisp.

Variations

- If using squid, clean and steam squid, then spoon sauce over.

- If using prawns, clean and cook in a little oil and onion. When pink, spoon sauce over and mix. Serve hot.

* Tip: If ground prawns (shrimps) are not available, grind roasted dried prawns in a coffee grinder or mortar and pestle.

Sambal Jambi Udang Kering (Dried Prawn Sambal)

In Malaysia, this strong-tasting *sambal* made from dried prawns (shrimps) is used as a spicy sandwich spread or as a topping for sticky rice savoury cakes *(pulut panggang bakar)*. If it is made and stored carefully in airtight bottles, it will last a year in the freezer.

Ingredients

Dried salmon-coloured large prawns (shrimps)	250 g
Dried chillies	15, soaked for 10 minutes
Cooking oil	250 ml
Red shallots	20, peeled and sliced
Tamarind paste *(asam jawa)*	50 ml, mixed with 450 ml water, strained
Sugar	3 Tbsp
Dried prawns (shrimp) paste *(belacan)*	5-cm square, dry-roasted, optional
Salt	to taste

Method

- Wash dried prawns and pat dry with kitchen paper. Pound them roughly so that they are softened and slightly broken up.

- Drain chillies and blend into a paste. Set aside.

- Heat half the oil in a wok and fry shallots until brown. Remove and drain, leaving oil in wok.

- Add pounded prawns and blended chillies to oil. Stir-fry until aromatic. Add tamarind liquid and sugar. Stir to mix sugar. Bring to the boil.

- If using dried prawns paste, crumble into wok and mix well.

- When liquid boils, add pounded prawns and stir well to blend all ingredients. Add salt to taste and gradually add remaining oil.

- Stir on low heat for about 20 minutes until mixtures is dry and flaky, not pasty. You may need to add a little oil around the edges of the wok to prevent sambal from sticking.

- Stir in fried shallots. Remove from heat, cool and store in bottles.

Kuah Lada (Annie's Pepper Fish)

This is a peppery hot and sour Nonya dish, eaten with rice and tiny servings of piquant sambals.

Ingredients

Aubergines (eggplants/brinjals)	2, medium
Dried prawn (shrimp) paste *(belacan)*	2-cm square, roasted
Candlenuts *(buah keras)*	2
Lemon grass *(serai)*	4 stalks, bruised
Galangal *(lengkuas)*	5-cm knob
Red chillies	2
Cooking oil	2 Tbsp
Black peppercorns	½ Tbsp, crushed
Tamarind paste *(asam jawa)*	2 tsp, mixed with 1 litre water, strained
Sting-ray *(pari)*	600 g, cut into 5-cm pieces
Salt	to taste
Sugar	to taste

Method

- Slice aubergines across into 5-cm wide rings. Halve them and slit the middle again. Cover and soak in water.

- Blend (process) dried shrimp paste, candlenuts, 2-cm stalk of lemon grass, galangal and red chillies into a paste.

- Heat oil in a pan and fry blended paste and remaining bruised lemon grass. Stir until aromatic. Add crushed peppercorns and tamarind liquid. Cook until gravy boils.

- Add aubergines. When they are soft and cooked, lower in fish into gravy carefully. Add salt and sugar to taste. When fish is cooked, remove from heat.

- Serve hot with rice and chilli *sambal*.

Sambal Udang (Amah's Prawn Sambal)

Ingredients

King prawns (shrimps)	600 g
Ground turmeric (kunyit)	1 tsp
Red shallots	10 or 3 medium brown onions, peeled
Ginger (halia)	2-cm knob, peeled
Garlic	5 cloves, peeled
Red chillies	10, seeded, if preferred
Lemon grass (serai)	1 stalk, optional
Candlenuts (buah keras) or macadamia nuts	4
Dried prawns (shrimp) paste (belacan)	1-cm square, roasted
Cooking oil	2 Tbsp
Vinegar	2 Tbsp
Sugar	1 tsp
Tomato sauce	2 Tbsp
Salt	to taste
Ground white pepper	to taste

Garnish

Coconut cream	2 Tbsp
Onions	3, peeled, finely sliced and crisp-fried

Method

- Cut legs and feelers off prawns with scissors and wash well. Take off heads and shells but leave tails. Devein carefully. Rub with turmeric.

- Blend (process) together shallots or onions, ginger, garlic, chillies and lemon grass. Add candlenuts and continue to blend mixture into a paste. Mix in dried prawn paste.

- Heat oil in a wok and sauté paste for about 5 minutes until aromatic. Turn heat up, add prawns and stir briskly, making sure prawns mix well into paste.

- Cover and cook for 5 minutes until prawns turn pink and curl up. Stir well. If mixture is too dry, add 50 ml water and stir.

- Add vinegar, sugar, tomato sauce, salt and pepper to taste. Bring sauce to the boil, then remove from heat. Before serving, pour coconut cream on top and sprinkle with fried onions.

Sambal Lengkong Melaka (Flaked Fish Sambal)

Ingredients

Red shallots	20 or 4 large onions, peeled
Garlic	5 cloves, peeled
Red chillies	6, seeded, if preferred
Chilli powder	3 Tbsp
Ground turmeric (kunyit)	1 tsp
Ground galangal (lengkuas)	1 tsp
Coconut cream	450 ml
Palm sugar (gula melaka)	2 tsp
Sugar	1½ Tbsp or to taste
Lime or lemon juice	175 ml
Mullet or any oily fish fillet	500 g, cut into 5-cm cubes

Method

- Blend (process) shallots, garlic and chillies together. Add chilli powder, turmeric and galangal and continue to blend into a paste.

- Mix 250 ml coconut cream with ground paste, palm sugar, sugar and lime or lemon juice. Place fish pieces in mixture.

- Transfer mixture and fish into an earthenware pot (belanga). Boil and then simmer until cooked. (Do not use aluminium ware for this.)

- Remove fish cubes and place in a bowl. Use a fork to break up and flake fish.

- Add remaining coconut cream to boiled mixture and simmer until reduced to half its original volume.

- Return flaked fish to thickened gravy. Stir and cook on low heat until fish is dry and flaky. (Alternatively you could place it in the microwave and bake for 10 minutes on MEDIUM or bake at 180°C for an hour or until dry and crisp.)

- Cool and bottle for use later as a sandwich spread or as a filling for savoury pancakes.

Ikan Goreng Masak Kicap dan Tauceo

(Fried Fish in Soy Sauce and Salted Soy Beans)

This dish is popularly cooked by the Malays in Indonesia and Malaysia. It uses soy sauce, salted soy beans and/or tomatoes, but if you choose to leave out the salted soy beans, use vinegar to balance the flavours. You may either use whole small fish or fillets of larger fish.

Ingredients

Whole chubb mackerel	6, small or 600 g perch, *kembong* or sand whiting cod fillets
Salt	3/4 tsp
Lime juice	2 tsp
Rice flour	100 g
Cooking oil	250 ml
Screwpine (*pandan*) leaf	1
Garlic	3 cloves, peeled and sliced
Red shallots	10, peeled and sliced
Red chillies	5, slit and seeded
Ginger (*halia*)	2-cm knob, peeled and sliced
Lemon grass (*serai*)	2 stalks, bruised
Salted soy beans (*tauceo*)	50 g, washed and mashed
Sweet dark sauce (*kicap manis*)	125 ml
Tomatoes	2, chopped
Ground white pepper	to taste
Sugar	to taste

Garnish

Onions	3, peeled, sliced and crisp-fried
Red chillies	2–3, sliced

Method

- Clean, scale or gut whole fish or cut fillets into 5-cm squares.

- Mix 1/2 tsp salt with lime juice to make marinade and pour over fish. Leave for 30 minutes to 1 hour and refrigerate.

- Mix rice flour and remaining salt and roll fish in mixture.

- Heat oil in a wok until it smokes. Quickly fry screwpine leaf until oil browns. Discard leaf.

- Brown fish pieces a few at a time in the same oil, stirring to allow them to turn golden. Remove and drain on absorbent paper.

- Remove all but 1 Tbsp oil from wok and heat again. Sauté garlic and shallots until brown. Add chillies, ginger and lemon grass and cook until aromatic.

- Add mashed soy bean seeds and 50 ml water. Bring to the boil. Stir until it cooks, then lower to simmer.

- Add sweet dark sauce, 250 ml water and tomatoes. Cook until tomatoes are soft and gravy is reduced and slightly thickened. Add salt, pepper and sugar to taste.

- Lastly, add fried fish and slowly ladle gravy over. Simmer for a short time before removing from heat. Garnish with crispy fried onions and red chillies.

Kari Sardin (Sardines with Pineapple in Coconut Milk)

Sardines and most darker fleshed fish are high in fish oils and are effective in lowering cholesterol levels, the modern penalty for over-indulgence. This is an Indonesian favourite.

Ingredients

Garlic	3 cloves, peeled
Ginger *(halia)*	3-cm knob, peeled
Red shallots	6 or 2 large onions, peeled
Turmeric *(kunyit)*	1-cm knob, peeled
Dried chillies	10, soaked to soften
Cooking oil	2 Tbsp
Lemon grass *(serai)*	1 stalk, lower portion bruised
Semi-ripe pineapple	150 g, peeled and cut into chunks
Coconut milk	350 ml
Canned sardines or pilchards	400 g, in tomato sauce
Sugar	to taste
Salt	to taste

Garnish

Lemons	3, cut into wedges

Method

- Blend (process) garlic, ginger, shallots and turmeric until fine. Add drained chillies and continue to blend.

- Heat oil in an earthenware pot (belanga). Stir-fry blended ingredients and lemon grass for about 5 minutes until aromatic. Lower heat and allow oil to separate from blended paste.

- Add pineapple chunks and coconut milk. Bring slowly to the boil, stirring so coconut milk does not curdle.

- Once gravy boils, lower heat and carefully lower whole sardines or pilchards and tomato sauce into gravy. (Omit tomato sauce if you prefer a tart taste.)

- Bring to the boil once more and add sugar and salt to taste. Remove from heat. Serve hot with lemon wedges.

Ikan Garing Cara Indonesia
(Crispy Indonesian-Style Fish)

Ikan garing is simple to make and requires no special skill from the cook. An earthenware pot (known as a *chatty* or *belanga*) would make this dish truly special as the flavours of the fish will be heightened.

Ingredients

Large tuna, Spanish mackerel or perch steaks	500 g, cut across the bone
Ground turmeric (*kunyit*)	1/4 tsp
Cooking oil	2 Tbsp
Garlic	4 cloves, sliced
Red shallots	6 or 2 medium brown onions, peeled
Red chillies	2–3, seeded, if preferred
Sour starfruit (*belimbing*)	2–3, small, halved
Dried prawn (shrimp) paste (*belacan*)	2-cm square, roasted
Galangal (*lengkuas*)	3-cm knob, peeled and pounded
Sweet dark sauce (*kicap manis*)	2 Tbsp
Tamarind paste (*asam jawa*)	2 tsp, mixed with 2 Tbsp water
Water	250 ml
Salt	to taste

Method

- Rub fish steaks with ground turmeric.

- Heat oil in a casserole dish and sauté garlic and shallots until brown. Add chillies, sour starfruit and prawn paste and stir well until aromatic.

- Add galangal, sweet dark sauce and tamarind liquid. Stir and add water. Bring mixture to the boil.

- Place fish in dish, arranging them such that they are level and not piled on top of each other. Ladle gravy over fish and cover dish.

- Simmer for 30–45 minutes until liquid is almost fully absorbed. Shake dish once in a while to make sure fish does not burn. Add salt to taste.

- Serve hot or cold with rice or bread.

Pendaram Udang (Prawn Cakes)

Pendaram udang are tasty prawn cakes, deep-fried in batter and eaten with chilli as a snack.

Ingredients

Small prawns (shrimps) or krill *(gerago)*	500 g
Ground coriander *(ketumbar)*	1 Tbsp
Ground cumin *(jintan putih)*	1/4 tsp
Ground sweet cumin *(jintan manis adas)*	1/4 tsp
Ground turmeric *(kunyit)*	1/2 tsp
Red shallots	4 or 1 medium brown onion, peeled
Garlic	3 cloves, peeled
Ginger *(halia)*	2-cm knob, peeled
Salt	to taste
Ground white pepper	to taste
Garlic chives	25 g, chopped
Coconut cream	250 ml
Rice flour	250 g
Cooking oil	450 ml
Screwpine *(pandan)* leaves	2, optional

Method

- Shell prawns or wash krill well and drain.

- Dry-roast ground coriander, cumin and sweet cumin for a few seconds in a dry pan. Add ground turmeric.

- Blend (process) shallots or onions, garlic and ginger together into a paste. Mix in roasted ground spices.

- Mix in prawns or krill, then add salt, pepper and garlic chives. The mixture should be thick and sticky.

- Whisk or blend coconut cream and half the rice flour to obtain a thick batter. If batter is too stiff, add some water. Mix prawn mixture into the coconut cream batter to form a thick mixture.

- Grease palms with a drop of cooking oil and shape mixture into cakes. Place a ball of mixture on one palm and shape into a flat cake with fingers. Put remaining rice flour on a plate.

- Heat oil in a wok and when it is heating up, place screwpine leaves in oil, if using. When oil browns, remove leaves. This will give the oil an aromatic flavour.

- Coat shaped cakes with rice flour and lower into hot oil to deep-fry. Fry 3–4 patties at a time, or as many as the wok will hold. Flatten cakes slightly between two spoons as you fry. When prawn cakes turn golden and float, push them down into the oil to crisp further. Remove and drain on kitchen paper. Continue until all the prawn cakes are done.

- Serve with chilli and tomato sauce.

Nonya Bunga Kantan Udang

(Ginger Flower Prawns)

Ingredients

Paste

Red chilli	100 g
Turmeric	20 g
Galangal	100 g
Lemon grass	100 g
Turmeric leaf	1/2
Ginger flower	50–80 g
Vietnamese mint	20 g
Screwpine (pandan) leaves	1
Dried prawn (shrimp) paste (*belacan*)	2 tsp, dry-roasted

Sambal

Light olive or vegetable oil	1 Tbsp
Garlic	2 cloves, peeled and finely chopped
Ginger	2-cm knob, peeled and finely chopped
Green tiger prawns (shrimps)	500 g, shelled, deveined and cleaned
Salt	to taste
Ground white pepper	to taste
Vinegar	1 Tbsp
Sugar	1 tsp or to taste

Method

- Blend (process) all paste ingredients until well-mixed and fine. This quantity (about 400 g) will be sufficient for cooking up to 2 kg prawns. Use it for four recipes or make a large quantity if you're having guests over. Store excess in an airtight container and keep refrigerated until needed.

- Heat oil in a wok and sauté garlic and ginger until brown. Add one quarter of paste and stir until aromatic.

- Add prawns and toss quickly until prawns turn red. Season with salt and pepper to taste and vinegar and sugar.

- Serve on top of a bowl of cooked egg noodles or with boiled rice.

Opor Sotong (Dry Squid Curry)

This dish of dry squid or *opor* has an Indonesian name but it could have originated on either side of the Melakan straits.

Ingredients

Small squid	500 g
Chilli powder	2 Tbsp
Ground turmeric (*kunyit*)	1 tsp
Cooking oil	125 ml
Garlic	4 cloves, finely sliced
Red shallots	8 or 3 medium brown onions, peeled and finely sliced
Tomato sauce	2 Tbsp
Dark soy sauce	1 tsp
Fish sauce	1 Tbsp
Tamarind paste (*asam jawa*)	1 Tbsp, mixed with 2 Tbsp water, strained
Sugar	1/2 tsp
Salt	to taste
Ground white pepper	to taste
Lemon juice	4 Tbsp

Garnish

Curry leaves	8
Lemon	1, cut into wedges

Method

- Wash and clean squid, discarding skin, ink sacs and quill. Clean out tubes. You can also use the tentacles and head after removing the eyes and beak. Cut squid tubes into 2-cm thin rings.

- Mix chilli powder and ground turmeric. Toss and rub rings in mixture to coat well.

- Heat oil in a wok and sauté garlic, then shallots or onions until brown. Add squid and fry on low heat, turning and stirring often so rings do not stick to each other. Add a little more oil if necessary. Add tomato sauce, dark soy sauce, fish sauce, tamarind liquid and sugar. Stir for 10 minutes, tossing until squid is cooked. Add salt and pepper to taste.

- Pour lemon juice onto squid and stir well before removing from heat. Serve hot, garnished with curry leaves and lemon wedges.

Ikan Goreng dengan Kuah Tomato

(Fried Fish with Tomato Gravy)

This unusual recipe that combines fish and tomato comes from an Indian Muslim palace chef.

Ingredients

Mackerel *(ikan tenggiri)*, threadfin *(serangin)* or any meaty fish fillets	500 g
Light soy sauce	125 ml
Ginger *(halia)* juice	1 Tbsp
Dried prawn (shrimp) paste *(belacan)*	3-cm square, roasted
Red shallots	4, peeled
Ginger *(halia)*	2-cm knob, peeled
Garlic	2 cloves, peeled
Red chillies	4, seeded, if preferred
Candlenuts *(buah keras)*	4
Plain (all-purpose) flour	125 g
Salt	to taste
Ground white pepper	to taste
Margarine	100 g
Cooking oil	3 Tbsp
Eggs	2, beaten
Potatoes	2, large, sliced
Tomatoes	5, diced
Vinegar	1 Tbsp
Sweet dark sauce *(kicap manis)*	1 Tbsp

Garnish

Coriander (cilantro) leaves

Method

- Clean, scale and gut fish, then cut into 6-cm pieces. Mix light soy sauce and ginger juice and place fish in to marinate for about 30 minutes.

- Blend (process) shrimp paste, shallots, ginger, garlic, chillies and candlenuts together. Set aside.

- Mix plain flour with salt and pepper.

- Heat margarine and oil together in a wok until it smokes. Dip each marinated piece of fish in egg, then in seasoned flour and deep-fry until golden. Remove, drain and keep warm.

- In the same oil, fry potato slices until golden. Drain and keep warm.

- Leaving 2 Tbsp oil in wok, sauté blended ingredients until fragrant. Add diced tomatoes. Bring to the boil then lower heat to simmer. Squash tomatoes until well-blended into ground ingredients.

- Add vinegar and sweet dark sauce, bring to the boil and remove from heat.

- To serve, arrange potato slices on the sides of a plate and fried fish in the centre. Pour gravy over fish and garnish with coriander leaves.

Cili Ketam (Chilli Crab)

Crabs sautéed with plump buds of garlic and mashed black beans is as wonderful a dish to prepare as it is to serve.

Ingredients

Mud crabs	2, about 1 kg
Garlic	6 cloves
Ginger (halia)	6-cm knob, peeled
Red chillies	14, seeded, if preferred
Cooking oil	1 Tbsp
Dried prawns (shrimp) paste (belacan)	2-cm square, roasted, optional
Salted soy beans (tauceo)	2 Tbsp, washed, drained and pulped
Sweet dark vinegar	2 Tbsp
Tomato sauce	3 Tbsp
Sugar	1 tsp
Salt	to taste
Cornflour (cornstarch)	1 Tbsp, mixed with 50 ml water

Garnish

Garlic chives or coriander (cilantro) leaves	1 bunch, cut into 3-cm lengths

Method

- Clean crabs thoroughly. Cut bodies into quarters and crack open claws (see pg 298).

- Blend (process) together garlic, ginger and chillies. Set aside.

- Heat oil in a wok until almost smoking. Crumble prawn paste and soy bean pulp into oil and cook for 1 minute, stirring quickly to prevent burning.

- Add blended paste and stir. Reduce heat and continue frying until aromatic. Add crab and stir, making sure gravy penetrates crab. Cover and cook in steam for 6–10 minutes.

- When crab flesh turns white, add vinegar, tomato sauce, sugar and salt to taste. Lower heat to simmer and continue to stir well for 5 minutes. Add cornflour mixture to thicken sauce slightly.

- Remove from heat and garnish with garlic chives or coriander.

Ikan Sumbat (Stuffed Fish)

Stuffed fish is popular all over Asia. For the stuffing, the Chinese use pork and pickled plums or onions and minced chicken, the Filipinos use rice, eggs and prawns (shrimps), the Malays use mainly herbs that will sweeten and tenderise the fish, while the Indians use onions or coconut and spices.

Ingredients

Black pomfrets, hardtails, mackerels or snappers	4–6, medium or about 400 g
Ground turmeric (kunyit)	1/2 tsp
Salt	1/2 tsp
Red shallots	8–10 or 2 large onions, peeled
Garlic	3 cloves, peeled
Ginger (halia)	2-cm knob, peeled
Candlenuts (buah keras)	2
Lemon grass (serai)	2 stalks
Red chillies	4, seeded, if preferred
Red ripe tomato	1, medium, cut in quarters
Tamarind paste (asam jawa)	1 tsp, mixed with 1 Tbsp water, strained
Basil (selasih) leaves	8
Cooking oil	125 ml
Salt	to taste

Garnish

Limes	2, sliced
Lime leaves	

Method

- Scale, gut and clean fish well. Rub with ground turmeric and salt.
- If using shallots, blend together with garlic, ginger, candlenuts, lemon grass, chillies and tomato.
- If using onions, blend (process) onions first and squeeze out excess juice. Reserve juice. Continue to blend with garlic, ginger, candlenuts, lemon grass, chillies and tomato.
- Add tamarind liquid and basil leaves to blended ingredients.
- Heat wok with 1/2 Tbsp oil and sauté ground ingredients, stirring frequently for about 5 minutes until mixture is aromatic and turns brown. Add salt to taste.
- Add reserved onion juice (optional) at the end of frying to add moisture. Remove from heat.
- Carefully stuff cavity of fish with fried mixture and sew or skewer up stomach to secure stuffing.
- Add remaining oil to wok and heat. When oil is hot, lower fish into wok with slit stomach toward you. Fry carefully until fish is golden on both sides. Remove and drain.
- Alternatively, brush some oil over stuffed fish and bake in a greased casserole dish at 180°C for 35 minutes. Open oven at intervals and oil fish as it bakes.
- Garnish with lime slices and leaves.

Variation

- This dish can also be made with fish fillets. Fry ground ingredients, basil leaves and tamarind liquid until aromatic. Then ladle over fish and place in microwave oven for 5 minutes on HIGH. Turn over and cook for 3 minutes on MEDIUM.

Ikan Masin (Nonya Fried Salted Fish)

Salted fish has a pungent flavour when cooked, and has been put into the same category of strong-smelling foods together with durian and some types of cheese. So do warn your neighbours beforehand when you plan to cook this dish.

Ingredients

Salted threadfin (ikan kurau)	250 g or 1 small whole salted fish
Cooking oil	250 ml

Method

- If using larger threadfin, cut into 2-cm chunks.

- If using whole salted fish, scrape off scales and clean stomach area. Soak for 5–10 minutes in water and rub off some of the salt. Drain and pat dry with paper towels or the water will cause the oil to splutter.

- Dry-roast fish for about 5 minutes under the grill, turning fish over when heated side turns golden and dries up.

- Heat oil in a wok until it smokes. Quickly fry fish pieces or whole fish. Turn fish over continuously until golden on both sides and take out the moment it starts to darken or fish could burn. Drain fish on absorbent paper.

- Serve fish with sambal belacan and a squeeze of lemon juice, garnished with cucumber slices.

Pindang Serani (Sour Spiced Fish)

Ingredients

Snapper, mackerel or cobia fillets	600 g, cut into 6-cm pieces
Salt	1/2 tsp
Lime juice	extracted from 1 lime
Galangal (lengkuas)	2-cm knob, peeled
Red chilli powder	1 tsp
Ground turmeric (kunyit)	1/2 tsp
Lemon grass (serai)	2 stalks
Cooking oil	2 Tbsp
Red shallots	6 or 2 brown onions, peeled and finely sliced
Garlic	3 cloves, peeled and finely sliced
Red chillies	3, sliced into 1-cm rings
Basil (selasih) leaves	6
Water	250 ml
Tamarind paste (asam jawa)	1 Tbsp, mixed with 125 ml water, strained
Sweet dark sauce (kicap manis)	1 Tbsp

Garnish

Lemons	2, cut into wedges
Cucumber	1/2, cut into chunks

Method

- Marinate fillet pieces in salt and lime juice for a few minutes.

- Pound galangal roughly with chilli powder, turmeric and lemon grass.

- Heat oil in a wok and sauté shallots, garlic and cut chillies. Add pounded ingredients and keep frying until fragrant.

- Add basil leaves, water, tamarind liquid and sweet dark sauce. When liquid starts to boil, add fish pieces. Stir and ladle sauce over fish as it cooks. Lower heat and simmer until fish is cooked and has absorbed the flavour of the spices. This should take no longer than 7 minutes or the fish could break up.

- Transfer to a serving bowl and garnish with lemon wedges and cucumber chunks.

Variation

- Add 2 Tbsp coconut cream to gravy before serving.

- Alternatively, bake fish. Place raw fish with cooked gravy in a casserole dish and cook at 180°C for 40 minutes. Garnish basil leaves and serve.

Ikan Panggang Pari (Grilled Sting-Ray or Eagle-Ray)

Ikan pari is a delicious fish, with firm and sweet flesh. The fins are gelatinous and have a particular flavour when grilled, especially in banana leaf. This is a popular dish throughout Malaysia.

Ingredients

Sting-ray *(pari)* or eagle-ray fillet*	500 g
Garlic	4 cloves, peeled
Red shallots	20 or 3 medium brown onions, peeled
Red chillies	5, seeded, if preferred
Candlenut *(buah keras)*	1
Lemon grass *(serai)*	1 stalk
Fresh saffron	2-cm strand
Dried prawns (shrimp) paste *(belacan)*	3-cm square, roasted
Light soy sauce	1 tsp
Cooking oil	50 ml
Dried prawns (shrimps)	2 Tbsp, coarsely chopped
Salt	to taste
Sugar	to taste
Tamarind paste *(asam jawa)*	1 Tbsp, mixed with 125 ml water, strained
Lime juice	extracted from 1 lime
Banana leaf	1 sheet or use foil as a substitute

Garnish

Onions	3, large, peeled, sliced and crisp-fried
Lemons	3, cut into wedges

Method

- Cut sting-ray into 3 thin slices lengthwise to obtain thin fillets. Wash and pat dry with paper towels.

- Blend (process) garlic, shallots, red chillies, candlenut, lemon grass and saffron until fine. Crumble in dried prawn paste and continue blending into a fine paste. Mix in soy sauce.

- Coat fish pieces with 1 Tbsp of paste.

- Heat oil in a pan and fry remaining paste until fragrant and aromatic. Add dried prawns and continue to stir until well-cooked.

- Add salt, sugar and tamarind liquid and stir to mix well. Reduce heat and keep sauce warm.

- Grease a grill-pan or oven-grill and place banana leaf on grill. Arrange fish pieces on banana leaf and cook slowly. When one side is cooked, turn fish over carefully on banana leaf. If using oven-grill, place another leaf on top of fish to avoid burning fish.

- When fillets are white and can be flaked easily, pour cooked sambal onto fish and grill for a few minutes longer. Remove from heat.

- Pour lime juice on fish. Snip off burnt edges of banana leaf and transfer onto plate. Serve hot with crisp onions and lemon wedges.

Paul's Pepper Crab

This is one of the dishes my friend Paul Lee taught me to prepare when I was guest chef at Club Med on the East Coast of Malaysia a few years ago. Paul's daughter, Yvette, who is studying Food Technology at William Angliss College, Melbourne, helped me prepare the dish for the photograph session. Enjoy.

Ingredients

Blue swimmer crabs	2 kg
Vegetable or light olive oil	450 ml
Butter	150 g
Garlic	100 g, peeled and crushed
Black peppercorns	1 tsp, crushed
Salt	to taste
Fish sauce	to taste

Marinade

Black peppercorns	1/2 tsp, crushed
Light soy sauce	3 Tbsp
Sugar	1 Tbsp

Method

- Clean crabs and cut into quarters. Remove claws.

- Combine marinade ingredients and leave crabs to marinate for at least 1 hour.

- Heat oil in a wok and deep-fry marinated crabs until they turn red. Remove and drain from oil. Keep warm.

- In another wok, melt butter and fry garlic. Add black peppercorns and heat well. Add crabs and stir to coat with sauce.

- Season with salt and fish sauce. Serve hot.

Poh Piah (Spring Rolls)

Fresh spring roll sheets are readily available in Malaysia and Singapore. In Australia, Vietnamese rice paper sheets are a good substitute. To use, wet a tea towel and wring dry. Place tea towel on table and gently peel a sheet from the pile of spring roll sheets. Place sheet on damp tea towel for a few minutes to soften it and make it pliable. Do not allow spring roll sheet to sit too long or it will be too soft to handle.

Ingredients

Eggs	5, beaten
Cooking oil	1½ Tbsp
Garlic	6 cloves, peeled, thinly sliced and crisp-fried
Black bean paste (haeko)	1 Tbsp
Prawns (shrimps)	200 g, small, cleaned, deveined and cooked
Pork	500 g, thinly sliced
Bamboo shoots	200 g, chopped
Yam bean	600 g, peeled and shredded
Light soy sauce	60 ml
Salt	to taste
Ground white pepper	to taste
Cos lettuce	1, washed, leaves separated and dried well
Sweet dark sauce (kicap manis)	30 ml
Chilli sauce	1 Tbsp or to taste, optional
Cucumber	1, cored and cut into thin strips
Crabmeat	200 g, lightly cooked
Coriander (cilantro) leaves	3 sprigs, chopped
Spring roll sheets	20 sheets

Method

- Cook eggs into a thin omelette. Roll up tightly then slice across to obtain fine strips. Transfer to a serving plate and set aside.

- Cook filling. Heat oil in a wok and fry garlic and black bean paste until aromatic. Increase heat and add prawns and pork. Fry for about 4 minutes until cooked and pork starts to darken.

- Add bamboo shoots, yam bean, soy sauce, salt and pepper to taste. Cook until bamboo shoots and yam bean are soft and mixture is almost dry. Transfer filling to a serving bowl and cool.

- Allow guests to assemble their own spring rolls. To assemble, take a lettuce leaf and lay it on a spring roll sheet. Brush dark sweet sauce and some chilli sauce, if preferred, on leaf.

- Spoon 2 Tbsp filling into a small sieve to drain excess liquid off. Spoon onto lettuce leaf and top with cucumber and egg strips, crabmeat and coriander leaves.

- Roll up by first folding side of sheet nearest you over filling. Then tuck left and right edges of sheet over the fold to enclose the filling.

- Roll enclosed filling over to form a neat spring roll parcel with loose edge tucked under filling. Guests may eat slice up the spring roll to eat or eat it as a hand roll.

Pasembor (Pasembor with Prawn Fritters)

Pasembor is a salad popularly available at Indian Muslim street stalls in the larger cities along the west coast of Malaysia. The crispiness of the prawn (shrimp) fritters gives this salad a special crunch that adds to the texture and flavour that is so much a part of the Malaysian food experience.

Ingredients

Salad

Squid tubes	100 g, cleaned
Lebanese cucumber	1, cored and shredded
Yam bean	1, medium, peeled and shredded
Bean sprouts	200 g, plucked
Water convolvulus (*kangkong*)	100 g, cut into 4-cm lengths
Cos lettuce	1, chopped
Firm bean curd	100 g, fried and diced
Unsalted peanuts (groundnuts)	100 g, dry-roasted and roughly chopped
Sesame seeds	30 g, dry-roasted

Prawn Fritters

Plain (all-purpose) flour	160 g
Rice flour	50 g
Salt	to taste
Water	450 ml
Prawns (shrimps)	200 g, shelled and minced

Sauce

Garlic	6 cloves, peeled and diced
Spanish onion	1, peeled and diced
Sambal oelek	1½ Tbsp
Water	60 ml
Tamarind paste (*asam jawa*)	1 Tbsp
Sugar	2 Tbsp
Salt or fish sauce	to taste
Cornflour (cornstarch)	1 Tbsp
Ground white pepper	to taste

Method

- Score squid and dip into boiling water for a few minutes to blanch. Slice into squares and set aside.

- Prepare prawn fritters. Combine plain flour, rice flour and salt with enough water to make a smooth batter. It should be rather thick and pour slowly. Coat prawns in batter.

- Heat some oil in a wok until it is almost smoking. Fry 3–4 prawn fritters at a time until golden brown and crisp. Continue until batter is used up. Drain on absorbent paper and slice into pieces.

- Leave 2 Tbsp oil in wok to cook sauce.

- Sauté garlic and onion on medium heat until aromatic. Add *sambal oelek* and some of the water. Stir for a few minutes then add tamarind purée, sugar, salt and remaining water. (If you prefer the sauce to be more liquid, add more water as necessary.)

- Bring to the boil and cook, stirring constantly, until sugar dissolves.

- Mix cornflour with 3 Tbsp water and stir well into sauce to thicken. Season with pepper and remove from heat.

- Assemble salad by arranging all the prepared salad ingredients except peanuts and sesame seeds on a serving platter. Place sliced prawn fritters on top and pour sauce over. Sprinkle with peanuts and sesame seeds to serve.

Udang Serai Mentega (Butter and Lemon Grass Prawns)

The flavours of Malaysia—lemon grass, chilli and coconut—are all present in this simple dish. Do not fry the coconut in anything but butter or the dish will not be as rich and flavoursome.

Ingredients

Green prawns (shrimps)	500 g, shelled, deveined and cleaned, with tails intact
Light soy sauce	1 Tbsp
Lemon grass (serai)	4 stalks, chopped
Garlic	2 cloves, peeled and chopped
Shallots	4, peeled and chopped
Butter	100 g
Hot black bean paste	2 Tbsp
Sugar	to taste
Grated coconut	1 Tbsp
Chilli or paprika powder	1 tsp

Method

- Brush prawns with soy sauce. Set aside.

- Blend (process) lemon grass, garlic and onion together until it forms a smooth paste.

- Heat 1 Tbsp butter on medium heat in a wok. Sauté paste until aromatic. Add hot black bean paste and sugar and cook for a few minutes more, being careful not to burn butter.

- Add prawns and cook on high heat for 4–5 minutes or until they change colour. Remove the prawns and keep warm.

- Add remaining butter to wok and, when hot, add coconut. Sprinkle chilli or paprika powder over and fry until aromatic. Remove from heat.

- Garnish prawns with fried coconut and serve hot.

Sotong Masak Hitam (Black Squid)

This dish is a speciality in northern Malaysia. The squid ink lends a fascinating flavour to the dish, which is quite unique. Squid is best bought fresh and cleaned at home before use. Pre-cleaned squid tubes, sliced from larger squid, toughen easily. I buy very small squid, no longer than 10 cm. These need to be cooked very quickly in a hot wok.

Ingredients

Squid	450 g
Cooking oil	3 Tbsp
Garlic	3 cloves, peeled and chopped
Spanish onion	1 small, peeled and puréed
Sambal oelek	3 Tbsp
Fish sauce	to taste
Tamarind pulp (asam jawa)	1 Tbsp, mixed with 3 Tbsp water
Palm sugar (gula Melaka)	2-cm piece
Lime juice	extracted from 1 lime

Garnish

Basil (kemangi) leaves	1 sprig, chopped

Method

- Clean squid and cut out eyes. Carefully remove tentacles, making sure ink sacs remain attached and unbroken. Discard quill and intestinal tract. Peel off skin and slice squid tubes across in half.

- Heat oil in a wok over high heat. Add garlic and onion and stir-fry until golden.

- Add sambal oelek and cook for 3–4 minutes until it loses its raw smell.

- Add squid tubes and tentacles, fish sauce, tamarind juice and palm sugar. Stir-fry and allow ink from sacs to spill out into gravy. Continue stirring until liquid reduces by half.

- Add lime juice. The squid ink may curdle when lime juice is added but the flavour will not be marred by this reaction. Remove from heat and toss with basil. Serve hot.

Thailand

Rendezvous with Temple Bells

> " In the swift stream
>
> You washed the fish
>
> Rubbed them with ocean salt "
>
> *Noto*

Water and watering thoroughfares are a fact of life in Thailand. In the large cities as well as in the country, the *klongs* that run almost parallel to the roads were in use long before the roads were constructed. These were the travel-ways and, more importantly, served as irrigation channels for rice fields that needed to be flooded during the growing season.

Water in the *klongs* is used for cooking and drinking as well as washing and cleaning oneself. This is a monsoon country, part of the mainland Southeast Asia which is directly affected by the wind systems that bring heavy downpours during the southwest monsoons from May to October.

Spend a day on the banks of the Chao Phraya in Bangkok and you will watch the city come alive. At dawn, the *sampans*, full of produce from orchids to vegetables, set off for the floating market. Another hour later, it could be forests of logs floating down to the sea and men riding the logs like rafts. Then as the day progresses, you may see a family *sampan* decked with washing drying in the sun, laughing bronzed-skinned children, floating market sellers, whistling express bus-boats and on special occasions royal barges...and as evening draws in, the twinkling of river and riverside lights creates a magical effect.

Most families live on fish and prawns (shrimps) from ponds in their compounds and on coconuts from their gardens. They shop everyday for fresh foods in markets, not relying on refrigerators or freezers. For fresh fish, there is a daily pre-dawn wholesale market on the banks of the Chao Phraya, where crowds of fish merchants haggle with restaurateurs and retailers over an astounding array of fresh fish from tuna, jewfish and mackerel to snapper, threadfin, perch, pomfret, hilsa, lobster, crab and squid. Near the market are barn-like seafood restaurants, where you can buy your seafood and have it cooked to your requirements in fish sauce, chilli, lemon grass or tamarind.

Thai food, influenced by early Chinese Tai tribes and neighbouring culinary practices, is sweet yet salty, bitter yet sweet, sometimes separately, sometimes combined together in an explosion of flavours that excites the palate. The scents of jasmine and rose subtly pervade rice and drinks, while kaffir lime and lemon grass intermingle with the bite of chilli cooked into fresh seafood.

The Thais are a deeply religious people and practice a religion that came to them from one neighbour by way of another. Though Buddhism originated in India, the Chinese brought it to Thailand. The script that the Thais adopted, however, was Sanskrit and Pali-influenced. It is easy to see that the deeply religious Buddhism practised in Thailand is not confined to the temples but is lived daily by the people.

Meat and vegetables are prepared and cubed or sliced thinly so that the diner does not need to use a knife, a sign of aggression to the Thais. Their passivity also extends to all things: it can be seen in the vow of poverty, very real to Thai Buddhists, whose male members begin life early as novice monks accepting the vow of poverty for a few weeks at a time to 'make merit'. As adult monks, they can be seen dressed in saffron-coloured robes going on their early morning rounds, with bowls in hand, begging for their meals, thus allowing others to 'make merit' with charitable giving.

The Thais are a very artistic people and have a deep understanding of the beauty of each ingredient that is served. Food never leaves the kitchen without being decorated and carved into lovely shapes. Ornamentation is elaborate and extensive, depending on the cook and the time available. There is an attempt to combine textures and colours so that the appetite is never jaded and a meal is a feast to the eyes as well as to the palate.

There is resilience in these people, seldom displayed, yet apparent in their resistance to foreign rule in all the years of European colonisation of the rest of Asia. Yet, no one can fault their hospitality and warmth when they are hosting guests, be it house guests or tourists, as they are warm and generous to a fault. The Thai always finds occasion to party, whether in celebration of the birth of a baby, the birthday of a friend or colleague, or one of the many religious and secular holidays in Thailand. It is always time for a family celebration and food is central to the celebration. Dinner begins with exquisite starter entrées, local beer and a series of beautifully and artistically prepared dishes, often ending with elaborately carved fresh fruit.

The hawker and his stall play an important role in the life of the man in the street. The Thais are not dessert but fruit eaters. Delicate and dainty tea-time sweets, sizzling kebabs and pickled and salted fruit served with hot chilli are common snacks. Even children nibble on pieces of sour mango or crunchy slices of guava dipped in chilli, soy and pounded peanuts (groundnuts), a veritable pleasure not to be missed.

Thailand's seafood dishes give a taste of the real delight of the country. The selection given below is just a small proportion of the wealth of tastes you can experience in the country itself.

Tord Man Pla (Thai Fish Cakes)

Tiny, dainty fish cakes or croquettes, just sufficient for one or two bites are made in all Asian countries. Try also the Indian fish *Koftas* (see pg 196), made quite differently with flaked fish or prawns (shrimps). Both recipes go well with light wines and could be made up for a wine-and-cheese evening with friends.

Ingredients

Coriander (*phak chee*) root	2-cm length
Black peppercorns	10
Garlic	4 cloves, peeled and chopped
Red chillies	2, seeded, if preferred and chopped
Ling or bream fillet or crab meat, prawns (shrimps) or squid	300 g
Breadcrumbs or rice flour	25 g
Fish sauce (*nam pla*)	2 Tbsp
Eggs	2, yolks and whites separated
Coriander (*phak chee*) leaves	25 g, chopped
Coconut cream (*hua ka-thi*)	3 Tbsp
Cooking oil	2 Tbsp

Method

- Blend (process) coriander roots with peppercorns, garlic and chillies into a paste. Set aside.

- Blend fish, crab meat, prawns or squid in a food processor and add blended paste. Add breadcrumbs or rice flour and mix until mixture leaves sides of container.

- Add fish sauce. Beat egg yolks and add. Add coriander leaves and bind mixture together. Gently stir in coconut cream.

- Place mixture in greased ramekins, patty tins or cupcake moulds. (Traditionally, this dish is steamed in Thai fish cake moulds or banana leaf cups. Do the same by making cones out of banana or lotus leaves.)

- Steam individual cups for about 15 minutes over hot water. Wipe any condensation away with a towel.

- When cakes are firm, remove from steamer and drain. Remove fish cakes from moulds and dip in beaten egg white.

- Heat oil in a wok and fry fish cakes until golden brown. Drain and serve.

Variation

- You may omit the steaming step but add more flour to the mixture to make it firm. Shape into balls and fry in hot oil.

- Alternatively, you may omit the frying step and serve the fish cakes steamed.

Pla Thu (Spicy Mackerel)

Ingredients

Mackerel (pla thu), perch, snapper or kingfish	500 g
Glutinous rice flour	75 g + extra
Salt	1 tsp
Ground white pepper	1/2 tsp
Water	80 ml
Cooking oil	250 ml

Garnish

Cucumber	1, sliced
Red shallots	4, peeled, sliced and crisp-fried

Mango Salad

Hot chillies	3–4, broken
Dried prawns (shrimps)	25 g, soaked for 10 minutes and pounded
Raw green mango	1, peeled and shredded
Shallot	1, peeled and shredded
Grated coconut	75 g, roasted
Cashew nuts	2 Tbsp, roasted and coarsely pounded
Fish sauce (nam pla)	2 Tbsp
Sugar	2 tsp

Method

- Clean, gut, scale and wash fish. Wipe dry with kitchen towel.

- Whisk rice flour, salt and pepper with water to make a smooth batter. Dip fish in batter and then coat in extra flour to dry it before frying.

- Heat oil in a wok until it smokes. Lower fish carefully into oil and fry until both sides are crisp and brown. Remove from wok, drain and place on dish arranged with cucumber slices.

- Garnish with crisp-fried shallots.

Mango Salad

- Dry-roast broken chillies with pounded shrimp for about 3 minutes until crisp or dark in colour.

- Toss with rest of salad ingredients and spoon around fish. Serve.

Gaeng Som Pu (Crab in Sour Tamarind Soup)

Ingredients

Crab	500 g
Chinese cabbage	125 g
Garlic	8 cloves, peeled
Red shallots	7 or 2 medium brown onions, peeled
Dried chillies	5–8, seeded
Prawn (shrimp) paste (kapee)	1 tsp
Salt	1/2 tsp
Water	250 ml
Fish stock	250 ml
Pickled mustard greens	50 g, sliced
Long beans	125 g, cut into 2.5-cm lengths
Tamarind paste (ma khaam)	1 Tbsp, mixed with 125 ml water, strained
Fish sauce (nam pla)	2 1/2 Tbsp
Ground white pepper	to taste

Garnish

Red capsicums (bell peppers)	3, finely chopped
Lemon rind	from 1 lemon

Method

- Wash and scrub crab, remove outer shell and cut body into pieces.
- Soak Chinese cabbage in cold water and after 5 minutes, squeeze out the water.
- Blend (process) garlic, shallots, chillies, prawn paste and salt.
- Mix blended paste with 250 ml water and fish stock. Bring to the boil slowly.
- Add crab and Chinese cabbage, mustard greens and long beans. Bring slowly to the boil, then lower heat to simmer.
- When crab flesh is white and vegetables are cooked, add tamarind liquid and fish sauce. Add pepper to taste.
- Garnish with chopped capsicums and lemon rind and serve hot with rice.

Thai Curries

Thai curries depend on the curry paste for colour, flavour and texture. These pastes are a combination of herbs and spices, and the proportions used determine the taste and colour of the completed curry.

The Thai word *gaeng* (liquid) is used to define curries and soups. The liquid is often twice or three times the quantity of the meat, as the *gaeng* is generously spooned onto rice and enjoyed.

Krung gaeng is a beautifully aromatic mixture of freshly ground herbs and spices. Each dish is a combination of different spices that will enhance the meat or fish cooked in it. *Krung gaeng ped* is red curry; *Krung gaeng khiaw wan* is green curry. The green colour comes from herb roots and green chillies, and this is a hot curry. *Krung gaeng som* is an orange curry paste: *Som* means sour or vinegar-flavoured and also refers to the sour orange or pomelo, a large citrus fruit with a thick green skin. *Mussaman* curry or Muslim curry, contains cinnamon, nutmeg and star anise. *Krung gaeng leung* is red curry paste with the addition of turmeric to make it yellow.

Each Thai family has its own recipe for curry, adapted according to preferences and there is no hard and fast rule. All Asian curries, however, need to be eaten with rice, which allows the hot and strong tastes to be savoured and enjoyed.

Haw Mok (Spicy Fish Steamed in Cups)

This is a delightful and novel way to serve fish—as an entrée in tiny ramekins.

Ingredients

Kingfish, sea perch or bass fillets	500 g
Egg	1, beaten
Coconut cream (hua ka-thi)	350 ml
Rice flour	1 Tbsp
Spring onions (scallions)	2, finely shredded
Red chillies	3, chopped
Green curry paste	2 Tbsp (see pg 306)
Cooking oil	1/2 tsp
Fish sauce (nam pla)	1 1/2 Tbsp
Kaffir lime leaves (bai makrut)	2, finely shredded

Garnish

Onions	2, peeled, sliced and crisp-fried
Coriander (phak chee) leaves	

Method

- Slice fish into fine strips, carefully removing bones with tweezers.

- Mix egg with coconut cream and rice flour. Stir fish strips and other ingredients except kaffir lime leaves into two-thirds of the coconut cream mixture.

- Grease little ramekins or patty tins, or make banana leaf cups by twisting banana leaf squares into cones. Pour mixture into each container. Do not fill to the brim. Place in a steamer carefully and steam for 7 minutes. Test to see whether cakes are firm. If not, steam a little longer.

- Add remaining coconut cream mixture and kaffir lime leaves into containers. Steam until firm once more and turn out onto a serving plate. Serve as individual entrées on a bed of coriander leaves, garnished with fried onions.

Microwave Method

- Alternatively, cook in the microwave oven. Preheat a browning dish for 6 minutes on HIGH. Add oil and continue heating for another 30 seconds. Add curry paste and cover. Cook on HIGH for 1 minute, stirring at the end of the cycle.

- Slice fish into fine strips, carefully removing bones with tweezers.

- Mix egg with coconut cream and rice flour. Stir fish strips and other ingredients except kaffir lime leaves into two-thirds of the coconut cream mixture in a banana leaf-lined microwave-safe container. Cover with plastic wrap and cook on MEDIUM for 10 minutes or until firm. Tilt container to move mixture around so it cooks evenly.

- Add remaining coconut cream mixture and cook covered for 5 minutes on HIGH. Place under a grill to brown if preferred. Garnish with fried onions and coriander leaves.

Gaeng Khiaw Wan Kung (Green Curry Prawns)

Green curry is very spicy as the unseeded green chilli packs quite a punch. The coconut milk however reduces bite while imparting a creamy flavour to the curry.

Ingredients

Coconut cream (hua ka-thi)	125 ml
Green curry paste	2 Tbsp (see pg 306)
Prawn (shrimp) paste (kapee)	1 tsp
Green king or medium white prawns (shrimps)	600 g
Coconut milk (ka-thi)	250 ml
Pea aubergines (eggplant/brinjal)	150 g or about 20
Basil leaves	8, rolled up and finely shredded
Kaffir lime leaves (bai makrut)	5, rolled up and finely shredded
Fish sauce (nam pla)	3 Tbsp
Palm sugar (nam tan peep)	1$\frac{1}{2}$ tsp

Method

- Bring coconut cream to the boil and cook until oil comes to the surface. Add green curry paste and prawn paste and stir over heat until mixture smells aromatic.

- Add prawns and half the coconut milk. Turn up heat as prawns should cook fast.

- Add remaining coconut milk, basil and kaffir lime leaves. Reduce heat and simmer to reduce liquid.

- Add fish sauce and palm sugar. Adjust for taste and add salt or sugar if necessary. Remove from heat and serve.

Tom Kung Gathi (Chalie's Spicy Prawns in Coconut Milk)

This recipe comes from Chalie, who was a chef and teacher at the cooking school of the Bangkok Oriental Hotel.

Ingredients

Canned coconut cream (*hua ka-thi*)	425 g
Water	250 ml
Prawns (shrimps)	500 g
Red shallots	6 or 2 medium onions, roasted, peeled and pounded
Lemon grass (*ta-khrai*)	3 stalks, tender bulbous section, sliced
Kaffir lime leaves (*bai makrut*)	5, rolled up and finely shredded
Dried chillies	4, roasted
Fish sauce (*nam pla*)	3 Tbsp
Sugar	1 tsp
Tamarind paste (*ma khaam*)	2 tsp, mixed with 50 ml water, strained
Lime juice (*ma-nao*)	1 Tbsp

Garnish

Kaffir lime leaves (bai makrut)	3
Red chillies	3, sliced
Coriander (*phak chee*)	4 sprigs, chopped

Method

- Mix coconut cream with water to get 750 ml coconut milk.

- Shell, clean and devein prawns. Reserve shells and boil in 125 ml coconut milk. Discard shells.

- Heat stock in a saucepan and add 350 ml coconut milk and prawns. Add pounded shallots or onions, lemon grass, lime leaves and dried chillies to soup, taking care not to bring the soup to the boil.

- Season with fish sauce, sugar, tamarind liquid and lime juice. Stir well.

- Bring to the boil then turn heat down at once. Add remaining coconut milk and leave on low heat to prevent curdling.

- Garnish with kaffir lime leaves, chillies and coriander. Serve hot.

Pla Duk (Chalie's Spicy Catfish Salad)

This catfish salad is a wonderful, flamboyant and effective dish, both to cook and to serve. It should be piled high in a compote and topped with a red hot chilli.

Ingredients

Catfish (pla duk), mackerel (pla thu), sea perch or bass	400 g
Lime juice (ma-nao)	1 Tbsp
Ground black pepper	1 tsp
Cooking oil	125 ml

Salad

Fresh lemon juice	50 ml
Fish sauce (nam pla)	1 Tbsp
Sugar	1/4 tsp
Ground black pepper	a dash
Red shallots	6 or 2 medium brown onions, peeled and sliced
Lemon grass (ta-khrai)	5-cm length, peeled and sliced
Red chillies	6, sliced
Peanuts (groundnuts)	75 g, roasted and pounded
Unripe mango	1/2, small, peeled and shredded

Method

- Scale, gut and clean fish. Scrape flesh from fish. Mix flesh well with lime juice and pepper.

- Spread fish on a tray to dry for 1 hour on a hot day, or grill under medium heat for 8–10 minutes. Turn fish over at regular intervals to prevent burning.

- Heat oil in a wok until it smokes. Sprinkle a little fish into wok at a time and fry until crisp and brown. Remove and continue frying until all the fish is done.

- Prepare salad. Mix together lemon juice, fish sauce, sugar and pepper.

- Combine remaining salad ingredients and toss with lemon juice mixture. Crumble in crisp fish pieces and toss again. Serve.

Fluffy Fish Salad

Suchithra Bhamonpon runs the Tan Tawan Thai restaurant in Mosman. The restaurant has a great menu and a wonderful selection of salads. Suchithra's skills have come to her from three generations of Thai cooks in her family. This particular dish, which she serves in her restaurant, is tasty yet simple to make.

Ingredients

Canned tuna in oil	185 g, pounded and blended with some of the oil
Green mango or apple	1, medium-sized, about 200 g, peeled, chopped and mixed with 2 Tbsp lime juice
Spanish onion	1, peeled and thinly sliced
Whole cashew nuts	50 g, dry-roasted
Coriander (phak chee)	2 sprigs, chopped
Shallot	1, peeled and chopped
Dried chillies	3, dry-roasted and pounded
Lemon juice	extracted from 1 lemon
Fish sauce (nam pla)	to taste
Sugar	to taste

Dressing

Sugar	1 Tbsp or to taste
Vinegar	60 ml
Lemon juice	extracted from 1 lemon
Salt	to taste

Method

- Heat oil in a wok and deep-fry pounded tuna in small batches. Drain on absorbent paper.

- Prepare dressing. Combine vinegar, lemon juice and sugar. Stir to dissolve sugar. Add salt to taste.

- Toss other ingredients together with fried fish and dressing and serve immediately.

Kung Thien (Sour Charcoal Broiled Prawns)

There is a Thai saying that as soon as prawns (shrimps) 'see' fire, they are done. This is a reminder not to overcook prawns, since they tend to toughen when overcooked.

Ingredients

Lime juice (ma-nao)	extracted from 1 lime
Fish sauce (nam pla)	2 Tbsp
Red chillies	3, sliced
Garlic	3 cloves, peeled and chopped
Coriander (phak chee) leaves	25 g, chopped
King prawns (shrimps), lobster or spiny-clawed prawns (shrimps)	600 g, large
Dark soy sauce	1 Tbsp
Strong Chinese wine	1 Tbsp

Garnish

Lettuce leaves	5–6
Coriander (phak chee) leaves	75 g
Chilli flowers	5

Method

- Place lime juice, fish sauce, chilli, garlic and chopped coriander leaves in a small bowl and stir well. The sauce should be hot and salty.

- Wash prawns or lobster and brush shells, removing claws. Using sharp scissors, cut through shell to devein prawns. This will also allow the marinade to penetrate prawns.

- Brush dark soy sauce into prawn or lobster claws, touching fleshy areas. Pour Chinese wine over carefully so that it seeps into flesh.

- Place prawns or lobster under a grill and cook until shells are only just turning red. Place on a cutting board and carefully split prawns from the back, cutting in half lengthwise with shells still intact. Brush with sauce and return to grill.

- To serve, pour remaining sauce on prawns or lobsters and arrange on a bed of lettuce leaves, garnished with coriander leaves and chilli flowers.

Kung Khai Pu (Coral Prawns and Crab Roe)

Roe is an important ingredient used widely in Asian cooking. Like caviar, it can be prepared in various ways.

Ingredients

Prawns (shrimps) with roe	500 g
Crab roe or any fish roe	50 g, optional
Pork fat	30-cm strip, thinly sliced
Lime juice (ma-nao)	extracted from 1 lime
Garlic	2 cloves, peeled and diced
Lime rind	from 1 lime
Red chillies	2, seeded and diced
Fish sauce (nam pla)	1 Tbsp
Tamarind paste (ma khaam)	1 Tbsp, mixed with 50 ml water, strained
Peanuts (groundnuts)	50 g, roasted

Garnish

Coriander (phak chee) leaves	25 g, chopped

Method

- Carefully devein prawns by inserting a skewer between head and body. Turn each prawn over and gently release coral roe from near the head into a bowl. Add to crab or fish roe if using.

- Marinate prawns in pork fat and lime juice for 30 minutes. Drain prawns and reserve liquid. Add liquid to roe.

- Heat wok and place pork fat in for about 3 minutes, adding a little water to help the fat dry up and turn to oil more quickly. Allow oil level to reduce and retain crunchy pork fat bits in wok.

- Add diced garlic, stir to brown. Add roe and marinating liquid. Bring to the boil.

- Add prawns, lime rind, chillies and fish sauce. Stir to heat through. Add tamarind liquid and peanuts and transfer to a serving dish.

- Serve hot garnished with coriander leaves. This dish is sometimes served with crisp rice crusts.

Pla Kaphong (Broiled Sea Perch)

Ingredients

Sea perch, pomfret (pla jalamet), kingfish or whiting (pla sai)	600 g
Ginger	3–5 cm knob
Light soy sauce	2 Tbsp
Ground white pepper	1 tsp
Lime juice (ma-nao)	1 tsp
Banana leaf	1, large, scalded

Sauce

Ginger	3-cm knob, sliced
Tamarind paste (ma khaam)	2 Tbsp, mixed with 2 Tbsp water, strained
Chilli jam (nam prik paad)	½ tsp or 2 red chillies, sliced
Light soy sauce	½ Tbsp
Palm sugar (nam tan peep)	2 Tbsp

Method

- Scale, gut and clean fish well. Pat dry with absorbent paper. Make cuts in flesh.

- Prepare marinade by blending (processing) ginger to extract 1 Tbsp juice. Discard pulp. Mix with soy sauce, pepper and lime juice. Brush inside and outside of fish with marinade. Leave fish in marinade for at least 1 hour.

- Wrap fish in banana leaf then seal again in aluminium foil.

- Place fish parcel on grill and cook for 15–20 minutes, turning package over every 5 minutes, being careful not to break parcel. Remove foil and transfer fish in opened banana leaf onto a serving plate.

- Prepare sauce. Mix ingredients together and serve with fish or pour over fish before serving.

Kung Kamkraan Pla (Thai-Style Barbecued Prawn or Lobster)

Char-grilling or broiling encapsulates a whole range of Asian cooking done in open hearth type fires or *hibachi*-like stoves. You can also grill, bake or roast this recipe, using the sauces as basting fluid, ensuring that the lobster or prawn (shrimp) remains moist. Use either sauce for either recipe.

Ingredients

Spiny-clawed prawns (shrimps) or slipper lobsters	2, each 250 g or crayfish, lobster tails, Balmain bugs or 500 g yabbies
Garlic	4 cloves, peeled and pounded
Kaffir lime leaf (*bai makrut*)	1
Lemon grass (*ta-khrai*)	1 stalk, bulbous section bruised
Coconut cream (*hua ka-thi*)	1 Tbsp

Sauce for Spiny-clawed Prawns (Shrimps)

Lime juice (*ma-nao*)	2¹/₂ Tbsp
Fish sauce (*nam pla*)	1 Tbsp
Lemon grass (*ta-khrai*)	3 stalks, chopped
Red chillies	2, seeded and chopped
Red shallots	2, peeled and sliced
Coriander (*phak chee*) leaves	25 g, chopped
Sugar	1 tsp
Chilli jam (*nam prik paad*)	1 tsp
Mint leaves	50 g

Sauce for Slipper Lobster

Red chillies	10, seeded, if preferred
Garlic	15 cloves, peeled
Lime juice (*ma-nao*)	2 Tbsp
Fish sauce (*nam pla*)	2 Tbsp

Dipping Sauce

Chilli jam (*nam prik paad*)	2 tsp
Garlic	1 tsp, peeled, crushed
Lime juice (*ma-nao*)	1 Tbsp
Fish sauce (*nam pla*)	1 Tbsp

Method

- If using prawns, wash and scrub clean, then break or cut off feelers. Slowly cut or split backs to devein. If using lobster, clean shells with soft brush and split backs open with a knife. Open tails to expose flesh.

- Blend (process) garlic and kaffir lime leaf. Stuff blended mixture into the space between shell and flesh of prawns or brush onto lobster meat.

- Grill prawns or lobsters, turning over often to prevent burning on one side.

- When grilling lobster, use lemon grass to baste meat with coconut cream.

- For prawns, mix lime juice and fish sauce with lemon grass, chillies, shallots, coriander leaves, sugar and chilli jam. Stir well. Pour over grilled prawns and serve garnished with mint leaves.

- For lobster, blend chillies and garlic, and stir together with lime juice and fish sauce. Pour over lobster and serve.

- Mix additional dipping sauce ingredients together and serve separately.

Or Chien (Mussel or Oyster Omelette)

The omelette originates from South China though it has been adapted to Thai, Laotian and Malaysian tastes with local ingredients added. This is a version from Pattaya, cooked on a large, well-oiled griddle heated by a strong gas flame.

Ingredients

Rice flour	2½ Tbsp
Ground white pepper	1 tsp
Water	250 ml
Eggs	4
Salt	½ tsp
Light soy sauce	1 tsp
Cooking oil	3 Tbsp
Garlic	2 cloves, peeled and sliced
Red shallot	1, peeled and sliced
Small oysters (fresh or in brine)	300 g
Spring onion (scallion)	1, sliced, up to 3-cm of green portion
Coriander (phak chee) leaves	10, chopped
Fish sauce (nam pla)	1 Tbsp
Red chillies	3, sliced lengthwise

Dipping Sauce

Vinegar	50 ml
Sugar	1 tsp
Small red chillies	2

Method

- Mix rice flour with half the pepper and water to make a thick batter. Beat eggs with remaining pepper, salt and soy sauce.

- Heat oil in a shallow heavy-based frying pan (skillet) until moderately hot. Sauté garlic and shallot until brown, then add batter, swirling the pan so batter spreads evenly. Turn heat down so batter does not burn.

- Spread oysters on batter, add chopped spring onion and coriander leaves. Cook for about 1 minute until batter turns opaque.

- Turn heat up, then add beaten egg to pan, swirling again to spread egg around. Turn heat down so that batter does not burn.

- Using a spatula, spread the egg until it sets, then break up omelette and add fish sauce and chilli. Transfer onto a serving dish.

- Mix dipping sauce ingredients together and serve in separate bowl with omelette.

Hoi Nang (Salted Soy Bean Oysters)

In this recipe the taste of oysters is heightened with the salted soy beans and herbs.

Ingredients

Oysters or cockles	10, large
Salted soy beans	4 Tbsp, rinsed and mashed
Coriander (phak chee) root	1 tsp
Garlic	5 cloves, peeled and each clove halved
Young ginger	5-cm knob, peeled
Tender galangal (kha)	2-cm knob, peeled
Margarine	125 g

Garnish

Onions	2, peeled, sliced and crisp-fried

Method

- Wash oysters or cockles and open either by carefully prying open with a knife or by steaming. Alternatively, arrange on a plate and heat covered with plastic wrap for 3 minutes on HIGH in the microwave oven.
- Mince coriander root finely and blend (process) with garlic, ginger and galangal.
- Heat margarine in a pan and sauté mashed soy beans. Spoon a little onto each oyster or cockle, then top with blended paste. Arrange oysters or cockles on a baking dish and bake in an oven at 190°C for 5–10 minutes. Remove from heat.
- Garnish with crispy fried onions and serve hot on individual entrée plates. This recipe can also adapted for scallops with shells.

Tamarind and Flaked Salmon Rice Salad

Ingredients

Cooked white jasmine rice	750 g, cold
Lemon grass (ta-khrai)	6 stalks, finely chopped at bulbous end
Spanish onions or red onions	2, peeled and finely chopped
Smoked salmon or canned tuna	150 g, flaked
Salt	to taste
Cucumbers	2, halved, seeded and soft flesh removed
Tamarind paste (ma khaam)	2 Tbsp mixed with 100 ml water
Ground black pepper	to taste

Method

- Drizzle some cold water through rice and fork through to separate grains. Set aside.
- Toss ingredients together except for tamarind liquid and pepper. Add tamarind liduid to moisten and finish with pepper. Serve salad with cold ham.

Issan Kung Foi (Prawns from the Northeast)

This dish originates from Korat, Thailand. Similar dishes can be found all over the Pacific and even in Spain and Peru, as *ceviche*.

Ingredients

Cooking oil	1 Tbsp
Garlic	1 clove, peeled and chopped
Minced chicken	50 g
Salt	1/2 tsp
Ground white pepper	1/2 tsp
Light soy sauce	1 Tbsp
King prawns (shrimps) with roe	500 g
Lime juice *(ma-nao)*	125 ml
Kaffir lime leaves *(bai makrut)*	3, rolled up and finely shredded
Lemon grass *(ta-khrai)*	5-cm length, thinly sliced
Vietnamese mint leaves	25 g, chopped

Sauce

Tamarind paste *(ma khaam)*	1 Tbsp, mixed with 50 ml water, strained
Fish sauce *(nam pla)*	1 Tbsp
Chilli jam *(nam prik paad)*	1 tsp
Coconut cream *(hua ka-thi)*	50 ml
Peanuts (groundnuts)	1 Tbsp, roasted and chopped

Garnish

Lettuce heart	1, finely shredded

Method

- Heat oil in a pan and stir-fry garlic and minced chicken until brown. Season with salt, pepper and soy sauce. Reserve, draining off as much of the oil as you can spoon out.

- Clean, shell and devein prawns, leaving the coral-coloured prawn roe near the abdominal cavity. Pat dry with absorbent paper.

- Marinate prawns in lime juice for 10 minutes.

- Knead prawns a little to squeeze out lime juice, reserving the liquid that collects in the bowl. Place prawns in another bowl and toss with kaffir lime leaves, lemon grass, mint and cooked chicken. Stir until well mixed.

- Make up sauce from prawn juices, tamarind liquid, fish sauce, chilli jam and coconut cream.

- Just before serving, pour sauce over salad and top with chopped peanuts. Garnish with shredded lettuce.

La Tieng (Prawns in Egg Nets)

These Thai 'nets', made with curved fingers dipped into egg then trailed over a griddle, are light and dainty egg pancakes, holding elegantly cooked prawns (shrimps).

Ingredients

Coriander (*phak chee*) root	2 Tbsp
Black peppercorns	1 tsp
Garlic	1 clove, peeled
Cooking oil	50 ml
Prawns (shrimps)	400 g, shelled, deveined and finely chopped
Fish sauce (*nam pla*)	2 Tbsp
Sugar	¹/₂ tsp
Kaffir lime leaves (*bai makrut*)	2, rolled up and finely chopped
Eggs	5, lightly beaten

Garnish

Coriander (*phak chee*) leaves	125 g, chopped
Red serrano chillies	3–4, cut into thin strips
Pickled garlic heads	3–4, sliced
Kalamansi limes	6, cut into wedges

Method

- Cut up coriander root roughly and blend (process) with peppercorns and garlic into a fine paste.

- Heat 1 Tbsp oil in a pan and sauté paste until aromatic. Add prawns and stir to mix. Quickly add fish sauce, sugar and kaffir lime leaves. Stir until prawns are cooked and mixture is bound together. Set aside.

- To make nets, lightly grease pan with a piece of absorbent paper dipped in oil and heat until hot but not smoking. Curl up hand and dip into bowl of beaten egg. Scoop up egg and drop-spreading it in a rotary fashion over pan. Continue doing this until you have a web-like net the size of a dinner plate. Ensure that the edges are reinforced with more egg so net can be lifted out quickly with a spatula. Continue making more nets until egg is used up.

- Transfer each net to a flat plate and place 4–5 coriander leaves in the centre. Top with 1 Tbsp prawn mixture, a few chilli strips and pickled garlic slices. Fold net into an envelope and arrange on serving plate. Serve hot or cold with a wedge of lime.

Hoi Narn Rom (Red Curry Oysters)

This oyster dish originates from Pattaya.

Ingredients

Oysters or cockles	500 g
Garlic	3 cloves, peeled
Ginger	2-cm knob, peeled
Cooking oil	2 Tbsp
Red curry paste	1 Tbsp (see pg 305)
Chilli jam (nam prik paad)	1 Tbsp
Sugar	1½ Tbsp
Fish sauce (nam pla)	2 Tbsp
Dried prawn (shrimp) and chilli powder	1 tsp
Lime juice (ma-nao)	50 ml

Garnish

Red chillies	3–4
Kalamansi limes	2, cut into quarters

Method

- Make chilli flowers for garnish by slitting chillies lengthwise and soaking in iced water. Chillies should open up into flowers. Set aside.

- Clean oysters or cockles. Take out abdominal tracts of cockles. Wash and pat dry.

- Pound garlic and ginger roughly.

- Heat oil in a wok. Sauté garlic and ginger until golden. Quickly fry oysters or cockles for 3–4 minutes. Remove from heat and transfer to a plate.

- In the same oil, sauté red curry paste and chilli jam. Add sugar, fish sauce, dried prawn and chilli powder and lime juice.

- Stir to cook and dissolve sugar. Add salt if necessary. Return oysters or cockles to wok and stir to mix well. Transfer to a dish.

- Garnish with chilli flowers and lime wedges. Serve hot.

Kung Mangkon (Lobster and Prawn Salad)

Ingredients

Lobster or crayfish tail	600 g
Prawns (shrimps)	200 g
Mandarin orange	1
Pineapple	200 g, peeled and cut into cubes
Red or green grapes	75 g, seeded
Red or green apple	1/2, cored and sliced
Chinese cabbage	125 g, shredded
Red shallots	4, peeled, sliced and crisp-fried
Garlic	2 cloves, peeled, sliced and fried
Desiccated or fresh grated coconut (ma-phraao)	2 Tbsp, toasted

Salad Dressing

Lime juice (ma-nao)	125 ml
Fish sauce (nam pla)	1 Tbsp
Sugar	1 tsp
Salt	1/2 tsp
Red chillies	2

Method

- Clean lobster or crayfish by removing head and inserting a knife in between head and body. Cut towards tail fin. Shell and devein prawns.

- Steam lobster tails and prawns until flesh turns white. Remove lobster meat and cut into large chunks. (Do not oversteam or meat will toughen.) Refrigerate until needed.

- Peel mandarin orange, taking out each segment and cutting down the back of each to form circles. Place circles on a plate.

- Prepare salad dressing. Mix salad dressing ingredients in a bottle and refrigerate until needed. Shake before pouring over salad.

- In a clear glass salad bowl, mix lobster or crayfish and prawn meat, mandarin circles, pineapple, grapes, apple and Chinese cabbage. Pour on salad dressing. Sprinkle fried shallots, garlic and toasted coconut on top. Serve at once. Toss salad just before eating.

Microwave Alternative

- Shallots can be browned in the microwave. Slice thinly, cover with oil in microwave-safe bowl and cook for 10–12 minutes on HIGH or until onions turn brown. Quickly drain from hot oil onto absorbent paper. Repeat process to brown garlic, but heat only for 6 minutes. It is important to watch shallots and garlic after the initial 5 minutes of cooking as it is impossible to give correct times for microwave oven onion-frying as the water content of shallots differs.

Som Tam (Papaya and Prawn Salad)

A simple microwave recipe.

Ingredients

Prawns (shrimps)	200 g, shelled and deveined
White Chinese cabbage (*phak kaat khaao*)	1/2 head, finely shredded
Small raw papaya (pawpaw)	1, skinned and thinly sliced
Red or green chillies	2, seeded, if preferred and sliced
Firm tomatoes	3, thinly sliced into half-moon silvers
Sour starfruit (*belimbing*)	4, thinly sliced
Peanuts (groundnuts)	2 Tbsp, roasted and coarsely crushed

Dressing

Palm sugar (*nam tan peep*)	2 Tbsp
Lime (*ma-nao*) juice	extracted from 3 limes
Fish sauce (*nam pla*)	2 Tbsp

Garnish

Spring onions (scallions)	2, sliced
Red chillies	2, sliced

Method

- Prepare dressing. Mix palm sugar, lime juice and fish sauce, stirring well until sugar dissolves.

- Cook prawns in a microwave-safe bowl covered with plastic wrap for 2 minutes on HIGH. Alternatively cook prawns in a pan with 50 ml water until they turn pink. Drain well.

- Combine cabbage, papaya slices, chilli, tomatoes and sour starfruit in a bowl, reserving 2–3 tomato silvers for garnish. Transfer to a serving dish. Sprinkle prawns and peanuts on top.

- Pour dressing over and toss lightly. Garnish with spring onions, chilli slices and reserved tomato slices.

Thai Salads

The Thai salad uses home-grown herbs and edible roots, namely coriander, Vietnamese mint, basil, lemon grass, turmeric and galangal. It is a simple task to put these herbs together into an aromatic salad along with prawns (shrimps), fish or squid and tender shoots from the yam plant, mango tree or *champoo* (*jambu*, roseapple).

Here are two salads, one using lightly cooked prawns and the other raw marinated scallops or jellyfish.

Yam Lo Chien and Yam Meng Kaprun
(Scallop Salad and Jellyfish Salad)

Ingredients

Fresh or salted jellyfish	250 g or 400 g fresh scallops
Red shallots	2, peeled, sliced and crisp-fried
Garlic	3 cloves, peeled, thinly sliced and fried
Grapes	6–8, peeled, halved and seeded

Dressing

Lime juice (ma-nao)	3 Tbsp
Fish sauce (nam pla)	1 Tbsp
Red bird's eye chillies	3–4, seeded, if preferred and chopped

Garnish

Tomatoes (for jellyfish salad)	2, cut into cubes
Lettuce leaves (for scallop salad)	6–8

Method

- If using fresh jellyfish, cut into thin strips, immerse in boiling water, then remove and plunge immediately in cold water. Drain. This will cook and firm the jellyfish so that it becomes crunchy. Preserved salted jellyfish comes in thin strips in packets and may need to be soaked in water for a few minutes to remove excess brine.

- If using scallops, marinate in some lime juice for at least 20 minutes.

- Prepare dressing. Mix lime juice, fish sauce and chillies. Toss jellyfish or scallops in dressing.

- Arrange jellyfish on a plate surrounded by tomato cubes. Arrange scallops on a bed of lettuce. Top with browned shallots, garlic and grapes to serve.

Pla Muek (Stuffed Squid)

Ingredients

Ingredient	Amount
Squid with firm tubes	600 g
Coriander (*phak chee*) with roots	125 g
Spring onions (scallions)	2
Garlic	5 cloves, peeled and pounded
White peppercorns	12
Cooking oil	1 Tbsp
Crabmeat	125 g
Minced pork	150 g
Cabbage	15 g, shredded
Egg	1, beaten
Salt	to taste
Lime peel	1 Tbsp, shredded
Sugar	½ tsp
Light soy sauce	1 Tbsp

Method

- Clean squid (see pg 299), keeping tubes intact.

- Pluck coriander roots and wash off mud and hair. Wash leaves separately.

- Slice coriander leaves with spring onions.

- Blend (process) garlic, coriander root and peppercorns with oil. Add crabmeat, minced pork and cabbage. Add egg, salt, coriander leaves, spring onions and lime peel.

- Stuff mixture into squid tubes, with more in the centre than at the sides. Make sure tubes are not too full. Make a small snip at the end of the tubes so they will not burst when cooking. Sew or use bamboo skewers to secure the open ends.

- Brush sugar and soy sauce on squids. Bake in an oven at 180°C for 40 minutes, basting from time to time with the liquid that collects at the bottom of the dish.

- Remove from oven and slice. Serve hot with chilli jam, fish sauce and cut onions.

Hoy Mang Poo (Spicy Hot Mussels)

These tiny hot-pot helpings of mussels in their luminescent green shells sitting in a hot lemony sauce can easily become addictive.

Ingredients

Mussels	15–20
Galangal (kha)	6-cm knob, peeled
Lemon grass (ta-khrai)	5-cm length
Coriander (phak chee) root	1 Tbsp
Kaffir lime leaves (bai makrut)	2, shredded
Sweet basil leaves (bai horapha)	25 g, coarsely broken
Chicken or fish stock	250 ml
Red chillies	4, seeded, if preferred and lightly crushed
Red shallots	5, peeled and coarsely pounded
Garlic	3 cloves, peeled and coarsely pounded
Fish sauce (nam pla)	3 Tbsp
Lime juice (ma-nao)	2 Tbsp
Cornflour (cornstarch)	1 Tbsp, mixed with 3 Tbsp water

Dipping Sauce

Lime juice (ma-nao)	2 Tbsp
Fish sauce (nam pla)	3 1/2 Tbsp
Red chillies	10, crushed
Garlic	7 cloves, peeled and crushed
Sugar	1/2 Tbsp

Garnish

Green chilli	1, sliced

Method

- Wash mussels in their shells, pulling at the beards until they are removed. Scrub shells well. Rinse in several changes of water.

- Blend (process) galangal with lemon grass and coriander root until mushy. Set aside.

- Prepare dipping sauce. Mix lime juice and fish sauce. Add chillies, garlic and sugar. Mix and pour into small individual bowls. Set aside.

- Place mussels in an earthenware pot or a heavy-based non-aluminium pan with blended ingredients, kaffir lime leaves, sweet basil leaves, stock, chillies, shallots, garlic, fish sauce and lime juice. Simmer for 5 minutes until mussels open.

- Remove mussels and keep warm. Allow sauce to reduce. Simmer for another 5 minutes to thicken sauce. Stir in cornflour mixture. Bring to the boil and stir. Add more stock if you prefer it thinner.

- Pour thickened sauce over mussels and give it a good stir to heat through. Serve hot with dipping sauce and freshly ground pepper. Garnish with green chilli.

Microwave Method

- Place mussels and with blended ingredients, kaffir lime leaves, sweet basil leaves, stock, chillies, shallots and garlic in a microwave-safe dish. Cover partly with plastic to prevent splattering. Cook for 8 minutes on MEDIUM until mussels open.

- Remove plastic. Stir once and ladle fish sauce and lime juice on mussels.

- Stir in cornflour mixture. Cook for 1 minute on HIGH. Stir and serve hot.

Pla Samli (Crispy Freshly Dried Fish)

It is a common sight to find fish pieces, prawn (shrimp) paste or sour mango pieces drying on zinc sheets in the backyards of homes in Thailand or in some parts of Malaysia. In a humid climate, mould grows easily, so sun-drying is the obvious solution to keeping food well-preserved.

Ingredients

Trevally, kingfish or tailor fish	600 g, scaled, gutted and cleaned
Lime juice *(ma-nao)*	5 Tbsp
Cooking oil	750 ml
Tomatoes	3, thinly sliced
Red shallots	2 or 1 medium brown onion, peeled and shredded
Green mango	1, skinned and shredded
Chilli jam *(nam prik paad)*	½ tsp
Fish sauce *(nam pla)*	4 Tbsp
Palm sugar *(nam tan peep)*	2 tsp

Garnish

Red shallots	3, peeled, sliced and crisp-fried

Method

- Using a sharp knife, slit fish from belly upwards then down so that fish is cut through but joined at the other side like a book. Open out fish and remove central bone if possible. Turn fish over flat and score flesh.

- Rub lime juice on fish and lay fish out on a metal tray in the sun to dry for 5 hours at least. Reserve excess lime juice. Turn fish over often so both sides will dry evenly. Alternatively, dry in an oven at 100°C.

- Heat oil in a large shallow wok—the oil should fill one third of the wok. Carefully lay fish flat in hot oil and fry until golden and crisp. Carefully turn fish over and fry the other side. Remove and drain on a bed of sliced tomatoes.

- Mix shredded shallots or onions, mango and chilli jam with fish sauce, remaining lime juice and palm sugar. Stir well. Pour over fish and garnish with fried shallots.

- Serve while fish is hot and crispy.

Paad Priew Wan Kung (Sweet, Sour and Hot Prawns)

An early treatise on Chinese cooking mentions five flavours: sweet, sour, salty, bitter and pungent. These flavours found their way into Thai cooking with the migration of the Chinese to the Kingdom of Siam, giving Thai food its exquisite flavours today.

Ingredients

Green prawns (shrimps)	500 g, medium
Rice wine	1 Tbsp
Rice flour	3 Tbsp
Cooking oil	250 ml

Sauce

Tamarind paste (ma-khaam)	2 Tbsp, mixed with 125 ml water, strained
Cornflour (cornstarch)	1 tsp
Vinegar	1 tsp
Fish sauce (nam pla)	2 Tbsp
Sugar	1 Tbsp
Chilli powder	1/2 tsp
Sesame seeds	1 tsp, roasted
Red shallots	6, peeled, sliced and fried
Garlic	3 cloves, peeled, sliced and fried

Garnish

Red shallots	3, peeled, sliced and crisp-fried

Method

- Clean and wash prawns, removing feelers and heads. Leave shells and tails intact. Devein by cutting carefully through shell on back. Soak prawns in rice wine for 15 minutes.

- Roll prawns in rice flour and coat well.

- Heat oil in a wok until it smokes. Deep-fry a few prawns at a time until crisp and golden. Drain on absorbent paper.

- Prepare sauce. Mix tamarind liquid, cornflour, vinegar, fish sauce and sugar. Add chilli powder, sesame seeds, shallots and garlic. Stir well and cook on low heat until sauce thickens. Serve in individual bowls for dipping prawns into. Garnish with crisp-fried shallots.

Variation

- This dish can be easily made using fried fish with the same sauce. Use pomfret (pla jalamet) or whiting (pla sai). Prepare fish by scaling, gutting and washing clean. Dry with absorbent paper and dust with rice flour.

- Fry fish in hot oil and serve with sauce as above.

Myanmar

More than Mohinga

> "On the road to Mandalay
> Where the flyin' fishes play,
> An' the dawn comes up like thunder
> outer China 'crost the Bay"
>
> *R. Kipling, MANDALAY*

Myanmar is a land of pagodas, saffron-robed Buddhist monks, light amber teak and tropical jungles covering verdant hillsides that slope in emerald steps until they plunge into the sea. A land of the barren, pitted Shan plateau traversed by hill tribes and opium poppies; of gems and elephants and long meandering rivers. It has a mysterious north, excitingly untouched as very little foreign intervention has been allowed in the years since World War II.

The food of Myanmar food is delicately spiced with garlic, onions, fish and prawn (shrimp) pastes, sesame oil and chickpea flour, ingredients common to its neighbouring countries, yet the taste is exclusively Burmese in character.

Myanmar's major rivers, which run parallel from north to south, terminating in large silt-laden deltas along its long coastline, provide an interesting variety of seafood and freshwater fish for the Burmese. A great deal of this seafood is preserved by sun-drying and by brining into the golden fish sauces or pastes *(nga pi)*. Seafood is a popular alternative to chicken and pork and most food is cooked with either vegetable or thin sesame oil.

The Indianisation of mainland Southeast Asia, begun long ago, intensified during the British colonial period in the mid-1800s, when Indians were encouraged to migrate to Southeast Asia with the promise of employment or business. This accounts for the use of Indian ingredients like chickpea flour and curry in Myanmar. Mohinga, a rich and creamy fish gravy eaten with many accompaniments, echoes the taste of Thai or Malaysian *laksas*. The use of river-bred hilsa (shad) as a preferred fish not only reflects common fishing areas within India but also Bengali eating preferences. Both in Myanmar and Bengal, people share beliefs that fish is a nerve tonic.

Most Burmese recipes call for the use of coconut milk and copious use of garlic, onions and ginger which are ground together into a paste and then stir-fried in some oil for a length of time (about 15 minutes) so that the whole mixture becomes thick and aromatic, separating from the oil. This is an essential first step in all Burmese cooking and it should be noted that if the oil starts to reduce and the mixture should catch at the bottom of the pan, the heat should be lowered and the mixture scraped from the side and bottom of the pan, a little bit of oil poured around the edges of the pan and the mixture stirred until the oil separation stage is reached. Only when this occurs should the rest of the ingredients be added.

Burmese cooking styles follow traditional methods and is family-oriented. Fish may be steamed all day until the bones become gelatinous. Whole families may be involved in making a stock of spicy fish crackers and banana stems are patiently soaked then chopped to get at the heart, transparent and bursting with a million sticky threads. When made into a salad with diced onions and chilli, the banana stem is believed to aid digestion and cure flatulence.

The Burmese eat all their meals either with rice or noodles. Usually, a hot clear soup is served in a large bowl and placed in the centre of the table. Family members serve themselves from this bowl, ladling a portion into their smaller individual bowls. There are other meat, fish and regular dishes, all placed on the table at the same time, the seafood and fish curried or added to vegetable, with fresh fruits to follow at the end. Food is either eaten with the fingers or with fork and spoon rather than with fork and knife. Fingers are rinsed in gold and black lacquered bowls of jasmine-spiced water and guests serve themselves during the meal, choosing from the many garnishes that follow any typical Burmese meal.

These garnishes—chopped mint, crisp-fried onions, hot chilli sauces or soy sauce, ground coriander leaves, crisp-fried dried fish cubes and spicy Burmese *Balachaung*—are part of the meal. This makes it possible for each person's individual taste to be catered for. One can add a bit of prawn paste to this mouthful or a crisp onion to the other, a sharper mint flavour to that soup or some chilli to a pinch of another vegetable dish. Each mouthful is different and enables the diner to experience the whole gamut of Burmese flavours in any one set meal.

Nga Nun Mie Kin (Easy Burmese Baked Crabs)

Ingredients

Mud crabs	4, medium, about 2 kg
Salt	to taste
Ground white pepper	to taste
Paprika	1 tsp
Ground cloves	1 tsp
Prawns (shrimps)	125 g, small, shelled and deveined
Onions	2, medium, peeled and sliced
Red chillies	2, seeded, if preferred and chopped
Eggs	2, beaten
Cooking oil	1 Tbsp
Breadcrumbs	125 g

Method

- Prepare crabs (see pg 298). Steam crabs for 5 minutes until claws turn pink. Reserve stock that accumulates on the steaming plate. Cool crabs and pick out flesh, taking care not to break shells. Remove gristle. Season crabmeat with salt, pepper, paprika and ground cloves.

- Chop prawn meat into tiny pieces.

- Heat oil in a wok and fry onion slices until golden. Add prawns and mix well until they turn red and are cooked. Add 2 Tbsp stock from steaming crabs, crabmeat and chillies. Mix well with cooked prawns.

- Remove mixture from wok and cool. Mix in half portion of beaten egg.

- Clean crab shells and fill with mixture. Brush exposed mixture with remaining beaten egg and scatter breadcrumbs on top. Bake filled shells in an oven at 180°C for 30 minutes until brown. Alternatively, place under a hot grill for 3–5 minutes. Serve hot.

Balachaung (Prawn Appetiser)

Ingredients

Dried prawns (shrimps)	250 g, washed
Ground turmeric (fa nwin)	1 tsp
Vegetable oil	350 ml
Sesame oil	1 tsp
Red chillies	3 or 1 tsp chilli powder
Ginger	5-cm knob, peeled
Lime juice	2$\frac{1}{2}$ Tbsp
Dried prawn (shrimp) paste (nga pi)	50 g
Salt	to taste
Ground white pepper	to taste

Garnish

Brown onion	1, large, peeled and sliced
Garlic	10 cloves, peeled and sliced

Method

- Pat-dry washed dried prawns with a towel. Dry roast in a clean wok then mix with ground turmeric.

- Mix vegetable and sesame oil and heat in a wok. Fry onions and garlic for garnish. Drain on absorbent paper towel and set aside.

- In same oil, fry prawns until crispy. Drain prawns together with dregs and set aside.

- Pound chilli into a powder. Blend (process) ginger. Add chilli powder and ginger to lime juice.

- Remove oil from wok and dry-fry prawn paste in oily wok for 1 minute until fragrant. Add blended chilli, ginger and lime juice. Stir to combine. Add crispy prawns to the mixture and add salt and pepper to taste.

- Transfer to a serving dish and garnish with fried onion and garlic. If preferred, add 1 Tbsp lime juice before serving.

Ohn-No Nga Kyaw Hin (Burmese Garlic Fish)

Ingredients

Bream, snapper or ocean trout	1 kg, scaled, gutted and cleaned
Garlic	6 cloves, peeled and thinly sliced
Fish sauce *(ngan pya ye)*	80 ml
Cooking oil	4 Tbsp
Red chilli	¹/₂, chopped
Lemon juice	extracted from ¹/₂ lemon
Sugar	2 Tbsp
Cornflour (cornstarch)	1 Tbsp, mixed with 125 ml water

Garnish

Lemon	1, cut into wedges
Vietnamese mint	1–2 sprigs, shredded
Garlic	3 large cloves, peeled, chopped and fried

Method

- Rub fish with some garlic slices. Season inside of fish with 1 Tbsp fish sauce.

- Heat oil in a wok until it smokes and slowly fry fish and half the remaining garlic slices. Turn fish over when browned and lower heat. Fry until fish is golden. Drain on absorbent paper and transfer to serving plate.

- In a saucepan, combine remaining garlic slices with chilli, lemon juice, sugar and remaining fish sauce. Add cornflour mixture and bring to the boil. Allow to thicken and pour over fish. Garnish with lemon wedges, Vietnamese mint and crispy garlic flakes to serve.

Ohn-No Nga Soak Hin (Fish Cakes in Cream)

Burmese fish cakes make a delicious entrée before a dinner of fish. They are simple to make and all you need to remember is to balance the liquid and flour content until you get a substance that leaves the sides of the bowl clean and can be made into fish croquettes easily.

Ingredients

Red chillies	3, seeded, if preferred and sliced
Garlic	3 cloves, peeled
Ginger	3-cm knob, peeled
Onion	1, peeled
Lemon grass (zabalin)	1 stalk
Chilli powder	1 tsp
Snapper or mackerel (nga yahn) fillets	500 g
Rice flour	4 Tbsp
Vegetable or sesame oil	450 ml
Coconut cream	250 ml

Garnish

Onions	2, peeled and thinly sliced
Coriander (cilantro) leaves	25 g, chopped

Method

- Blend (process) chillies, garlic, ginger, onion and white part of lemon grass. Add chilli powder. Blend with fish and half the rice flour. Mix thoroughly.

- Divide mixture and shape into croquettes or cakes. If mixture is too wet to shape well, add 1–2 tsp more rice flour. Roll each croquette in a plate of remaining rice flour to coat before frying.

- Heat oil in a wok until very hot. Quickly fry 3–4 croquettes at a time until golden. Drain well.

- In the same oil, fry half the sliced onions and reserve for garnish.

- Cool and slice fish croquettes into thin slices using a sharp knife.

- Heat coconut cream in a saucepan to just below its boiling point but do not boil. Lay fish slices in heated coconut cream and cover. Allow fish to steam gently in coconut cream for 5 minutes.

- Serve garnished with raw onion slices and coriander leaves.

Mohinga (Burmese Fish Soup)

To make this dish, it is important to first obtain a banana stem and prepare it before starting other preparations. Bamboo shoots are an acceptable substitute.

Ingredients

Banana stem	40-cm long, about 500 g or 500 g bamboo shoots
Fish fillet	700 g
Ground turmeric	1/2 tsp
Lemon grass (zabalin)	3 stalks
Water	500 ml
Red chillies	4
Ginger	2-cm knob, peeled
Garlic	6 cloves, peeled
Oil	1 Tbsp vegetable oil mixed with 1 Tbsp sesame oil
Dried prawn (shrimp) paste (nga pi)	1 Tbsp, roasted
Onions	7, medium, peeled and thinly sliced
Chickpea flour	2 Tbsp mixed with 1 Tbsp rice flour
Chicken stock	500 ml
Dried prawns (shrimp)	2 Tbsp
Salt	to taste
Ground white pepper	to taste
Fish sauce (ngan pya ye)	1 tsp
Thin rice noodles	500 g

Garnish

Coriander (cilantro) leaves	6–7 sprigs, chopped
Hardboiled eggs	2, shelled and sliced
Lemon	1, cut in wedges
Dried chillies	3, pounded

Method

- If using banana stems, remove outer layers and soak tender inner stem in salted water for 3 hours. Slice banana stem or bamboo shoot thinly across the grain.

- Brush fish with turmeric.

- Remove leaves from lemon grass, use thick bulb only. Place in water and bring to the boil. Add fish and cook until opaque. Flake fish if desired. Set fish and soup aside. Remove lemon grass and slice.

- Blend (process) chillies, ginger and garlic.

- Heat oil in a deep saucepan. Fry blended mixture, shrimp paste, lemon grass and sliced onion until golden. Add fish and soup, and banana stem or bamboo shoot. Cover and simmer for about 20 minutes to reduce.

- Meanwhile mix chickpea flour to a smooth paste with 125 ml water.

- Add chicken stock, dried prawns, fish fillet and flour paste to simmering fish soup in saucepan. Stir until stock thickens. Leave simmering to heat evenly. Season to taste with salt, pepper and fish sauce.

- Cook noodles as directed on packet.

- Serve hinga or soup, noodles and garnishes in separate bowls. Guests use smaller bowls and help themselves to noodles, soup and prepared garnishes.

The Philippines

Food Talks

> " ...As a gift it is always proper, it says the right things. It curries favour, stores up goodwill. "
>
> *Doreen Fernandez, SARAP*

The 7,000 islands of the Philippines, a beautiful tropical setting surrounded by abundant waters, stretches of sandy beaches and thick tropical forests have made Filipinos dependent on the environment for their food. One is never far away from the water in the Philippines. There are more coastlines accessible to the Filipino than in any other nation of its size.

No wonder then that most Filipino dishes revolve around fish and seafood. Not only do Filipinos enjoy or prefer seafood, they savour every morsel—some relish the flesh, some the fins, yet others the dark flesh adjacent to the jawbone. All shapes, sizes and colours of crabs are eaten, the most unusual of all being the tiny soft-shelled *talangka* whose delicate orange fat is prised from under the shell and eaten as a delicacy. The golden snail, the juicy crustacea, the *kapiz*, the shark, the lobster, the squid, the octopus and even the king or robber crab are all favoured foodstuffs. All things unusual are savoured and served up as delicacies by the Filipino from the *barrio* (village) or the sophisticate from the city.

Chinese food, because of its ease of preparation and the fact that it was less costly, found its way to the ordinary homes of the Filipinos, where it is widely adapted and prepared today. The Chinese influence on Filipino cuisine has been most obvious in the introduction of the *panci* or noodles in its many forms. These noodles were adopted to local tastes. For instance, Southeast Asians will recognise the Filipinisation of the Chinese names in *bihon (beehoon), sotanghon, mami, lomi lumpia* (spring rolls) *siopao* and *siomai* (dim sum dishes) or *mahmee, lohmee, siew paw* and *siew mai.*

The Spanish influence is also present though because of the elaborate preparation required and the many imported products, Spanish-influenced cuisine is today eaten during festivals and celebrations and in formal dinners. The American influence, too, is evident in the legacy of fast food chains and the instant food markets found in urban and even rural Philippines.

Together with these external influences, a thriving native fare exists, where subtle herbs like lemon grass or turmeric and galangal are mingled with seafood, where *camias* (sour starfruit) or tamarind leaves are used for souring broths and refreshing the fresh raw dishes in *kinilaw* (a raw dish similar to *ceviche*). Rice is the staple and acts as a bland foil for the sour sinigang or the salty *bagoong* (fish paste), for the hot peppers or the subtle *sawsawan* (sauces). Rice is boiled, or flavoured and steamed into rice cakes; rice washings are used to thicken *sinigang* soups and to make flat white wafer-thin *keping* or translucent wafers like rice *pappadams*. Fish and seafood are kept simple and eaten without marring their freshness or natural tastes. Heavy sauces are not part of

Filipino cooking; rather seafood is eaten raw—as in oysters—or marinated in souring kalamansi limes or *camias*—as in *kinilaw* or *sinigang*—or steamed as in *halabos na hipon* or roasted over coals or open fires.

An important element in Filipino cooking is the *sawsawan* (sauce). The diner is invited to participate and to add to the main dish with the provision of sauce dishes. If the diner so wishes, he could add a drop of soy sauce or a drop of vinegar or garlic to the dish. The simplicity of native cuisine allows for the inclusion of *sawsawan* and each spoonful could become a different flavour or combination, depending on individual tastes.

Open-air markets where seafood is sold fresh each day and night are popular with Filipinos and tourists. There are large, barn-like seafood markets where fresh lobsters, crabs, prawns (shrimps) and a good variety of fish sit on crushed ice. Customers make their choices and take them to one end of the market where food stalls await to prepare and cook them into a succulent meal.

The Filipinos are a warm and spontaneous people who enjoy entertaining family and friends. Nothing is too difficult to do for a guest—when they invite someone to a meal, they give of all they have, even slaughtering the last chicken or using up the last stocks of rice and onions in the kitchen. Parties are large, happy affairs. Being an artistic and sensitive people, food is laid aesthetically on tables, with cutlery and crockery and beautifully carved fruit and vegetables as garnishes.

Filipinos eat either with fork and spoon or with their fingers, but whenever fingers are used, especially for fish, the food is pinched delicately between thumb and finger, dipped in sauces and eaten with morsels of rice.

Kinilaw na Bangus (Raw Fish Salad)

Kinilaw is an uncooked fish dish and therefore requires very fresh fish. Any delicate fish or crab may be used in place of milk fish. This dish is popular on the islands of Samar, Leyte, Bohol, Cebu and Panay. The souring (acidifying) ingredient is usually kalamansi lime juice but sometimes mango juice, *camias* fruit or vinegar may be used.

Ingredients

Milk fish *(bangus)*, pomfret or perch fillets	400 g
Vinegar	250 ml
Ginger	3-cm knob, peeled and shredded
Onions	3, medium, peeled and finely sliced
Salt	2$\frac{1}{2}$ tsp
Freshly ground black pepper	$\frac{1}{4}$ tsp
Kalamansi lime juice	extracted from 2 large kalamansi limes
Lettuce *(letsugas)* leaves	6, small, cup-shaped

Garnish

Red chillies *(sili labuyo)*	3, chopped

Method

- Skin fillets with a sharp knife, then wash and cut into 5-cm cubes. Add half the vinegar and leave for a few minutes, then gently squeeze vinegar out. This will firm the fillets.

- Mix fillet cubes with ginger, onions, salt and pepper in a bowl. Add remaining vinegar and lime juice and mix well. Refrigerate for at least 1 hour.

- Drain some of the vinegar off before spooning salad into lettuce cups. Garnish with chopped chillies and serve as an entrée.

Ginataang Lapu Lapu (Filipino Coconut Fish Stew)

Add chilli to this blend of spices, herbs and fish and it could almost pass off as the South Indian fish *moulie* (see pg 204).

Ingredients

Grouper *(lapu lapu)* or other fish fillets	350 g
Coconut milk	500 ml
Water	250 ml
Kalamansi lime juice	2 Tbsp
Lemon grass	1 stalk
Butter	1 Tbsp
Filipino or Chinese sausages	3–4, thinly sliced
Garlic	2 cloves, peeled and sliced
Onion	1, peeled and sliced
Sweet potatoes	150 g, boiled, peeled and cubed
Dried prawns (shrimps) with chilli	1 Tbsp
Salt	to taste
Ground white pepper	to taste

Garnish

Mint leaves	3–4 sprigs, shredded
Kalamansi limes	2, cut in half

Method

- Put fillets in a saucepan with half the coconut milk and water. Bring to the boil, then add lime juice and stir. Do not over boil. Remove from heat after about 6 minutes when fish turns white. Cool fish and flake meat. Reserve stock.

- Mash bulbous part of lemon grass slightly with the back of a knife. Set aside.

- Heat butter in another saucepan and sauté sausages, garlic and onion until brown.

- Add sweet potatoes, quickly stir-fry until golden. Do not mash.

- Add fish and dried prawns with chilli. Stir quickly.

- Gradually add reserved fish stock and simmer for about 5 minutes with mashed lemon grass. Add remaining coconut milk and stir gently to mix well. Allow to cook slowly for 5 minutes. Add salt and pepper to taste and remove from heat.

- Garnish with mint leaves and kalamansi lime halves. Serve hot with rice.

Kilawin sa Manga (Fish and Mango Salad)

If you are unable to obtain mango or guava, improvise with kiwi fruit or tangerine slices. In any case, the sour-sweet taste will need to be simulated. I serve this salad with a dish of Chinese crystal prawns—the combination is colourful and stunning.

Ingredients

Milk fish *(bangus)* or white pomfret *(duhay)* fillets	200 g
Salt	1/2 tsp
Ground white pepper	1/2 tsp
Orange	1
Almost ripe mangoes	3, medium
Kiwi fruit or ripe guavas	2
Kalamansi lime	1
Coconut cream	125 ml

Garnish

Lemon rind	from 1 lemon

Method

- Clean and wash fish fillets. Place in a bowl and cook in the microwave oven for 3–5 minutes on HIGH. Alternatively, bring to the boil with water, salt and pepper. Remove from heat after about 5 minutes, as soon as fish is cooked.

- Flake cooked fish with fork or with fingers into a bowl, discarding skins if any.

- Peel orange and divide into segments. Peel off thin membrane from each segment. Submerge lemon rind and orange peel in iced water to create curls for garnish.

- Wash and pare skin off mangoes. Cut flesh into thin diagonal slices. Discard seeds.

- Peel kiwi fruit or guavas. Slice into lengths. Squeeze lime juice over fruit to prevent from darkening.

- Gently toss fish and fruit together, being careful not to mash fruit. Pour coconut cream into mixture. Add salt to taste, then refrigerate.

- Garnish with lemon rind and orange peel curls. Serve with rice.

Ginataang Hipon (Prawns in Coconut)

Ingredients

Prawns (shrimps)	500 g, shelled if preferred and deveined
Young green coconut	1
Cooking oil	2 Tbsp
Garlic	3 cloves, sliced
Red shallots	4 or 2 medium brown onions, peeled and sliced
Ginger	3-cm knob, peeled and sliced
Red chillies (*sili labuyo*)	3, seeded, if preferred and chopped
Coconut cream	250 ml
Salt	1 tsp

Garnish

Desiccated coconut	25 g, toasted, optional

Method

- Wash prawns in 450 ml water and $1/2$ tsp salt. Drain.

- Cut open coconut and, using a butter curler, peel out strips of flesh. Measure 75 g of coconut flesh and set aside.

- Heat oil in a wok and sauté garlic, shallots and ginger until golden.

- Add chillies and lower heat. Add coconut cream and prawns and simmer. Add $1/4$ tsp salt and coconut flesh. Stir gently. Add salt to taste.

- Garnish with toasted desiccated coconut (optional) or with a few strips of coconut flesh. Serve hot with rice, steamed cabbage or stir-fried water convolvulus.

Variation

- Add green or ripe mangoes (skinned and sliced) just before coconut flesh is added, or use it to replace coconut flesh completely.

Inihaw na Tambakol (Roasted Tuna Jaws)

Barbecued fish on coals or *inihaw* using giant yellow fin tuna jaws which I relished at Millie Reyes' restaurant, Aling Asiang, in Makati, Manila. Tuna jaws can be obtained from large fish markets. They are big fish and will need to be cleaned and cut to size by the fishmonger.

Ingredients

Garlic	5 cloves, peeled and crushed
Red shallots	10, peeled and crushed
Dark soy sauce	125 ml
Light soy sauce	125 ml
Freshly ground black pepper	to taste
Yellow fin tuna jaw	1, about 1 kg or use tuna, mackerel or cod cutlets
Salt	to taste

Vinegar Sauce

Vinegar	50 ml
Sugar	1 tsp
Red shallots	2, peeled and finely sliced
Red chillies (*sili labuyo*)	2, seeded, if preferred and finely sliced

Garlic-chilli Sauce

Garlic	3 cloves, peeled and mashed
Chilli sauce	50 ml
Sugar	$^1/_2$ tsp

Method

- In a bowl, combine garlic, shallots, dark and light soy sauce and pepper to make marinade. Sit fish in marinade for at least 2 hours.

- Prepare vinegar sauce. Mix vinegar and sugar over heat until sugar melts. Remove from heat and stir in shallots and chillies. Transfer to a sauce bowl.

- Prepare garlic-chilli sauce. Combine garlic, chilli sauce and sugar. Mix well. Transfer to a sauce bowl.

- Place fish on a barbecue grill and smoke slowly. Turn over and baste with marinade. Repeat for about 30 minutes until fish is cooked. Add salt and pepper to taste.

- If using yellow fin tuna jaw, use a large cleaver and carefully chop fish jaw into pieces. Serve hot with vinegar and garlic-chilli sauce (*sawsawan*).

Lapu Lapu Relleno (Stuffed Deboned Fish)

This dish requires the skill of a carver as well as that of a chef, for the central bone has to be expertly sliced out through the stomach and the resulting void stuffed. An easy fish to debone and stuff would be the milk fish *(bangus)*.

Ingredients

Grouper *(lapu lapu)*, milk fish *(bangus)* or any white-fleshed fish	600 g
Kalamansi lime juice	extracted from 3 kalamansi limes
Cooking oil	1 Tbsp
Garlic	2 cloves, peeled and sliced
Brown onions	2, peeled and sliced
Minced pork	125 g
Hardboiled eggs	2, shelled and roughly mashed
Stuffed green or black olives	6, chopped
Plain (all-purpose) flour	75 g
Ground white pepper	to taste
Salt	to taste

Spanish Tomato Sauce

Olive oil	3 Tbsp
Garlic	2 cloves, peeled and blended
Onion	1, peeled and diced
Tomato sauce	50 ml

Garnish

Parsley	1 sprig, chopped
Stuffed green or black olives	6, chopped

Method

- Clean, scale and gut fish. Remove gills. Pound fish carefully to soften flesh and break bones so they can be removed easily. Carefully scrape flesh around stomach with a sharp knife to remove spine bone. If some flesh comes out with the bone, remove it as well. Keep skin, head and tail intact and soak fish in 50 ml lime juice to firm fish skin.

- Heat oil and fry garlic and onions until brown. Add minced pork and brown well, then add mashed hardboiled eggs, chopped olives and 1 Tbsp lime juice. Remove from heat and season with pepper and salt to taste.

- Stuff minced pork mixture into fish and shape fish as it is filled. Sew up stuffed cavity using a fine needle and thread. Be careful not to pull too hard or the skin could tear. Alternatively, use a bamboo skewer to seal cavity.

- Mix flour with $1/4$ tsp salt and $1/2$ tsp pepper and coat fish. Place fish on a greased baking dish.

- Prepare Spanish tomato sauce. Heat olive oil and brown garlic. Add diced onions and pour in tomato sauce. Remove from heat.

- Pour sauce over fish and bake in an oven at 180°C for 30 minutes or until done. Remove fish from oven and brown under a hot grill for 6–8 minutes.

- Serve hot, garnished with chopped parsley and olives.

Sinigang (Sour Fish Soup)

This versatile recipe is often adapted to include fish or prawns. Its characteristic sour broth is achieved with the addition of ripe guavas, sour starfruit *(camias)*, green tamarind pods or the juice of kalamansi limes and tomatoes. It is a perfect meal to serve with rice.

Ingredients

Milk fish *(bangus)*, pomfret *(duhay)*, perch, trevally *(talakitok)*, prawns (shrimps), cockles, clams or lobsters	600 g
Limes	2 or 4 sour mango pieces
Sour starfruit, tamarind pods or guava	5
Water from washing rice	1.25 litres
Tomatoes	2, cut into quarters
Aubergine (eggplant/brinjal)	1
Water convolvulus	3 stalks
Salt	to taste
Ground white pepper	to taste

Method

- Gut, scale and clean fish, then cut into 5-cm pieces.

- Squeeze limes for juice or cut up sour mango pieces.

- Boil sour starfruit, tamarind pods or guava in one-fifth of the water from washing rice until soft. Mash softened fruits in the water and set aside.

- Place mashed fruit and water in an earthenware pot or non-aluminium saucepan over low heat. Keep temperature constant by adding ingredients slowly, one at a time. Add remaining rice water, then lime juice or sour mangoes, then tomatoes and then aubergine. Cook for 12–15 minutes until vegetables are soft.

- Slowly add fish or other seafood and cook for 5 minutes.

- Finally add water convolvulus and salt and pepper to taste. Cook for about 2 minutes and remove from heat. Serve hot with rice.

Bangus en Tocho (Nora's Fish with Salted Beans)

Nora Daza is a renowned chef in the Philippines. She was among the first to standardise and publish Filipino recipes.

Ingredients

Milk fish (bangus), bream or silver dory fillets	600 g, cut into 5-cm pieces
Salt	1 tsp
Cooking oil	125 ml
Firm bean curd square	1, cut in cubes
Garlic	3 cloves, peeled and chopped
Onion	1, large, peeled and chopped
Tomatoes	4, chopped
Ginger	3-cm knob, peeled and shredded
Salted soy beans (tocho)	2 Tbsp, washed and mashed
Vinegar	2 Tbsp
Sugar	to taste

Method

- Rub fish pieces with salt and leave for 15–20 minutes. Then drain and pat dry with absorbent paper.

- Heat oil in a wok and fry fish until golden. Drain fish and set aside.

- In the same oil, fry cubes of bean curd until golden then drain and set aside.

- In remaining oil, sauté garlic, onion, tomatoes and ginger. Add mashed salted soy beans and stir well for 1 minute then add a little water.

- Bring mixture to a gentle boil and add vinegar and sugar. Stir well. Add fish and bean curd and bring to the boil. Taste and adjust seasoning with more sugar, pepper or salt if required.

Langat na Hipon (Prawns with Sour Starfruit)

Ingredients

Prawns (shrimps)	500 g, large, shelled and deveined
White vinegar	50 ml
Gin	1 tsp
Onions	2, medium, peeled and sliced
Lemon grass	1 short length, sliced in rings
Salt	1 tsp
Sugar	1/2 tsp
Lemon pepper	1/2 tsp
Black peppercorns	1 tsp, crushed
Cooking oil	3 Tbsp
Garlic	4 cloves, peeled and crushed
Sour starfruit or small green tomatoes	8, sliced in rounds
Spring onions (scallions)	2, coarsely broken

Method

- Place prawns in a mixture of vinegar, gin, onions, lemon grass, salt, sugar, lemon pepper and peppercorns. Set aside.

- Heat oil in a wok and sauté garlic until brown. Add prawn mixture and wait for mixture to boil before stirring thoroughly. Mixing or stirring before this will cause prawns to taste too much of vinegar.

- Cook until prawns turn pink. Add sliced sour starfruit or tomatoes and spring onions and bring to the boil. Stir once. Remove from heat and serve hot or cold with rice.

Pescado Al Horno (Baked Fish)

Ingredients

Kalamansi lime juice	5 ml
Salt	1 1/2 tsp
Ground white pepper	a pinch
Paprika	1/2 tsp
Grouper *(lapu lapu)*, rock cod or sea bass	350 g, scaled, gutted and cleaned
Prawns (shrimps)	250 g, shelled and cleaned with tails intact
Red capsicum (bell pepper)	1, cored and diced
Red shallots	4, peeled and sliced
Brown onion	1, medium, peeled and sliced
Sugar	1/2 tsp
Breadcrumbs	25 g
Olive oil	50 ml
Tomato sauce	125 ml
Cheddar cheese	75 g, grated
Banana leaf	1, optional

Garnish

Parsley	25 g

Method

- Prepare marinade. Combine lime juice, 1/2 tsp salt, pepper and 1/4 tsp paprika.

- Allow fish and prawns to sit in the marinade for 15 minutes.

- Combine capsicum, shallots, onion, sugar, remaining salt and remaining paprika to make stuffing. Stuff fish stomach then coat fish and prawns in breadcrumbs.

- Place fish in a casserole dish and arrange prawns around it. Pour olive oil and tomato sauce around fish. Sprinkle remaining breadcrumbs and grated cheese on top.

- Bake in an oven at 180°C for about 45 minutes until done, basting occasionally. Serve on a plate garnished with sprigs of parsley.

- Alternatively, grill fish and prawns on a banana leaf on an open-air grill. Add olive oil, tomato sauce, breadcrumbs and grated cheese once fish is cooked and transfer to a microwave-safe dish. Place in the microwave oven for 2 minutes on HIGH to cook oil and melt cheese. Serve garnished with parsley.

Pinais (Prawn Casserole)

Pinais (pronouced 'pee-na-ees') is a rich prawn (shrimp) casserole and is interestingly reminiscent of Thai *haw mok* (see pg 71).

Ingredients

Prawns (shrimps)	600 g, small, shelled and deveined
Red shallots	4 or 2 medium onions, peeled and sliced
Ginger	3-cm knob, peeled and sliced
Garlic	2 cloves, peeled and mashed
Red chillies (*sili labuyo*)	2, seeded, if preferred
Banana leaf	1, large or 2 *gabi* leaves, optional
Coconut cream	450 ml, refrigerated
Salt	to taste
Ground white pepper	to taste

Method

- Chop prawns roughly.

- Blend (process) shallots, ginger, garlic and chillies together to form a paste.

- Tear up banana leaf or *gabi* leaves into broad strips and arrange at base of casserole dish. Alternatively, butter casserole dish.

- Take coconut cream out of the refrigerator and collect the thick cream on top. Mix thick coconut cream, prawns, blended paste and salt and pepper to taste. Pour mixture into casserole dish.

- Simmer casserole on low heat for about 30–40 minutes until *pinais* develops a custard-like consistency. Serve hot or cold with rice.

- Alternatively, cook casserole in the microwave oven for 10 minutes on MEDIUM or until mixture becomes custard-like. Serve hot or cold with rice.

Vietnam, Cambodia & Laos

Along the Mekong

> "The host said not a word,
> the guest was dumb
> And silent too the white chrysanthemum."
>
> *Ryota*

There is evidence that rice has been cultivated in the rice bowl of Asia—Vietnam, Cambodia, Laos, Myanmar and Thailand—since the 3rd century B.C. It is a beautiful part of the world. In the watery reflections of the never-ending paddies, lakes and rivers, there is greenery everywhere. The inland lake called the Tonle Sap in Cambodia is particularly fascinating, as this is where a special kind of paddy, the floating variety, grows, its stems holding ripening rice stalks aloft as it struggles to keep abreast of waters that are bound to rise and fill the Mekong. The ripe grains have to be harvested from boats. In the dry season, this lake with its outlet to the Mekong will dry up, leaving a bounty of fish that flop and gasp in tiny pools and eddies until the scant water is sucked up by the thirsty land, and farmers scoop up shoals of fish to smoke, dry or make into a *lop (sambal)* to last until the following 'wet'.

It is impossible to truly separate Vietnam, Cambodia and Laos, for many of their traditions have the same roots. These countries had boundaries that moved with each wave of invasion for centuries and part of what is now North Vietnam passed off a few hundred years ago as South China. Within the region, the people are at one with the land. They are a hardy farming people making a living in a harsh environment.

The food in this region reflects many cross-cultural influences. There was the Chinese influence until the early Tang Dynasty and the Indianisation of the mainland. In the 16th century, the Portuguese occupied Central Vietnam briefly, and later, in the 18th century, the French colonised Laos and Vietnam. Vietnamese food can be traced to all these cultures, yet it retains its own subtle identity.

As in the rest of Asia, seafood is the staple protein source, mainly because of its availability and accessibility. Fishing is done in rivers, traps are set in inlets and estuaries. Boats are put daily out to sea, except in the monsoon season, when fishermen repair nets, salt fish or make pastes from their excess catch.

Fish is prepared and served in a variety of ways: fresh and raw; steamed or boiled into soups and casseroles, utilising heads, tails and the in-between; dried and salted, and pickled in brine. The clear, amber fish sauce that is produced—called *nuoc mam*—is used to flavour most of their food, be it beef, chicken, vegetable or fish. *Pong pla* or *pla ra* or *lop* (depending on which country you are in) is a fish relish eaten with rice. If fish, the main ingredient of this sauce, is unavailable, then anything on hand pounded into lemon grass would surely have to suffice, even if it had to be locusts. In Kampoon Boontawee's *A Child of the Northeast*, the making of this relish is described. 'He knew how *pong pla* was made; he had watched his mother. She put about a cupful of water in a pot with a little fermented fish, not too much or it would make the *pong pla* too salty. Then she added pieces of fish. While she waited for the water to boil, she threaded, then dried peppers and onions and roasted them. When the fish had cooked, she mixed it with the crispy pounded onion. If they were fortunate to have fresh coriander leaves, she would sprinkle some on top.'

The spices that are used are common to most of these areas: lemon grass, Thai ginger *(kha)*, root ginger, turmeric and tamarind, eaten with sweet leafy vegetable and fish.

The Laotians, Cambodians and Vietnamese prefer to eat fresh food rather than chilled and do not believe in refrigeration. Vegetables and herbs are readily available, sometimes garden grown: lemon grass is wild and grows as grass, aubergines (eggplants/brinjals), tomatoes, various leaves for frying with fish or shellfish, the banana stem for salads and soup, the leaf to bake, the fruit to eat and the flower to curry. These people prefer sticky rice served in woven bamboo baskets with fish sauce and sliced raw onions. Spoons are used to serve from the main dish to individual dishes, but to eat the sticky rice, the only way is to reach in with the fingers, roll it up into a ball and dip it in the sauce as an appetiser.

Vietnam is today awakening to a new life. Much of the old grand cuisine remains dormant, waiting to be revived by the tourist dollar and astute entrepreneurs who may bring prosperity and peace to the region.

Chao Tom (Prawns on Sugarcane Sticks)

Chao Tom is one of Vietnam's happy surprises.

Ingredients

Prawns (shrimps)	500 g, shelled and deveined
Salt	1/2 tsp
Sugar	1/2 Tbsp
Pork fat	50 g, cut into cubes
Garlic	6 cloves, peeled
Egg white	from 1 egg
Cornflour (cornstarch)	1 tsp
Fish sauce *(nuoc mam)*	1 tsp
Ground white pepper	1 tsp
Sugarcane sticks	6

Sweet Sauce

Red chillies	1 Tbsp, chopped
Fish sauce *(nuoc mam)*	2 tsp
Sugar	2 Tbsp

Method

- Season prawns with salt. Rub sugar into pork fat. Leave both for 30 minutes.
- Blend (process) prawns, pork fat and garlic. Add egg white, cornflour, fish sauce and pepper to bind mixture together.
- Wet fingers and divide mixture into 6 portions. Shape mixture into oval shapes, the size of a large egg. Press mixture around sugarcane sticks to form popsicle-like meat sticks. Make 6 meat sticks.
- Prepare sauce. Mix chillies with fish sauce and sugar.
- Grill meat sticks under a domestic grill or over a charcoal fire. If you want the *chao tom* to remain golden and unburnt, brush with a mixture of salted water as you grill.
- Serve hot with sweet sauce.

Tom Riem Beurre (Prawns in Butter)

Although Vietnam was colonised by China from 1st century B.C. to early 9th century A.D., Vietnamese food remains distinctive, with its own particular style. With the French colonisation of Vietnam later, the basic rules of haute cuisine were applied to the local food and the blend produced a subtle, sophisticated and exquisite cuisine.

Ingredients

Prawns (shrimps)	1 kg, shelled and deveined
Ground white pepper	a dash
Salt	1/4 tsp
Sugar	1 tsp
Dark sweet soy vinegar	1 tsp
Cooking oil	1 Tbsp
Garlic	6 cloves, peeled and finely chopped
Butter	1 Tbsp

Garnish

Chives	6, chopped

Method

- Marinate prawns with pepper, salt, sugar and sweet soy vinegar.
- Heat oil in a wok and sauté garlic until brown. Add prawns and marinade and stir on moderate heat until most of the liquid evaporates. Lower heat and cover for 3 minutes to cook prawns.
- Stir once, then add butter. Remove immediately and serve garnished with chives.

Tom Riem Beurre (Prawns in Butter)

Muc Don Thit Chien (Vietnamese Squid with Stuffing)

Ingredients

Squid	600 g, about 10
Bean threads or glass noodles	25 g, soaked in warm water for 30 minutes
Dried Chinese mushrooms	10, soaked in warm water for 30 minutes
Water chestnuts	6
Prawns (shrimps)	125 g, shelled and deveined
Minced pork	125 g
Salt	to taste
Ground white pepper	to taste
Light soy sauce	1 Tbsp
Brown onions	2, medium, peeled and finely chopped
Garlic	1 clove, peeled and finely chopped
Sugar	1/2 tsp
Fish sauce (nuoc mam)	1 Tbsp
Eggs	2, beaten
Plain (all-purpose) flour	2 Tbsp
Cooking oil	125 ml

Method

- Clean squid, remove ink sacs and purple skins, and keep tubes whole. Set aside.

- Check that soaked bean threads or glass noodles and mushrooms are soft. Drain and chop up bean threads or glass noodles, mushrooms and water chestnuts, separately. Then combine chopped ingredients and chop again. Set aside.

- Chop up prawns and add to minced pork. Add salt, pepper and soy sauce to mixture.

- Mix chopped bean threads or glass noodles, mushrooms and water chestnuts, prawn and pork mixture, onions, garlic, sugar, fish sauce and half the beaten egg together.

- Fill squid tubes with mixture, taking care not to overfill. Make a small slit near pointed end of squid so squid tube will not burst when cooked. Secure top end of squid with bamboo skewers or sew carefully with thick thread.

- Arrange squid tubes in a steamer. Steam for 10 minutes until squid is just cooked. Remove from steam.

- Combine remaining beaten eggs with flour to form a batter.

- Heat oil in a wok. Dip squid tubes in batter then deep-fry 2 at a time until golden. Drain.

- Slice squid tubes and arrange on a plate to serve.

Ca Nau Ngot (Cambodian Tomato Fish Head Soup)

Ingredients

Catfish or snapper fish head	1, large, about 1 kg
Water	2 litres
Salt	1/4 tsp
Fish sauce (nuoc mam)	2 Tbsp
Sugar	1 tsp
Ripe tomatoes	3, cut into quarters
Spring onions (scallions)	6, roughly broken up
Ground white pepper	1/2 tsp
Red chillies	2, seeded, if preferred
Coriander (phak hom pom) leaves	25 g
Lime juice	extracted from 1/2 lime

Method

- Wash and scale fish head. Split fish head in half, but cut into smaller pieces if the pot you are using is small.

- In the pot, boil water and add salt, fish sauce and sugar. When water boils, add fish head and bring to the boil once more. Do not over-boil as fish head could break up too early.

- Leave fish head to simmer for 10 minutes, then remove. Keep soup warm and allow liquid to reduce by simmering for another 10 minutes.

- Add tomatoes and bring to the boil for 10 minutes. Add spring onions, pepper and chillies and cook soup for another 10–15 minutes to reduce further.

- When soup is slightly thick, add fish head and bring soup to a simmer. Allow fish head to cook in soup for another 10 minutes. During this time, ladle soup over fish head at regular intervals.

- Test for taste. The soup should be spicy, sweet and tart. Sprinkle coriander leaves and add lime juice just before serving.

Lop Pla Ra (Fresh Salad)

A dish from Issan, the northeastern region that borders Thailand, Vietnam, Laos and Cambodia. *Lop* means long fingernails, referring to the long nails needed to shred the fish for this dish.

Ingredients

Catfish, mackerel or other firm fish fillets	300 g, skinned
Lemon grass *(bai mak nao)*	2 stalks
Spring onions (scallions)	5
Galangal *(laos)*	5-cm knob, peeled
Red chillies	3
Rice flour	1 Tbsp
Fish sauce *(nuoc mam)*	1 Tbsp
Lime juice	extracted from 1 lime
Salt	to taste

Method

- Using a cleaver and chopping block, mince fish by chopping, mixing and turning the fish over after every few chops.

- Wash and scrape skin off bulbous part of lemon grass. Peel outer layers from bulbs of spring onions and reserve roots and green stems. Combine lemon grass, spring onions, galangal and chillies and blend (process) until well mixed.

- Add blended ingredients to minced fish and mix well with rice flour, fish sauce, lime juice and salt to taste. The lime juice will pickle the raw fish, a common practice in North Thailand, as in Peru and Fiji.

- The people of Issan eat this with rice. I use this as a dip, garnished with mint leaves, or as a filling for tiny lettuce rolls served as an entrée.

Canh Ca Nuoc Dua (Cambodian Coconut Fish Soup)

The flavours of this unusual dish are delicate and very subtle. For this recipe, you need a special ingredient called Black Jack or *nuoc mau*. If unavailable, use caramel sauce instead.

Ingredients

Black Jack *(nuoc mau)*	2 tsp or 50 ml caramel sauce*
Mullet, bream or snapper	350 g, cut into 6-cm pieces
Salt	1/2 tsp
Spring onions (scallions)	3, roughly broken up
Coconut water	425 g can
Garlic	1 clove, peeled and chopped
Fish sauce *(nuoc mam)*	3 Tbsp

*Caramel Sauce

Sugar	1 Tbsp
Water	185 ml

Garnish

Spring onion (scallion) curls	2
Onions	2, peeled, sliced and crisp-fried

Method

- Prepare caramel sauce if Black Jack is unavailable. Heat sugar and one-third of water to dissolve sugar. Boil until solution changes colour, then lower heat and add remaining water. Stir to mix, remove from heat and store in a jar until needed. Alternatively, heat sugar and one-third of water in the microwave oven for 2 minutes on HIGH. Add remaining water, stir and return to microwave oven for another 2 minutes on HIGH. Remove, cool and store in a jar.

- Marinate fish in Black Jack or caramel sauce and salt for at least 1 hour.

- In the meantime, prepare spring onion curls for garnish by making many long vertical cuts down the length of spring onions and soaking in iced water.

- Bring coconut water and garlic to the boil over moderate heat. When boiling, lower in fish and marinade. Submerge fish completely. Add spring onions.

- Boil for 5 minutes and skim off any scum from surface. Reduce heat and simmer for 20 minutes and allow liquid to reduce. Add fish sauce. Serve in soup bowls with garnish of spring onion curls and crisp-fried onions.

Cang Cua Boc Tom (Cambodian Crab Claws)

Ingredients

Meaty crab claws	500 g
Prawns (shrimps)	250 g, shelled and minced
Red shallots	2, peeled and sliced
Salt	¼ tsp
Ground white pepper	¼ tsp
Sugar	¼ tsp
Dark soy sauce	1 Tbsp
Cornflour (cornstarch)	3 Tbsp
Egg white	from 1 egg, lightly beaten
Cooking oil	3 Tbsp

Sauce

Garlic	2 cloves, peeled and chopped
Onion	1, large, peeled and chopped
Pickled onions	5, chopped
Ginger	2-cm knob, peeled and chopped
Light soy sauce	1 Tbsp
Oyster sauce	1 Tbsp
Dark sweet soy vinegar	1 Tbsp

Method

- Steam crab claws for 7 minutes or until flesh turns white (not opaque). Collect stock from steamed crab claws and reserve.

- Combine prawns, shallots, salt, pepper, sugar and dark soy sauce. Mix well and add 1 Tbsp cornflour and half the egg white to bind mixture.

- Divide mixture into portions according to the number of crab claws. Cover meaty part of each claw with mixture, leaving the actual claw free to be used as a grip when eating.

- Combine 50 ml of crab stock with remaining cornflour and set aside.

- Make sauce by heating 1 Tbsp oil in wok. Sauté garlic, onion, pickled onions and ginger. Add light soy sauce, oyster sauce, sweet dark soy vinegar and cornflour-crab stock mixture. Bring to the boil then simmer. Add some crab stock and stir until sauce thickens. Transfer to a sauce bowl.

- Heat remaining oil in a wok and dip each prepared crab claw in remaining egg white. Fry 3–4 crab claws at a time until golden.

- Arrange claws on a serving dish and pour sauce over or serve sauce as a dip.

Ca' Qua (Vietnamese Fish 'Hotpot')

Ca' Qua (pronounced 'cha-ka') is an interesting Vietnamese dish that is served only in one restaurant in Hanoi. You climb up dark stairs into a huge windowed room filled with tables. The diners will all be eating this one dish served to them by eager waitresses running up and down the stairs, making sure the 'hotpots' are full of tasty stock and the herbs are constantly being topped up. The meal I had there was quite an experience and imagine my surprise when I returned to Sydney and dined with Angie Hong who runs one of the nicest Vietnamese restaurants in Sydney. We had Ca' Qua a la Newtown!

Ingredients

Extra light olive oil	1 Tbsp
Dried prawn (shrimp) paste	1 tsp, dry-roasted
Garlic	2 cloves, peeled and chopped
Fennel seeds	2 tsp, dry-roasted and ground
Chilli paste	1 tsp
Coconut milk	450 ml
Ground turmeric	$1/2$ tsp
Coconut cream	250 ml
Ground white pepper	to taste
Lime juice	extracted from 1 lime
Fish sauce (*nuoc mam*)	to taste
Bream or other firm-fleshed fish	500 g, chopped into pieces

Garnish

Fennel or dill leaves	
Peanuts (groundnuts)	1 Tbsp, chopped
Garlic chives	
Spring onions (scallions)	
Thin rice noodles (dried)	200 g

Method

- In a clay pot or wok, heat oil and brown prawn paste and garlic until aromatic. Add ground fennel and chilli paste and cook for 1 minute.

- When fennel smells aromatic, add coconut milk and turmeric.

- Allow coconut milk to simmer slowly so that it absorbs the flavours.

- Add coconut cream and stir to mix well. Taste for seasoning and add pepper, some lime juice and fish sauce if necessary.

- Leave sauce on the boil and add fish and your preference of garnishes. In Hanoi, we had our own small individual pots of sauce. The fish and garnish were served on separate plates. We then added the garnish as we preferred, according to each mouthful. You may choose to add fennel leaves in the pot of sauce at the beginning or at the end.

- For a more complete meal, enjoy this dish with thin rice noodles. Freshen noodles in hot water, drain and blanch just before serving.

Pa Ling Sousi (Fried Catfish in Thick Sauce)

Pa ling is the catfish used in Lao and Cambodian cooking because of its abundance in the inland lakes, rivers and streams. Any firm-fleshed fish, however, can be substituted to make this innovative dish.

Ingredients

Catfish (pa ling), snapper, hilsa or trout fillets	400 g, cut into 5-cm pieces
Salt	1 tsp
Red chillies	5, seeded, if preferred
Red shallots	7, large or 2 medium brown onions, peeled and sliced
Pork bones	200 g
Lard	125 g
Coconut cream	250 ml
Kaffir lime leaves	3, shredded
Fish sauce (nuoc mam)	2 Tbsp
Ground black pepper	1/2 tsp
Coconut milk	125 ml

Garnish

Spring onions (scallions)	2, chopped
Coriander (phak hom pom) leaves	6–8, chopped

Method

- Season fish with salt.

- Blend (process) chillies with shallots or onions and set aside.

- Prepare 125 ml stock by boiling pork bones in 450 ml water and leaving to simmer until reduced. Strain and set aside.

- Heat lard in a wok until it is smoking. Fry a few pieces of fish at a time until golden. Remove and drain.

- In another wok, heat coconut cream on low heat until the cream separates. Add blended shallots or onions and chillies to the oily cream mixture and stir well until aromatic. Add some kaffir lime leaves.

- Add stock to cream. Stir well and allow liquid to reduce by simmering on low heat for about 20 minutes.

- Add fish sauce, pepper and coconut milk. Stir and gradually add fried fish. Ladle sauce over fish so fish absorbs sauce. Serve garnished with spring onions, coriander leaves and remaining kaffir lime leaves.

Sa Ton Pa Va (Laotian Marinated Fish Salad)

Fish salads are best made with as fresh a fish as you can purchase. Serve this Laotian dish as a dip with tiny water-biscuits, or as an entrée with pieces of fish wrapped in lettuce leaves.

Ingredients

White pomfret, cod, ling, perch or any white fish fillet	200 g
Lime juice	extracted from 5 limes
Salt	1/2 tsp
Garlic	2 cloves, peeled and chopped
Red shallots	5 or 2 large onions, peeled and chopped
Galangal (laos)	3-cm knob, peeled
Lemon grass (bai mak nao)	3 stalks
Dried chillies	2
Kaffir lime leaves	3
Fish sauce (nuoc mam)	2 Tbsp
Fish roe	125 g
Spring onions (scallions)	2, chopped
Coriander (phak hom pom) leaves	3 sprigs, chopped

Method

- Skin fish fillets and slice thinly into 2-cm long strips. Combine lime juice and salt to make marinade. Soak fish in marinade for 1–2 hours.

- Pound or blend (process) garlic, shallots, galangal, lemon grass, dried chillies and kaffir lime leaves together into a paste.

- Lift fish fillets from marinade and drain. Place into a salad bowl. Reserve a little marinade.

- Add pounded ingredients and fish sauce, a little at a time, and gradually stir in fish roe.

- Taste and adjust seasoning. The salad should taste sour and just a little salty. Add 1 Tbsp of reserved marinade to the mixture and stir in chopped spring onions and coriander. Serve.

Sam Rok Krung (Spiced Shellfish)

This dish has a peanut (groundnut) sauce but it has a decidedly different flavour from that of Malay *satay*.

Ingredients

Cockles, scallops, oysters, clams or mussels	250 g
Lemon grass (*bai mak nao*)	2 stalks
Garlic	4 cloves, chopped
Galangal (*laos*)	2-cm knob
Cooking oil	2 Tbsp
Peanuts (groundnuts)	1½ Tbsp, roasted and coarsely pounded
Fish sauce (*nuoc mam*)	1 Tbsp
Sugar	1 tsp
Ground black pepper	1 tsp

Garnish

Lemon rind curls	from 2 lemons
Coriander (*phak hom pom*) leaves	25 g, chopped

Method

- Scrub and wash the shellfish well. If you are using mussels, pull off the 'beards'.

- Pour boiling water over shellfish. As soon as they begin to open, drain water and any sand that may collect. Prise clams, oysters or mussels from their shells and place them in a dish together with the liquid from the shells.

- Discard all but bulbous root of lemon grass and blend (process) with garlic and galangal.

- Heat oil in a wok and sauté blended mixture. Stir until aromatic.

- Add shellfish and cook for about 3 minutes, stirring well until fragrant.

- Add peanuts, fish sauce, sugar and pepper, stirring well to ensure peanuts are well blended into mixture. Remove from heat immediately.

- Alternatively cook in the microwave oven. Preheat a browning dish for 6 minutes on HIGH and add 1 Tbsp oil. Continue to heat for 30 seconds on HIGH, then add garlic and blended ingredients. Cook for 2 minutes on HIGH, stirring once.

- Stir shellfish into mixture and cook for another 1 minute. Add peanuts, fish sauce, sugar and pepper. Stir well. Cook for a further 2 minutes on HIGH and remove.

- To serve, arrange shellfish in their shells and garnish with lemon curls and coriander leaves.

Ca Nung Tut Luat (Cambodian Grilled Fish)

The custom of wrapping food in one of the ingredients and eating it is very Asian, from the pan or betel leaf chewed along with lime paste to *sang choy bau* or the practice of serving minced pork in lettuce. Similarly, the Vietnamese and Cambodian have rice paper which is translucent and fries into light, crunchy rolls.

Ingredients

Black pomfret or kingfish	1, about 1–1.5 kg
Salt	to taste
Ground white pepper	to taste
Belly pork	200 g, thinly sliced
Cucumber	1, sliced
Lettuce	1, shredded
Onion	1, peeled and sliced
Vietnamese mint leaves	15–20, roughly broken up
Garlic chives	50 g, roughly broken up
Rice paper squares	10–12 sheets

Sauce

Garlic	3 cloves, peeled and chopped
Cooking oil	1 Tbsp
Sweet soy sauce	4 Tbsp
Sweet chilli sauce	1 tsp
Fish sauce (*nuoc mam*)	1/2 Tbsp
Vinegar	2 Tbsp
Sugar	2 Tbsp
Peanut butter	2 Tbsp
Water	250 ml
Sesame seeds	25 g, roasted

Method

- Scale, gut and clean fish. Brush with salt and pepper.

- Place fish on grill and cook until flesh turns white, not opaque. Remove and keep warm in foil.

- Cook belly pork in a frying pan (skillet) with 2 Tbsp water but no oil, as the fat will provide the grease. Remove pork from heat when oil appears in pan.

- In the same pan, fry onion in remaining pork fat until brown. Add garlic chives. Reserve as garnish.

- Prepare sauce. Sauté garlic in hot oil until golden. Add sweet soy sauce, chilli sauce, fish sauce, vinegar, sugar, peanut butter and water. Stir well until sugar melts. Remove and sprinkle roasted sesame seeds on top. Serve sauce in individual bowls, one for each guest.

- Place fish on a plate of shredded lettuce and serve with cucumber, pork and Vietnamese mint leaves in separate bowls.

- Prepare rice paper by brushing each sheet individually with wet fingertips thoroughly.

- Guests make their own 'rolls' by placing some lettuce, cucumber slices, mint leaves and a slice of fish on a sheet of rice paper and rolling it up like a spring roll. Dip in sauce before eating.

The Colonial Influence

From Memsahib's Kitchen

> "Attempts to anglicise the cuisine beyond a point were much frustrated by India ... preceding chicken, there would in all probability be mulligatawny soup."
>
> *Charles Allen, PLAIN TALES OF THE RAJ*

Marco Polo's tales of the exotic East fired the imagination of Europeans in the 14th century. He wrote of lands rich in spikenard, galangal and cloves, and of merchants reaping handsome profits. Other travellers reinforced these accounts with lush tales of gold, silk, perfume and most important of all, spices from the legendary Spice Islands.

The race for spices had begun. Spices had of course travelled the Buddhist route earlier, creating an impact in Sichuan, China, but now wealthy European houses discovered that spices enhanced stale and unpalatable food, extended the life of meat and fish and imparted a sense of well-being to its users. Thus these precious spices were locked away and used in minute portions. When exploited by astute Arab traders as economic collateral, however, they took on awesome proportions. The East became the focus of trade and prosperity for countries who chose to exploit it.

Magellan and the Portuguese were the first of the Europeans to arrive in Asia, taking 'Coelan', Sri Lanka, Goa, Melaka and, finally, Macau. The French, then the Dutch, followed, planting spice estates as they carved out empires.

With the arrival of the British East India Company came the merchant *boxwallahs* or traders, civil servants and that most wondrous of colonial institutions, the *memsahib* or lady who bravely tried to carry on British traditions in spite of numerous frustrations. Allen in *Plain Tales* recounts a story of one *memsahib* who discovered her cook straining the soup through one of her husband's socks. When chastised, he replied, 'But pardon, *Memsahib*, don't worry, it's not one of his clean ones!'

Trading centres grew in the style of the 'home country' and ports mushroomed like clones of their colonial originals. It was not a mere adoption of a new culture, but more of a cultural overlay, of one dominant culture imposing its influence on an ambient, accommodating host culture. Jao de Barros in 1640 wrote that the Portuguese arms and boundaries were material, time might destroy them, but it would not destroy the religion, language and customs they left behind. Today Goa, Melaka and Macau remain very Portuguese and modern-day Ho Chi Minh City (Saigon), Vientiane (Laos) and Pondicherry (India) are charming French anachronisms.

The British left more than roads, railways and a judicial system; they left a train of food customs and manners that are carried on in '*pukka*' British tradition in Calcutta, Delhi, Hong Kong, Penang and Kuala Lumpur. Clubs in some of these countries today still function in true British style, members choosing to dine on Sunday curries, formally suited with black tie and dinner jackets in the sweltering heat of the tropics.

The colonial character in architecture, street names and, of course, food remains, the imported customs, religion and way of life are still in evidence, though they have, along with physical characteristics of the colonials, altered with intermarriage. Similarly, the cooking styles have become transposed, including new and old ingredients. Food influences run like threads, weaving into local traditions and trends, appearing as a method here, a name there, or as a herb somewhere else.

Food influences are the most enduring of cultural influences, as this part of the culture is contained within the home environment, and is largely matrilineal. One eats what mother dictates. Familiar food traditions help to keep a migrating people secure and food introduced by the colonials has endured in modern times though origins have long been forgotten. Macau, Goa and Melaka are ports where the colonial influence is most apparent. There are interesting parallels in the food patterns. Goans serve a dish called *Bibinca*, almost identical to Egg *Bibinca* served in the Philippines and *Bibikkan* served in Sri Lanka. Given the physical distance between the countries, this coincidence could only have originated with the tenuous but significant Portuguese link. Goa exists in a time warp of Portuguese culture, quite separate from the parent Indian culture that surrounds it. A Goan cookbook cites the most unlikely of combinations in names and situations as an example of this influence. In which other city would you find an Indian looking 'M*iss Devine Visitation*,' sipping some cashew *feni* (the local liqueur) with '*Miss Conception D'Rodrigo*', in a Portuguese-style taverna? In abstemious India? As names go, the British added to this rich heritage with baptismal fonts brimming full of Huntsmen, Macintyres, Livingstons and Danforths.

Prawn (shrimp) dishes of Goa are peppered with names as prawn baffad, though the ingredients include red chillies. Prawn *balchao* is duplicated in a recipe from Macau that uses prawn paste in a prawn dish: a non-Chinese or Indian ingredient that could only have travelled the colonial route from Malacca. *Carpa recheada* from Macau is reminiscent of *Lapu lapu rellenos* (see pg 123) in the Philippines, and that famous British dish, the mulligatawny soup, had humble Indian beginnings as a simple rassam. Fish kedgeree cooked with rice and eggs started off as the *kitchri*, an Indian dhal (lentils)-and-rice meal.

Cross-cultural food experiences never end. Today, English and Americans, Australians and Europeans have turned to Asian food with enthusiasm. They have discovered that there is nothing really mystical about it, that it can be adapted for Western palates and lifestyles. Spices and herbs still pack in that same verve and punch!

These few recipes give a taste of the richness of the culinary heritage left by the colonials and are well worth trying.

Ikan Bilis Spice Mix (Whitebait Spice Mix)

This is commonly served in clubs and restaurants with drinks or as a side dish with *nasi lemak* (coconut rice).

Ingredients

Whitebait *(ikan bilis)*	300 g, head and centre bone removed, "fillets" separated
Rice flour	2 tsp
Cooking oil	400 ml
Peanuts (groundnuts)	300 g, cleaned and roasted
Sugar	1 Tbsp
Chilli powder	2 tsp or to taste

Method

- Dust whitebait with rice flour.

- Heat oil in a wok until bubbles appear when a wooden *satay* skewer is dipped in oil.

- Fry a handful of whitebait at a time, quickly removing with a slotted spoon as they turn brown. Drain on absorbent paper to ensure whitebait is dry. Continue until whitebait is done. Do not allow whitebait to burn or brown too much.

- Drain oil from wok but do not wash wok. Toss peanuts into hot oily wok to brown lightly. Add whitebait, sugar and chilli powder, tossing to mix well. Sugar will melt and blend with chilli powder to coat whitebait.

- Leave to cool before storing in airtight jars. Use as required. (To re-crisp whitebait, grill lightly on low for 5 minutes.)

Rassam (Prawn and Drumstick Soup)

This peppery and watery stew (known as *moolagu-thanni* in Tamil) is eaten with fish curry and rice. It is the forerunner of the *mulligatawny* soup which the British colonialists introduced to their home country and colonial outposts.

Ingredients

Drumsticks or 2-cm thick long beans with fleshy pith	4
Tamarind paste	1 Tbsp, mixed with 2 Tbsp water, strained
Water	250 ml
Coriander seeds	1/2 Tbsp
Fennel seeds	1/2 tsp
Black peppercorns	1 tsp
Rice water or starch from cooked rice	250 ml
Ghee (clarified butter) or cooking oil	1 Tbsp
Brown onions	2, large or 5 red shallots, peeled and sliced
Garlic	3 cloves, bruised with skin intact
Green chillies	2, slit lengthwise
Ginger	2-cm knob, peeled and bruised
Prawns (shrimps) or school prawns	250 g, deveined
Ground turmeric (*haldi*)	1/2 tsp
Salt	to taste
Ground white pepper	to taste

Garnish

Lime	1, finely sliced and twisted

Method

- If using drumsticks, scrape off the skin and clean. Cut drumsticks or long beans into 6–8 cm lengths.

- Mix tamarind liquid with water and strain.

- Coarsely grind coriander seeds, fennel seeds and black peppercorns together.

- Prepare rice water by scrubbing raw rice grains firmly together and reserving the resulting whitish liquid, or use the water from boiling rice. This is mainly starch and helps to thicken soups and stews.

- Heat ghee or oil and add onions, garlic, chillies and ginger. Stir-fry for 2 minutes or until onions are soft. Add ground coriander, fennel and pepper.

- Add tamarind liquid and another 450 ml water and bring to the boil. Add prawns and drumsticks or long beans and continue to boil for 5 minutes.

- Add rice water and stir for 3 minutes. Lower heat and add turmeric powder, salt and pepper to taste. Remove from heat and serve garnished with twists of lime.

Onaku Konju (Dried Prawn Sambal)

This is a delightful Keralan and Goan recipe which is very popular. It almost echoes the *sambal* recipes I found in Melaka, Pattaya and even Japan, although the Japanese recipe uses grilled and shredded squid.

Ingredients

Dried prawns (shrimps)	150 g
Vegetable oil	3 Tbsp
Red shallots	15 or 4 medium brown onions, peeled and finely sliced
Green chillies	5–6, seeded, finely sliced
Red chillies	3, seeded, finely sliced
Lime juice	extracted from 1 lime
Sugar	to taste
Salt	to taste

Method

- Roast dried prawns over coals, under the grill or in a heavy-based frying pan (skillet) or wok until they turn crisp and golden. Pound lightly until they crumble.

- Heat oil and fry shallots or onions and chillies until shallots or onions are golden brown.

- Add pounded dried shrimps and stir-fry for about 5 minutes on medium heat until the aroma is strong.

- Remove from heat and cool. When shrimps are cooled, add lime juice, sugar and salt to taste. Toss well and serve cold with vegetable dishes and white rice.

Carpa Recheada (Stuffed Carp)

This recipe reflects the Portuguese influence again. Though somewhat different, it is reminiscent of the Filipino *Lapu lapu relleno* (see pg 123). There is a heavy dependence on soy sauce in this recipe. The Filipino recipe utilises a stuffing of eggs and olives.

Ingredients

Carp, snapper, bream or small trevally	1, about 750 g
Garlic	2 cloves, peeled
Onions	2, large, peeled
Portuguese sausage or Chinese pork sausage	50 g
Dried prawns (shrimps)	50 g, soaked for 30 minutes and drained, then chopped
Light soy sauce	1 tsp
Dark soy sauce	1 tsp
Cornflour (cornstarch)	2 tsp
Salt	to taste
Ground white pepper	to taste
Rice flour	1 tsp
Cooking oil	750 ml

Garnish

Lettuce leaves	5–6, shredded
Tomatoes	2, sliced

Method

- Clean, scale and gut fish. Make a slit from the head down to the stomach. Using a sharp knife, carefully remove the central bone and some of the thick flesh from the fish. Do not cut too close to the skin. Remove fish meat, debone and chop or mince well.

- Mince garlic, onions and sausage. Place in a bowl with chopped prawns and fish meat. Add soy sauces, cornflour, salt and pepper. Mix well.

- Stuff mixture carefully into fish, shaping the fish as you go. Secure the slit with bamboo skewers or sew up carefully. If sewing, do not pull thread too hard or the fish skin could tear. Rub rice flour on skin to firm skin.

- Heat oil in a wok. When it is smoking, lower fish in carefully. When one side is brown, gently turn over and fry for another 6–8 minutes until fish is golden. Drain on absorbent paper.

- Remove gently and place on a bed of shredded lettuce and sliced tomatoes to serve.

Chatinie Bacalhau Doraido (Chatinie Golden Cod)

The *bacalhau doraido* or cod is popular in Macau. I find dishes that remind me of other times and other places fascinating, as the cultural overlay on the food of Southeast Asia is in reality a historical account of people who influenced these places. The preference for cod is purely European; the use of coconut milk definitely an influence from the other Portuguese colonies of Goa and Melaka; and this recipe, discovered in their third Asian outpost, Macau, is reminiscent of a salad served in Melaka utilising krill.

Ingredients

Cod, catfish or snapper fillets	500 g
Cooking oil	2 Tbsp
Garlic	2 cloves, peeled and minced
Onions	2, peeled and minced
Coconut milk	175 ml
Salt	to taste
Ground white pepper	to taste

Garnish

Lemon	1, cut into wedges

Method

- Place fish in a saucepan with sufficient water to cover it. Boil for 3–5 minutes or until fish becomes firm. Alternatively, cover fish in plastic wrap and cook in the microwave oven 3 minutes on HIGH.

- Flake fish and discard any bone and skin.

- Heat oil and sauté garlic, then onions until golden brown. Add flaked fish and mix well with garlic and onion.

- Pour in coconut milk and stir. Allow to simmer and stir continuously, breaking up fish as you go along so fish remains separate and does not burn.

- Remove from heat when fish shreds are separated, fried, golden and aromatic. Add salt and pepper to taste.

- Serve garnished with lemon wedges. Use as a sandwich filling or serve with rice.

Portuguese Codfish Balls

Ingredients

Salted cod fish	450 g
Potatoes	450 g
Olive oil	1 Tbsp
Onion	1, large, peeled and sliced
Garlic	3 cloves, peeled and sliced
Salt	to taste
Parsley	1 sprig, chopped
Eggs	3, separated, optional
Ground black pepper	1 Tbsp
Plain (all-purpose) flour	100 g

Method

- Soak cod fish in water overnight, changing water twice to remove salt. Boil cod fish in water for 2 minutes and cool. Reserve water. Remove skin and bones from fish and shred as thinly as possible.

- In water used for boiling cod fish, cook unpeeled potatoes. Then cool, peel and mash.

- Squeeze out any excess liquid from shredded cod fish and add to mashed potatoes. Pound into a paste with a mortar and pestle.

- Heat 1 Tbsp olive oil in a pan and cook onion until transparent. Add garlic and cook for 1 minute. Take off heat and stir mixture into mashed potato.

- Add salt to taste. Then add parsley, egg yolks and pepper. Stir to combine.

- Whip egg whites until they form soft peaks and fold into potato mixture.

- Flour hands and make dumplings with potato mixture.

- Heat remaining olive oil in a pan until it is smoking. Drop 3–4 dumplings into hot oil and deep-fry until golden. Drain on absorbent paper and serve warm.

Casquinhas (Baked Stuffed Crab)

Casquinhas is a dish from Macau similar to the baked stuffed crab from Malaysia. Olives and the white (béchamel) sauce differentiate it from the Goan and Melakan versions. Compared to the Myanmarese baked crab recipe (see pg 104) which uses paprika or chilli, cloves and small prawns, this recipe has a very European slant with the use of large onions, black olives and breadcrumbs.

Ingredients

Crabs	4, about 1.2 kg, with well-formed shells
Cooking oil	1 Tbsp
Garlic	2 cloves, peeled and minced
Onions	2, large, peeled and minced
Black olives	8, minced
Egg	1, beaten
Breadcrumbs	75 g

Béchamel Sauce

Butter	45 g
Plain (all-purpose) flour	30 g
Milk	600 ml
Onion	1, large, peeled and chopped
Clove	1
White peppercorns	8–10
Lime juice	1/2 tsp

Garnish

Stuffed green olives	8, sliced, optional

Method

- Wash and clean crabs (see pg 298). Steam crabs and pick out crabmeat. Shred crabmeat, wash and reserve crab shells.

- Prepare bechamel sauce. Melt two-thirds of the butter in a pan. Add flour and whisk or stir for about 2 minutes, being careful not to burn mixture.

- Meanwhile boil milk in another pan.

- Remove whisked butter and flour mixture from heat and slowly stir in boiling milk, preventing any lumps from forming.

- Return to heat. Add onion, clove and peppercorns. Stir until sauce boils and allow to simmer for 15 minutes.

- Remove and blend well in blender (processor). Return to pan and stir in remaining butter and lime juice on a low heat. Remove at once.

- Heat oil in a wok and sauté minced garlic and onions until golden. Add olives, crabmeat, 60 ml béchamel sauce and stir well. Allow to cook for 5 minutes more, then remove from heat.

- Fill crab shells with cooked crabmeat mixture and brush with beaten egg. Cover with breadcrumbs and place under a hot grill for 3 minutes or until golden. Garnish with sliced stuffed olives as desired.

India, Pakistan, Bangladesh & Sri Lanka

The Coromandel Fishermen

> " Fill our heaving nets
> With living harvests yet
> Warm from the green floating
> Groves of the tides. "
>
> *Sarojini Naidu, SONG OF THE COROMANDEL FISHERMEN*

Wherever Indians gather, the talk invariably centres around food. Much of India is vegetarian and ancient food taboos live on in each ethnic and religious group. Hindus forbid the eating of beef and this partly stems from a recognition of the cow's usefulness. Muslims forbid the eating of pork as the pig was a scavenger. Buddhists and Jains forbid the taking of life and therefore advocate vegetarianism in one form or other. Chicken and vegetables are the only foods deemed acceptable by the majority across the country, apart from fish.

The bounty of the sea is the focus of regional specialities in select coastal provinces. (Transport difficulties denied those living inland an equal opportunity with fresh seafood.) The recipes found here are from Bengal, Bombay, Goa, Tamil Nadu and Kerala. They are, to an extent, representative of India. Apart from regional differences, there are also vertical barriers of class and society that also dictate what, when and how one eats. Only the poor eat shellfish or salted fish in India, and the Muslims avoid shellfish. Some higher caste Indians prefer white-fleshed fish. Bengalis prefer freshwater fish while Bangladeshis prefer seafood to freshwater fish. And in certain societies, being vegetarian does not deter one from eating fish. Similar food traditions and contradictions are present in Pakistan and Sri Lanka.

An Indian meal is an experience in itself. Most Indians eat three large meals a day—a heavy cooked breakfast of fermented pancakes (*dosai, iddli, apom* or *roti*), a heavy lunch which is the main meal of the day, and a light dinner consisting of leftovers from lunch. There is a healthy dependence on milk foods and dairy products. Most breakfasts are painstakingly time-consuming to make, as breads and pancakes need pre-soaking, grinding and time to rise.

For most middle-class Indians, lunch is the heaviest meal of the day, with at least two meat or fish dishes and three or four vegetables, a dhal and an appetiser, and *rassam* (pepper water) in the south or *lassi* (buttermilk) in the north. Indians, Bangladeshis, Sri Lankans and Pakistanis all traditionally eat while seated on the floor but in most city homes, food is eaten in a western-style dining room.

Eating is steeped in tradition. Food is eaten with fingers of the right hand and it is important that the palm stays clean. Food is served in individual *thaals*, round silver or stainless steel (which Indians call 'eversilver') trays with little silver bowls arranged around it, containing chutneys, pickles, appetisers and *pappadams*. Rice, *roti* or *chappati* is placed on the *thaal* itself and each person has his own set of food dishes. True vegetarians will not touch a drinking vessel with their lips, choosing to pour the drink from an undetermined distance into an open mouth than risk contamination from non-vegetarian lips. In 'modern' homes, where the older generation is vegetarian and the younger generations have been introduced to meat or fish, the house could support two separate kitchens, each with its own set of ovens, equipment, utensils and even cooks who specialise in one or the other type of food.

When discussing Indian, Pakistani and Sri Lankan foods, it helps to remember that India's vastness and food styles can be equated to the food, cultures, ethnic differences and vastness of Europe. Spices and herbs and styles differ from north to south—northern food is Moghul-influenced, sophisticated and lavish, with a dependence on wheat and dairy foods. Southerners and Sri Lankans live in a tropical environment and depend on the sea, the coconut and other tropical products. Sri Lankan and South Indian curries are traditionally much hotter, and their food is quite varied, having Arab and colonial influences.

The rich creamy *masalas* and *korma* cooked by the Muslims in Pakistan are different again from the Muslim food cooked in Bangladesh, which is hotter, with more chilli added, though it has the subtly blended herbs, spices and mustard oil of the Bengali. North Indian Hindu food is rich, subtle and herby with coriander, cumin, garam masala and little chilli, while food in Hyderabad is Muslim in character. Seafood in Kerala and in Goa is particularly unique. Keralans are 'rovers' and the food has more of an abandon, a bite, to it, reflecting the adventurous spirit that prompted these energetic people to set up wonderful foodstalls in far-flung destinations, while Goa reflects its Portuguese customs and food styles.

Sri Lankan food is similar to that cooked by the Malayali of Kerala, both countries sharing roughly the same latitude and climatic conditions. Both cuisines lean heavily on coconut and seafood. These people pride themselves on being good cooks and spend hours in the kitchen preparing breakfast, lunch or teatime snacks. As in India, breakfast and lunch are the main meals, while dinner is lighter. Northern Sri Lankans are traditionally farmers and eat frugally as farming communities do. Everything in the arid north is put to use: the total utilisation of the coconut tree is a good example of northern thrift. Coconut water sours bread and makes a refreshing drink; the flesh is squeezed for milk or dried as copra from which oil is extracted; coconut shells are used as fuel to smoke copra or made into ladles; husks are made into coir mattresses and ropes; the sap at the top of the tree is tapped for sugar and toddy; the thin stems of leaves are used to make brooms; and the leaves are woven into mats.

The Sinhalese of Sri Lanka use an interesting condiment, the flesh of the skipjack tuna *(katsuwonis pelamis)* that is smoked and dried into rock-hard consistency. This fish, called 'Maldive fish' because the centre of production used to be in the Maldives, is pounded and added to soups, curries, sautéed with vegetables and made into my favourite Sri Lankan *sambol*, the *pol* or coconut *sambol*. It is exported to Japan as bonito flakes *(katsuobushi)*.

Tandoori Maach (Pakistani Tandoori Fish)

This dish is a delicacy of cooks who migrated from Peshawar to India. If you do not have a *tandoori* oven, use an ordinary oven.

Ingredients

Pomfret, threadfin or red snapper (whole or steaks)	500 g
Lime or lemon juice	3 Tbsp
Salt	1/4 tsp
Garlic	8 cloves, peeled and crushed
Ginger	5-cm knob, peeled and crushed
Coriander (*dhania*) seeds	2 tsp or 4 tsp ground coriander (*malli*)
Ground turmeric (*haldi*)	1 tsp
Garam masala	1 tsp
Chilli powder	1 Tbsp
Mango powder (*amchur*)	2 tsp
Ground fennel (*perinseeragam*)	1/2 tsp
Vinegar	1 Tbsp
Yoghurt	3 Tbsp
Tomato purée	1 Tbsp
Cooking oil	1 Tbsp
Mango powder or lemon juice	1 tsp

Garnish

Mint leaves	25 g
Coriander (*dhania*) leaves or fenugreek (*methi*) leaves	25 g
Lemons	2, cut into wedges

Method

- Scale, gut and clean fish, making slashes on the thickest part. Rub 1 Tbsp lime or lemon juice and salt over fish and leave for 30 minutes.

- Blend (process) garlic and ginger with coriander seeds or coriander powder, turmeric, *garam masala*, chilli powder, mango powder, fennel, vinegar, yoghurt, remaining lime juice and tomato purée into a paste.

- Rub paste all over fish and into fish stomach cavity. Leave fish to season for at least 2 hours.

- Skewer fish lengthwise using a metal or bamboo skewer. (If microwaving, use a bamboo skewer.)

- Traditionally, a *tandoori* oven was used, but for domestic cooking, a grill, a barbecue or an oven can be used. Place skewers on a greased baking tray. Bake or grill for 15 minutes at 180°C, turn fish over and bake for another 15 minutes.

- Alternatively, cook in the microwave oven. Preheat browning dish for 7 minutes on HIGH. Heat oil in dish for 30 seconds and place fish in to sear in the heat. Cook for 6 minutes on HIGH and 2 minutes on MEDIUM.

- Dredge fish with mango powder or lemon juice as you remove it. Serve with mint and coriander or fenugreek leaves and lemon wedges.

Elish Maacher Jhol (Fish Gravy)

Jhol is the Bengali name for watery stew, and *maacher jhol*, spiced fish stew, is almost a national dish in Bengal.

Ingredients

Tamarind paste *(imli)*	5-cm square
Water	250 ml or 2 Tbsp vinegar
Turmeric *(haldi)*	2-cm knob, peeled or 6 dried chillies
Whole mustard seeds	2¹/₂ Tbsp
Shard, hilsa, mackerel, bream or black pomfret fillets	600 g
Mustard oil	2 Tbsp
Salt	to taste
Sugar	¹/₂ tsp or to taste
Green chillies	4, slit and seeded

Garnish

Green chillies	2, chopped

Method

- Mix tamarind paste with water or vinegar and stir with a fork. Strain and reserve liquid.

- Grind turmeric or dried chillies into a paste. Add 2 Tbsp mustard seeds and grind into a paste once more.

- Cut fish into 5-cm pieces, dry with absorbent paper and coat with some turmeric paste. Mix remaining paste in a bowl with 250 ml water. Set aside.

- Heat mustard oil in a pan or *dekshi* until it becomes hazy. Sauté remaining whole mustard seeds until they splutter. Lower in fish pieces carefully and keep moving them around in the oil to prevent them from sticking to the bottom of the pan.

- When fish is brown, pour in bowl of liquid paste carefully so oil does not splutter. Add tamarind liquid and bring to the boil. Simmer for 15 minutes and add salt, sugar and slit green chillies to taste.

- Garnish with additional chopped chillies and eat with rice and yoghurt.

Chingri Vindaloo (Bengali Prawn Vindaloo)

The Bengali penchant for adding ground mustard or mustard oil to all their recipes contributes a distinctive taste to their cuisine.

Ingredients

Ginger	3-cm knob, peeled and sliced
Garlic	4 cloves, peeled and sliced
Mustard seeds	2 Tbsp
Mustard oil	3 Tbsp
Ground turmeric (*haldi*)	1¹/₂ tsp
Chilli powder	2 tsp
Ground coriander (*malli*)	2 tsp
Ground cumin (*jeera*)	2 tsp
Prawns (shrimps)	600 g, shelled and deveined
Vinegar	4 Tbsp
Water	125 ml
Salt	to taste
Sugar	1 tsp or to taste

Garnish

Green chillies	6, seeded and chopped

Method

- Pound or blend (process) ginger, garlic and mustard seeds into a paste.

- Heat mustard oil in a pan and add paste, ground turmeric, chilli powder, ground coriander and ground cumin. Stir until ingredients are well-mixed and cook for about 5 minutes.

- Add prawns and stir well until they turn pink. Add vinegar and stir-fry until vinegar is absorbed. Add water and bring to the boil.

- Season with salt and sugar to taste and remove from heat. Serve garnished with chopped green chillies.

Pol Sambol (Herbert Fernando's Maldive Fish and Coconut Sambol)

Fish and coconut *sambol* is a must with every Sri Lankan meal. The Sri Lankans and the Maldive islanders use the dried variety of skipjack tuna, a rather small tuna. The Japanese also use this dried fish, which they call *katsuobushi,* or dried bonito flakes, to flavour their soups and stocks.

Ingredients

Onions	2, large
Maldive fish or dried prawns (shrimps)	1 Tbsp
Grated coconut	from 1 coconut or 125 g desiccated coconut mixed with 2 Tbsp coconut cream
Chilli powder	1 tsp
Paprika	2–3 Tbsp
Lime juice	extracted from 3 limes
Curry or bay leaves	3, crushed
Salt	to taste
Ground white pepper	to taste

Method

- Boil water and plunge onions into boiling water for 1 minute to take away any bitterness. Drain, peel and slice into thin pieces.

- If Maldive fish or dried prawns are in large pieces, soak for 10 minutes in warm water, then drain and pound. Set aside.

- Crush and break up onion roughly in a blender, then add grated coconut gradually along with chilli powder and paprika.

- Continue mixing, and add lime juice and Maldive fish or dried shrimps. Mix well but ensure that paste does not become too fine.

- Finally, add crushed curry or bay leaves, and salt and pepper to taste.

- The paprika and chilli will give this *sambol* a bright red colour. It keeps for 3–4 days and can be freshened with the addition of more lime juice. Store in an airtight container.

Meen-Thalai Kari (Kerala Fish Head Curry)

Traditionally, an earthenware pot *(chatty)* or deep pan *(dekshi)* was used to cook fish curry. These pots or pans were reserved only for fish and the curry produced was unbelievably tasty.

Ingredients

Curry leaves	1 stalk, plucked
Green chillies	4, seeded and sliced
Raw green mangoes	2 or 4 tart tomatoes, sliced
Ground coriander *(malli)*	½ Tbsp
Ground turmeric *(haldi)*	½ tsp
Chilli powder	1 Tbsp
Fish stock	250 ml
Cooking oil	1 Tbsp
Onions	2, large, peeled and sliced
Garlic	2 cloves, peeled and sliced
Ginger	5-cm knob, peeled and sliced
Snapper or mackerel fish head	500 g, cut in half lengthwise
Grated coconut	75 g, dry-roasted and finely blended
Coconut milk	250 ml
Salt	to taste

Garnish

Curry leaves

Method

- Mix curry leaves, green chillies and mangoes or tomatoes in a bowl.

- Mix ground coriander, ground turmeric and chilli powder with fish stock.

- Heat oil and sauté onions until golden. Add garlic and ginger and stir-fry until soft. Add curry leaves, green chillies, mangoes or tomatoes and fish stock mixture.

- Bring to the boil. Cover and cook spices for 5–8 minutes. Lower to a simmer for about 10 minutes until gravy is reduced. Add fish and simmer for 5 minutes.

- Add roasted ground coconut and stir carefully. The gravy can be thin or thick according to your liking. For a thinner gravy, add more stock or coconut milk at the end. The gravy matures with prolonged simmering. If you prefer it strong, remove the fish halfway through, thicken gravy and replace fish at the end.

- Taste for salt and remove from heat. Garnish with curry leaves and serve with boiled rice or sour pancakes *(dosai)*. Fish curry improves with keeping.

Patrani Machhi (Fish Parcels Parsi Style)

This famous Parsi dish is served at weddings and feasts.

Ingredients

Banana leaves or foil	same number as fish pieces, cut into 20-cm squares
Raw green mango	1 or $1/4$ tsp tamarind paste *(imli)*
Grated coconut	150 g or 100 g desiccated coconut mixed with 50 g coconut cream
Coriander *(dhania)* leaves	25 g
Garlic	6 cloves
Cumin seeds *(jeera)*	1 tsp
Sugar	$1/2$ tsp
Salt	to taste
Pomfret, snapper or threadfin fillets	500 g, cut into 6-cm pieces
Lime or lemon juice	extracted from 1 lime or lemon
Cooking oil	50 ml or 2 Tbsp ghee or margarine

Garnish

Mint leaves	
Green chillies	4, sliced lengthwise, seeded and soaked in cold water to form chilli flowers

Method

- If using banana leaves, soften them by dipping into very hot water. Wipe dry as they become pliant.

- If using mango, remove seed and chop flesh into pieces. If using tamarind paste, combine with 2 Tbsp water and strain liquid.

- Grind or blend (process) grated coconut, coriander leaves, garlic, mango or tamarind liquid, cumin seeds and sugar into a paste. Mix in salt to taste.

- Place banana leaf or foil squares on a plate. Apply paste liberally to both sides of each piece of fish, then sprinkle some lime or lemon juice on fish. Place one fish piece on one banana leaf or foil square and wrap up, tying firmly with string.

- Heat oil, ghee or margarine in a shallow pan over low heat. Shallow-fry fish parcels on one side for about 5 minutes, then turn parcels over and fry for a further 5 minutes. If using banana leaves, they will darken and seem to shrink. Cover pan for a few minutes to cook fish further.

- Alternatively, bake parcels in a conventional oven. Grease a baking dish and place fish parcels in without overlapping. Smear parcels with ghee or margarine and bake at 180°C for 30 minutes.

- You may also cook the parcels in the microwave oven. Place the banana parcels in a microwave-safe dish and smear with ghee or margarine and cover with plastic wrap. Cook for 6 minutes on MEDIUM and another 2 minutes on HIGH.

- Remove fish parcels and serve the opened parcels on a plate, garnished with mint leaves and green chilli 'flowers'. Eat with rice and lime pickles or green vegetables.

Meen Curry (Southern Fish Curry)

This recipe is a blend of Keralan and Sri Lankan recipes. The addition of tamarind should be one of the last steps in making a curry. If you do not like your curry too sour, halve the amount of tamarind. Tamarind is not only a souring agent, it stops the cooking process in meat or fish and helps preserve it. Fenugreek, lime juice and vinegar are used to 'sour' a fish curry. If you like your curry tart, try adding some green tomato or mango as they do in southern India.

Ingredients

Cooking oil	2 Tbsp
Mustard seeds	$^1/_2$ tsp
Black gram dhal	1 tsp
Brown onions	$2^1/_2$, medium or 10 small red shallots, peeled and thinly sliced
Garlic	6 cloves, peeled and sliced
Ginger	3-cm knob, peeled and sliced
Fenugreek seeds (methi)	$^1/_4$ Tbsp, lightly pounded
Mixed or fish curry powder	2 Tbsp
Water	250 ml
Tamarind paste (imli)	1 Tbsp, mixed with 250 ml water, strained
Tomatoes	2
Trevally, mackerel or snapper steaks or fillets	500 g, sliced into 6-cm pieces
Coconut cream	125 ml
Salt	to taste
Ground white pepper	to taste
Lime or lemon juice	1 Tbsp

Method

- Heat oil in a deep saucepan or *dekshi* and stir-fry mustard seeds and black gram dhal. (The mustard seeds will pop.)

- Add onions or shallots and sauté until brown. Add garlic and stir-fry until golden.

- Add ginger and fenugreek seeds and stir quickly or the fenugreek could turn bitter.

- Add curry powder and brown quickly. Add water and cook curry on low heat for 3 minutes. Stir in tamarind liquid and add tomatoes. Allow tomatoes to simmer in curry. If curry becomes too dry, add 125 ml water.

- Allow curry to reduce a bit and thicken, then lower in fish fillets. Allow curry to come to the boil for 3–5 minutes, then add coconut cream and stir well on low heat. Add salt, pepper and lime juice and remove from heat.

- Serve hot. This curry keeps well overnight and tastes even better the next day when all the spices have matured.

Kathrika Pahi (Dried Fish and Aubergine)

This strongly flavoured dish from South India may not appeal to all. For a milder flavour, use fried whitebait in place of dried fish. Serve in small quantities.

Ingredients

Aubergines (eggplants/brinjals)	500 g, slit lengthwise into 4–6 pieces
Ground turmeric (haldi)	a pinch
Salt	1/2 tsp
Tamarind paste (imli)	50 g
Vinegar	50 ml
Chilli powder	1 Tbsp
Ground coriander (malli)	1 1/2 Tbsp
Ground fennel (perinseeragam)	2 tsp
Salt	to taste
Cooking oil	250 ml
Dried seer or threadfin	300 g, cut into 2-cm cubes
Garlic	10 cloves, peeled and sliced
Red shallots	10 or 1 1/2 medium brown onions, peeled and sliced
Red or green chillies	4, slit and seeded
Cinnamon stick (karuva pattai)	1
Coconut cream	125 ml
Sugar	to taste

Method

- Rub cut aubergines with ground turmeric and salt. Set aside on absorbent paper and allow any liquid to seep out. Pat dry.

- Mix tamarind paste with vinegar and enough water to form 175 ml liquid and strain. Mix in chilli powder, ground coriander, ground fennel and 1/4 tsp salt. Set aside.

- Heat oil until it is smoking. (Because aubergine is spongy, it will absorb a lot of oil unless cooked in very hot oil.) Fry aubergine pieces quickly, removing them as they turn golden and drain on absorbent paper.

- Fry dried fish cubes until golden, then remove. Fry garlic, shallots or onions and chillies separately in the same oil, removing and draining separately.

- Remove oil and pour in tamarind liquid mixture. Add cinnamon stick. Mix well and bring to the boil slowly. If it becomes too thick, add 125 ml water.

- Lower heat and add fried garlic, shallots or onions, chillies and dried fish. Allow gravy to thicken and reduce for 5 minutes, stirring on low heat.

- Add aubergines and stir in coconut cream. Add sugar and salt to taste. Remove from heat after 2–3 minutes, when oil separates from gravy. Serve hot or cold, with a mild curry.

Sookha Bombla (Bombay Duck from Gujerat)

The *sookha boomla* or *bambloe* fish, a small fish found in the Bay of Bengal, is a strong flavoured fish known to the rest of the world as 'Bombay Duck'. It is prepared by cutting a slit down the side of the fish, lying the fish flat, open and removing the central bone. Bombay Duck is thoroughly washed, salted, then dried before export. To prepare it for cooking, wash well, then wrap in absorbent paper and lay between two plates with a weight on top for about 10 minutes to remove the excess moisture from the fish. It can then be wiped dry and shallow-fried with some curry pastes.

Ingredients

Cumin seeds *(jeera)*	1 tsp
Coriander *(dhania)* seeds	1/2 tsp
Cloves	1/2 tsp
Black peppercorns	1/2 tsp
Cinnamon stick *(karuva pattai)*	2-cm length
Chilli powder	1 Tbsp
Garlic	10 cloves, peeled and sliced
Vinegar	125 ml
Dried Bombay duck	15 pieces, soaked in warm water for 30 minutes
Vegetable oil	125 ml
Red shallots	6, peeled and sliced
Ground turmeric *(haldi)*	1/2 tsp
Salt	to taste

Method

- Dry-roast cumin and coriander seeds over high heat for 5–6 minutes or cook in the microwave oven for 2 minutes on HIGH. Add cloves, peppercorns, cinnamon stick and chilli powder and pound or blend (process) together with garlic slices. Add a few drops of vinegar to ease blending if necessary.

- Squeeze water out of soaked dried Bombay Duck and wipe dry with paper towels.

- Heat oil, then fry dried Bombay Duck until crisp. Remove and drain.

- In the same oil, sauté shallots until brown. Remove all but 2 Tbsp oil and add blended paste to browned shallots. Stir-fry and add vinegar and turmeric and bring to the boil.

- Add crisp dried Bombay Duck and cook, stirring until fish is tender and oil separates. Test for salt and add salt if necessary. Remove from heat and cool.

- Store in bottles and use as an appetiser or pickle.

King Prawn Balchaun

Goans enjoy eating both rice and *roti* (Indian bread and ordinary loaf bread). Bread is a Portuguese legacy and it is used to scoop up delicious sauces using the fingers. If serving this dish, it might be a good idea to provide finger bowls filled with weak tea or water and slices of lemon or lime.

Ingredients

Ground turmeric	1 tsp
Salt	to taste
King prawns (shrimps)	500 g, shelled, deveined and cleaned
Coriander *(dhania)* seeds	1 Tbsp
Red chillies	8
Cumin seeds *(jeera)*	1 tsp
Cloves	6
Black peppercorns	1 Tbsp
Garlic	12 cloves, peeled
Ginger	2-cm knob, peeled
Olive oil	2 Tbsp
Red or Spanish onions	6, medium, peeled and finely sliced
Tomatoes	6, medium, seeded and cubed
Tomato purée	2 Tbsp

Garnish

Coriander *(dhania)* leaves	2 sprigs, chopped

Method

- Apply ground turmeric and salt to prawns and keep aside.

- Blend (process) coriander seeds, red chillies, cumin seeds, cloves, peppercorns, garlic and ginger into a fine *masala* paste.

- Heat olive oil in a wok and deep-fry prawns until cooked. Keep aside.

- In the same oil, fry onions until soft. Add *masala* paste and fry until aromatic.

- Add tomatoes and sauté until well-combined. Add prawns and season to taste with salt.

- Add tomato purée and cook covered for about 5 minutes. Remove cover and simmer to reduce sauce until thick. Garnish with coriander leaves and serve warm with bread.

Kabab Tikkah Machhi (Fish on Skewers)

Ingredients

Ling, tuna or other firm-fleshed fish	1 kg, skinned and cut into small cubes
Light olive oil	1 Tbsp
Besan (gram flour)	½ Tbsp
Ginger	3-cm knob, peeled and blended into pulp
Plain yoghurt	5 Tbsp
Ground cumin	2 tsp
Freshly ground black pepper	2 tsp
Paprika	a pinch
Cloves	4, ground
Salt	to taste
Onions	4, small, peeled and thickly sliced in rounds
Ghee (clarified butter)	2 Tbsp, melted
Lime juice	extracted from 1 lime

Method

- Rub fish with olive oil then wash well and rub with *besan*. Wash again to remove slime from fish.

- Mix ginger pulp with yoghurt, cumin, black pepper, paprika, cloves and salt. The mixture should be light red in colour. Leave fish to marinate in mixture for 1 hour.

- Thread skewers through onion rounds and fish cubes, alternating the two. Brush with ghee and place under grill to brown. Bast frequently with juices from grill-pan and turn skewers over at least twice during grilling.

- Moisten with lime juice and serve hot on skewers.

Raal Peretal (Amma's Dry Prawn)

Raal peretal is a method of fry-cooking fish, prawn (shrimp) or meat. The curry is slowly stirred in special gingelly oil until all the spices are intermingled with the fish, prawns or meat, leaving a dry, tasty blend that is easy on the palate. If potato is added, its soft texture when cooked, goes well with the chewier prawn, while absorbing the full flavours of the sauce.

Ingredients

Potato	1, large, cut into 8 cubes, optional
Gingelly or vegetable oil	3 Tbsp
Garlic	4 cloves, peeled and pounded
Ginger	2-cm knob, peeled and pounded
Red shallots	25, small or 2 large brown onions, peeled and sliced
Ground coriander (*malli*)	1 Tbsp
Ground cumin (*jeera*)	1/2 Tbsp
Ground turmeric (*haldi*)	1/2 tsp
Chilli powder	1 Tbsp
School prawns (shrimps)	500 g, shelled and deveined
Sugar	to taste
Salt	to taste
Tamarind paste (*imli*)	1 Tbsp, mixed with 3 Tbsp water, strained
Curry leaves	1 stalk, plucked

Method

- If using potato, parboil potato cubes for 6–8 minutes. Drain water and reserve cubes.

- Heat oil in an earthenware pot or *dekshi*. Sauté garlic and ginger until golden. Add shallots or onions and stir-fry until golden and soft.

- Add ground coriander, cumin, turmeric and chilli powder and stir-fry until aromatic. Stir prawns and potato cubes into mixture and mix well. Add sugar and salt to taste.

- The prawns should be coated with the curry mixture. If the mixture is too dry, add 1 Tbsp water.

- When prawns are curled and cooked, add tamarind liquid and stir well. Add curry leaves, stir once more and remove from heat. Serve hot.

Palchura Varai (Selva's Spicy Flaked Baby Shark)

This Sri Lankan fish preparation is a flaked fish stir-fry made from the very tasty *palchura* or baby shark. As the fish is stirred, onions, garlic, ginger and turmeric are added, plus a large amount of toasted coconut which gives the dish a nutty flavour.

Ingredients

Young shark, mackerel or gemfish fillets or cutlets	500 g
Ground white pepper	1¼ tsp
Salt	1¼ tsp
Ground turmeric *(haldi)*	1½ tsp
Cooking oil	2 Tbsp
Star anise	1, broken up
Cinnamon stick *(karuva pattai)*	1, broken up
Garlic	6 cloves, peeled and sliced
Brown onions	3, medium, peeled and sliced
Ground cumin *(jeera)*	1 Tbsp
Chilli powder	2 tsp
Grated coconut	200 g, dry-roast 125 g
Garam masala	1 tsp
Ground white pepper	to taste

Garnish

Onions	2, peeled, sliced and crisp-fried

Method

- Cover fish in 250 ml water and bring to the boil with 1 tsp pepper, 1 tsp salt, and ½ tsp turmeric. Drain water when fish turns opaque. Cool and then flake fish, removing any bones and skin.

- Heat oil in a wok or large frying pan (skillet). When hot, add star anise, cinnamon stick and garlic. Stir until garlic turns golden. Add sliced onions and stir until softened.

- Add flaked fish and mix thoroughly with onion. Add cumin, remaining turmeric and chilli powder and toss thoroughly.

- After 3 minutes, add all the grated coconut, stir and toss well for 10 minutes.

- Sprinkle *garam masala* over entire contents of pan. Add pepper and salt to taste and keep tossing until ingredients are well-mixed and coconut smells aromatic.

- Remove from heat and garnish with fried onions.

A Sri Lankan-Keralan Recipe

Ingredients

Cumin seeds *(jeera)*	1 tsp, dry-roasted and finely ground
Garlic	1 clove, chopped or ½ tsp garlic powder
Ground turmeric *(haldi)*	1½ tsp
Salt	1 tsp
Chilli powder	1 tsp
Lime juice	extracted from ½ lime
Threadfin or black pomfret cutlets	500 g, cut into 6-cm pieces
Cooking oil	250 ml

Method

- Mix ground cumin with garlic, turmeric, salt, chilli powder and lime juice to make a paste. Smear over fish and leave for 30 minutes.

- Heat oil and shallow-fry 2–3 fish pieces at a time. Turn to brown both sides. Remove and drain on absorbent paper. Serve.

A Malaysian-Indonesian Recipe

Ingredients

Ground turmeric *(haldi)*	2 tsp
Salt	1 tsp
Chilli powder	1 tsp
Spanish mackerel	500 g, cut into 6-cm pieces
Cooking oil	250 ml

Garnish

Lemon or lime juice	from 1 lemon or lime
Red shallots	3–4 or 1 medium brown onion, peeled, sliced and crisp-fried

Method

- Mix turmeric and salt with some water to form a paste. Add chilli powder and smear paste over fish. Leave for 30 minutes.

- Heat oil and shallow-fry 2–3 fish pieces at a time. Turn to brown both sides. Remove and drain on absorbent paper.

- Sprinkle with lemon or lime juice and garnish with fried shallots or onions and serve.

Parra Karavadu (Salted Fish Pickle)

This is a beautiful but rather strong-tasting salted fish pickle. It is eaten in tiny amounts with mounds of rice and vegetables.

Ingredients

Salted fish (threadfin or any thick-fleshed salted fish)	1 kg, washed and cut into 1-cm cubes
Cooking oil	350 ml
Shallots	15, small or 4 large brown onions, peeled and chopped
Garlic	6 cloves, peeled and chopped
Ginger	6-cm knob, peeled and chopped
White vinegar	750 ml
Fennel seeds (perinseeragam)	1½ Tbsp
Cumin seeds (jeera)	2 Tbsp
Chilli powder	2 Tbsp
Ground turmeric (haldi)	1 dsp
Curry leaves	3–4 stalks, plucked
Tamarind paste (imli)	1 Tbsp
Sugar	½ Tbsp or more
Salt	to taste
Fenugreek seeds (methi)	1 tsp, dry-roasted
Mustard seeds	1 Tbsp

Method

- Dry salted fish cubes in the sun or a warm oven until crisp. Heat oil and fry a few pieces at a time and drain.

- Blend (process) shallots or onions, garlic and ginger with 50 ml vinegar. Set aside.

- Similarly, blend fennel and cumin seeds with 50 ml vinegar to make a fine paste. Set aside.

- Mix chilli powder and ground turmeric with 50 ml vinegar to form a paste.

- Mix tamarind paste with 125 ml vinegar and strain.

- Re-heat oil in a pan and add blended shallot, garlic and ginger mixture. Sauté until golden. The oil should be visible at all times. Add a little more if necessary.

- Add fennel and cumin paste and sauté until aromatic.

- Stir in chilli and turmeric paste quickly. If necessary, add a little more oil.

- Add curry leaves, tamarind liquid, salt and sugar to taste. Cook for 2 minutes.

- Meanwhile combine roasted fenugreek seeds with mustard seeds and bruise slightly. Add to pan then remove quickly from heat.

- Quickly mix in salted fish and taste for sugar, chilli and salt. The pickle should be hot, sweet and tasty, but not too salty.

- Leave to cool and store in airtight bottles. This pickle will keep for up to 1 year. Serve with rice and vegetables.

Nandu Masala Chettynaad

(Vellasamy's Crab or Prawn Masala from Chettynaad)

This recipe comes from the small province of Chettynaad in South India. Use either crabs or prawns (shrimps) for this dish, not both.

Ingredients

Crabs	2, large or 1 kg prawns
Vegetable oil	50 ml
Brown onions	4, large, pounded, juice extracted and reserved
Ginger	6-cm knob, peeled and pounded
Garlic	10 cloves, peeled and pounded
Tomatoes	2, large, cut into quarters
Green chillies	4, sliced lengthwise in half, seeds removed
Fennel seeds (*perinseeragam*)	1 Tbsp, ground
Chilli powder	1½ Tbsp
Ground coriander (*malli*)	1 Tbsp
Grated coconut	150 g, dry-roasted
Poppy seeds	1 Tbsp
Salt	to taste
Water	50 ml

Garnish

Curry or coriander (*dhania*) leaves	75 g

Method

- If using crabs, clean and cut each crab into four pieces. Crack claws and break off legs. If using prawns, shell, leaving tail intact and devein.

- Heat oil in a deep saucepan or *dekshi* until it is hazy. Sauté onions until brown.

- Add ginger and garlic and stir until brown. Mix in tomato quarters, green chillies, ground fennel seeds, chilli powder and ground coriander. Cook for 5 minutes until aromatic.

- Add roasted grated coconut and stir-fry until fragrant and oil begins to separate from spices.

- Put in crabs or prawns, onion juice, poppy seeds, salt to taste and water. Bring to the boil, then reduce to a simmer. Keep stirring for 5 minutes for curry to penetrate crab claws.

- Remove from heat and garnish with curry or coriander leaves.

Gabolli (Hot and Sour Mullet Roes)

We had these lovely entrees in a tiny restaurant which was open only 3–4 nights a week because the owner, Martin, was busy with other enterprises. He opened it for us because he had heard that we were anxious to savour his lovely cooking and were going to bring a tour to Goa the following year. The restaurant was a tiny little house opening out into a beautiful garden surrounded by coconut and palm trees. There were tables laid out and it was a bright moonlit night which brought the best of Goan cuisine to us. We could hear the waves close by and glasses of *feni* (cashew nut liqueur) set the mood for the evening.

Ingredients

Fish roes (mullet)	2, large, about 10 x 3-cm
Chilli powder	1 tsp
Ground turmeric	1 tsp
Dried cocum*	4 pieces, pounded
Ground white pepper	to taste
Salt	to taste
Spanish or red onions	2, medium
Grated coconut	50 g

Garnish

Mint	1 sprig, chopped
Coriander (*dhania*) leaves	1 sprig, chopped
Kalamansi limes	3, cut into halves

Cocum is a sour fruit, dried and used mainly in cooking fish dishes. It is similar to assam nipis. *If cocum is unavailable, use as a substitute.*

Method

- Wash roe carefully to remove some of the sticky residue but try not to remove the membrane itself.

- Mix chilli powder, ground turmeric, cocum, pepper, salt, onions and grated coconut into a thick mixture.

- Heat a pan with 250 ml water and place mixture in. Cook until onion becomes soft and roe becomes compact. Remove from heat and cool roe. Take roe and freeze for 1 hour to compact it further.

- Remove roe from freezer and slice thinly. Serve roe with mayonnaise or the sauce in which it was cooked. Garnish with chopped mint, coriander or kalamansi limes.

Koftas (Prawn and Fish Cakes)

This recipe for prawn (shrimp) or fish is found all over Asia. *Kofta* is a North Indian term. South of the Deccan it is called a *vadai*, or sometimes 'cutlet' or 'croquette'. The Sri Lankan and the Kerala versions are very similar, Keralans using fresh rather than dried chillies, and Sri Lankans using Maldive fish as flavouring.

Ingredients

Prawns (shrimps)	500 g or mackerel, seer or blackfish cutlets
Dried chillies or fresh green chillies	3
Salt	¹/₂ tsp
Grated or desiccated coconut	125 g, dry-roasted
Ginger	5-cm knob, peeled and finely grated
Maldive fish	1¹/₂ tsp, ground, optional
Fennel seeds *(perinseeragam)*	2 tsp, roasted and ground into paste or use 2 tsp *garam masala*
Curry leaves	1 stalk, plucked and shredded
Red shallots	10, peeled and finely chopped
Lime juice	extracted from 1 large lime
Eggs yolks	2, beaten
Plain (all-purpose) flour	1 Tbsp
Ground white pepper	¹/₂ tsp
Cooking oil	250 ml

Method

- Shell prawns or fillet fish. In a pan, fill enough water to cover prawns or fish and chillies. Add salt and bring to the boil for about 5 minutes. Alternatively, cook in the microwave oven for 4 minutes on HIGH. Remove, drain and reserve liquid. Blend (process) prawns or fish and chillies into a paste.

- Mix meat paste with coconut, ginger, Maldive fish, fennel or *garam masala*, curry leaves, shallots and lime juice.

- Add a little egg yolk at a time until mixture is pliable and can be shaped easily into balls. The mixture should not be too sticky, but should leave the sides of the bowl easily without sticking to your palm. If it is too wet, add some flour to make it firm.

- Make up 20 oval shapes, then flatten them slightly and dip in a flour and pepper mixture.

- Heat oil in a *dekshi* or deep pan. When oil becomes hazy, gently lower in *koftas* a few at a time, quickly turning as they turn golden. Remove with a slotted spoon and drain.

- Alternatively, cook in the microwave oven. Preheat a browning dish for 6 minutes on HIGH and add 2 Tbsp oil. Heat for 1 minute on HIGH and cook 6–8 patties for 2 minutes on HIGH. Turn patties over. Cook for a further 2 minutes on MEDIUM, then remove and allow to stand for a few minutes before serving.

- Serve as an entrée or as part of a main meal.

Fried Fish

These fried fish recipes are some of the most delicious, especially if the fish is fresh and the spices are well-blended. A whole mound of rice can be eaten with just a single piece of fried fish and some salted vegetables.

To fry fish properly, you will need a good heavy-based pan or *dekshi*, preferably with a curved bottom. The fat or oil should be sufficient to cover the fish. Fish should be dried with absorbent paper, seasoned with turmeric, pepper or salt and dipped in egg white or breadcrumbs, or rubbed over with a mixture of flour and ground cumin, before being fried in very hot oil.

Here are recipes for three kinds of fried fish from Goa, Sri Lanka, Malaysia and Indonesia.

A Goan Recipe

Ingredients

Onions	2, peeled and finely sliced
Garlic	1 clove, peeled
Ground turmeric *(haldi)*	a pinch
Chilli powder	$1/2$ tsp
Mustard seeds	$1/4$ tsp
Cumin seeds *(jeera)*	$1/4$ tsp
Mackerel, trevally or sea bass	500 g, cleaned and gutted
Cooking oil	1 Tbsp
Water	125 ml
Salt	to taste

Method

- Blend (process) half the onions, garlic, turmeric, chilli powder, mustard seeds and cumin seeds into a paste. Smear over fish and leave for 30 minutes.

- Heat oil and fry remaining onion until slightly brown.

- Carefully place fish in and fry until golden on one side before turning over.

- Add water, then cover and simmer for about 5 minutes. Season with salt.

- Transfer to a serving dish and leave for 10 minutes until fish is soft before serving.

Goan Prawn Curry

Among all the crustaceans available in Goa, prawns (shrimps) are the most popular. Prawns found in streams and rivers close to the sea are most tasty. In Goa, prawns are cultivated in salt pans called *khazanas* which are opened at high and closed at low tide. These prawns are costly but very much in demand and highly regarded among the Goans who cook it when entertaining and during festivals. If you are unable to obtain raw mangoes, use drumsticks or lady fingers instead.

Ingredients

Grated coconut	100 g
Chilli powder	1 Tbsp
Ground turmeric	1 tsp
Red onion	1, medium, peeled and sliced
Tamarind paste *(imli)*	1 Tbsp
Cooking oil	2 Tbsp
Tiger prawns (shrimps)	500 g, shelled, deveined and cleaned
Asafoetida	a pinch
Green mango	1, small, about 100 g, peeled and cut into cubes
Salt	to taste
Ground black pepper	to taste

Method

- Blend (process) grated coconut, chilli powder, ground turmeric, half the onion and tamarind paste into a fine paste.

- Heat oil in a large pan and fry ground paste until aromatic. Add in remaining onion, prawns, asafotieda and 450 ml water.

- Cook mixture for 3–4 minutes then add 1 litre water. Add mango pieces and cook for 3 minutes.

- Season with salt and pepper and serve with steamed rice.

Kanava Porial (Radha's Squid)

Squid is not very popular in India, but it remains a regional specialty in Kerala and Sri Lanka. This recipe comes from the Indians who live in Malaysia. This method of cooking squid is almost identical to that of the Fijian Indians.

Ingredients

Squid	500 g (cleaned weight)
Garlic	2 cloves, peeled
Ginger	2-cm knob, peeled
Ground turmeric *(haldi)*	1 tsp
Chilli powder	2 tsp
Ground cumin *(jeera)*	1 tsp
Ground fennel *(perinseeragam)*	1 tsp
Potato	1, large
Cooking oil	2 Tbsp
Brown onions	2, large, peeled and sliced
Curry leaves	3 stalks, plucked
Cinnamon sticks *(karuva pattai)*	2, roughly broken
Cloves	4, roughly broken
Cardamom pods	5, roughly broken
Almond meal	1 Tbsp
Salt	to taste
Sugar	a pinch
Fennel seeds *(perinseeragam)*	1/2 tsp
Lime juice	extracted from 1/2 lime

Method

- Clean squid. Remove head, tentacles and quill and peel off skin. Slice body tube and tentacles into 2-cm pieces.

- Grind or blend (process) garlic and ginger. Mix with ground turmeric, chilli powder, ground cumin and ground fennel. Stir squid pieces into mixture. Leave to stand.

- Cut potato into slices similar in size to squid pieces. Parboil potato in 250 ml water for 6 minutes.

- Heat oil and cook onions for about 5 minutes until golden brown. Add curry leaves, cinnamon sticks, cloves and cardamom pods. Stir-fry.

- Add squid with the ground paste to stir-fry. Mix well. Pour in 250 ml water and add potato. Cook on medium heat and stir slowly for 8–10 minutes until squid and potato are cooked and liquid has reduced in volume.

- Add almond meal and stir. Cook for 1 minute more.

- Add salt to taste, a pinch of sugar, fennel seeds and lime juice. Remove from heat and serve.

Ari Kadaka (Fried Mussels)

Traditionally, this recipe used rice flour and toasted coconut to form a firm dough. This dough was then rolled and stuffed into the shells of the mussels, secured tightly with string and then steamed. The steamed dough and mussel balls were then removed and fried with chilli powder. Here I have adapted the recipe for use in a modern kitchen.

Ingredients

Mussels	20, large
Rice flour	125 g
Desiccated or grated coconut	50 g, dry-roasted
Ground cumin (jeera)	1½ tsp
Salt	½ tsp
Cooking oil	2 Tbsp
Onion	1, large, peeled and sliced
Ground turmeric (haldi)	¼ tsp
Chilli powder	1 tsp

Garnish

Red shallots	3 or 1 medium brown onion, peeled, thinly sliced and crisp-fried

Method

- Wash and scrub mussel shells and pull out the "beards". Place them in a bowl and steam very briefly. As soon as the mussels open, remove from shells and keep warm.

- Dry-roast rice flour in a dry frying pan (skillet), turning and stirring for about 3 minutes until it looks cooked and takes on a slightly darker hue. Alternatively, cook rice flour in the microwave oven for 1–2 minutes on HIGH.

- Combine coconut, rice flour, ground cumin and salt in a bowl. Boil 180 ml water and add gradually to mixture to form a stiff dough. You may not need to use all the water.

- Make small marble-sized balls of dough and flatten them. Place a mussel in the centre of each dough piece and enclose, allowing part of the mussel to be seen.

- Heat oil and fry onion until brown. Remove fried onion and reserve for garnish.

- Continue heating oil and when it smokes, gently lower in a few mussel balls at a time. Sprinkle in some ground turmeric and chilli powder with each batch and stir to brown mussel balls quickly. Mussels turn tough if overcooked, so remove immediately when brown.

- Serve hot, garnished with fried onions and shallots. This dish goes well with mint chutney.

Maach Malad (Peanut Fish)

Anglo-Indian food has a definite place in the cuisine of India, having taken the best from British and Indian cuisine to become what it is today.

Ingredients

Threadfin, trevally, perch or hilsa fillets	600 g
Ground turmeric (haldi)	½ tsp
Salt	1 tsp
Grated coconut	25 g, dry-roasted
Peanuts	2 Tbsp, dry-roasted or 2 pieces peanut brittle
Ginger	3-cm knob, peeled
Brown onions	3, medium, peeled
Garlic	4 cloves, peeled
Vinegar	1 Tbsp
Lime juice	2 Tbsp
Mustard oil	50 ml
Ground coriander (malli)	1 tsp
Ground turmeric (haldi)	½ tsp
Tomato purée	1 Tbsp
Banana leaf or foil	1 large sheet
Red chillies	6, seeded or 2 tsp chilli powder
Coriander leaves (dhania sabz)	25 g

Garnish

Green chillies	3
Lime juice	a few drops

Method

- Rub fish with turmeric and salt, then cut into 6-cm pieces.

- Pound or blend (process) roasted grated coconut and peanuts into a fine powder then add ginger, onions and garlic and blend into a paste. Add vinegar and lime juice to facilitate grinding. If the mixture is still too dry, add some water and blend again.

- Heat mustard oil in a deep saucepan or *dekshi* until it becomes hazy. Fry fish until golden and remove to drain on absorbent paper.

- In the same oil, fry blended paste until aromatic. Add ground coriander, ground turmeric and then tomato purée. Stir well and remove from heat.

- Line a casserole dish with banana leaf or foil, leaving some leaf or foil to hang over the edge of the dish to cover casserole. Place fish pieces into casserole dish and spread paste around fish. Stuff red chillies into or sprinkle chilli powder and some coriander leaves around fish.

- Cover with leaf or foil and bake at 180°C for 20–25 minutes or until fish is cooked. Garnish with remaining coriander leaves, green chillies and lime juice. Serve hot or cold, with rice or *chappatis*.

Fish Moulie (Casserole of Fish in Coconut Cream)

This smooth-textured casserole with its rich coconut milk is sometimes called a 'white curry' in southern Indian circles and in Sri Lanka.

Ingredients

Pomfret, snapper or threadfin fillets or steaks	500 g
Salt	1 tsp
Ground white pepper	½ tsp
Ground turmeric (haldi)	1 tsp
Brown onions	2, medium, peeled
Garlic	3 cloves, peeled
Ginger	2-cm knob, peeled
Almonds or cashew nuts	10
Cinnamon stick (karuva pattai)	2-cm length, pounded
Ground cumin (jeera)	½ Tbsp
Chilli powder	1 tsp
Coconut milk	350 ml
Cooking oil	2 Tbsp
Curry leaves	1 stalk
Vinegar	2 Tbsp
Coconut cream	125 ml

Garnish

Garlic	3 cloves, peeled, sliced and crisp-fried
Red shallots	6 or 2 medium brown onions, peeled, sliced and crisp-fried

Method

- Pat dry fish and brush with salt, pepper and turmeric.

- Grind or blend (process) onions, garlic, ginger and almonds or cashews together into a paste.

- Heat oil in a deep saucepan or *dekshi*. Sauté onion paste until aromatic. Add cinnamon, curry leaves and vinegar and stir.

- Mix cumin and chilli powder with coconut milk and add to pan. Bring to the boil, stirring continuously. Once gravy boils, reduce heat.

- Add fish slowly, ladling gravy over. Simmer for about 10–15 minutes until fish turns whitish and gravy is reduced in volume to your liking.

- Finally, add coconut cream and stir carefully to avoid breaking up fish. Remove from heat and serve hot, garnished with fried garlic and shallots or onions.

- Alternatively, cook using the microwave oven. Put sautéed paste into a microwave dish and add half the coconut milk. Mix well with all other ingredients except coconut cream and cook in the microwave oven for 6 minutes on HIGH. Stir well, then cook for a further 2 minutes on MEDIUM.

- Add coconut cream and stir. Cook for another 2 minutes on MEDIUM or longer if you want to reduce the gravy further. Serve hot, garnished with fried garlic and shallots or onions.

Meen Chutney (Fresh Pickled Fish)

This is one way to keep fish fresh, as it goes through a novel drying process before being pickled. This pickle can be kept for a month. Cut down on chilli if you prefer it milder.

Ingredients

Pomfret, threadfin, bream or ling	600 g, cut into 5-cm pieces
Plain (all-purpose) flour	2 Tbsp
Vinegar	750 ml
Ground turmeric *(haldi)*	1½ tsp
Salt	1 tsp
Red shallots	6, peeled
Garlic	4 cloves, peeled
Ginger	6-cm knob, peeled
Ground cumin *(jeera)*	½ Tbsp
Mustard oil or peanut oil	250 ml
Chilli powder	3 Tbsp
Fenugreek seeds *(methi)*	1 tsp, roughly pounded
Cloves	½ tsp, roughly pounded
Ground cinnamon *(karuva pattai)*	½ tsp, roughly pounded
Sugar	1½ tsp

Method

- Carefully pick out any bones from fish. Rub fish with flour and wash off to reduce any fishy smell.

- Firm fish flesh by soaking in 125 ml vinegar for 5 minutes then drain and dry. Brush 1 tsp turmeric and salt on fish, then marinate in another 125 ml vinegar for 2 hours. Drain well.

- Grind or blend (process) shallots, garlic, ginger and cumin into a paste.

- Heat enough oil to cover fish in a small pan until it becomes hazy. Deep-fry 2 pieces of fish at a time until golden. Remove and drain on absorbent paper.

- Heat oven to 100°C. Spread fish on baking tray and dry fish pieces in oven for 4 hours. Alternatively dry them in the sun for 4–5 hours.

- Meanwhile, mix remaining turmeric, chilli powder, fenugreek, cloves, and cinnamon. Reheat 1 Tbsp oil in pan until very hot. Sauté blended paste, then add blended spices and cook until mixture is golden.

- Lower dried fish into mixture and stir quickly. Add remaining vinegar and allow to boil for 2 minutes. Add sugar and salt to taste. Stir well, then remove from heat.

- When cool, store in airtight container or serve with cucumber *raita* (yoghurt and cucumber) and rice.

Venthiam Colombu (Amah's Fish Curry)

The innocent-looking tiny, toffee coloured fenugreek seed, 'venthiam' as it is known in Tamil, packs quite a flavour. It is sour, verging on the edge of bitter. My old Cantonese amah cooked a much better traditional *venthiam colombu* in spite of the fact that she was never taught how to do it by my aunts who felt threatened by a Cantonese invading their kitchens. Amah's ingredients were not always the same but the final dish was always stunning and beautifully presented. 'Columbu' refers to the consistency of the gravy—thick and flavoursome.

Ingredients

Ground turmeric *(haldi)*	¹/₂ tsp
Salt	¹/₂ tsp
Ling fillets	600 g
Cooking oil	2 Tbsp
Fenugreek seeds *(methi)*	1 Tbsp, coarsely pounded
Whole mustard seeds	1 Tbsp
Garlic	1 clove, peeled and crushed
Spanish onion	1, peeled and diced
Chilli powder	1 tsp
Cumin seeds *(jeera)*	2 tsp, dry-roasted and ground
Fennel seeds *(perinseeragam)*	2 tsp, dry-roasted and ground
Coconut milk	450 ml
Tamarind paste *(imli)*	1 Tbsp
Tomato purée	1 tsp

Garnish

Curry leaves or
  crisp-fried onion

Method

- Combine ground turmeric and salt and coat fish fillets.

- Heat oil in a wok until it smokes. Cook fenugreek and mustard seeds until they pop.

- Add garlic and onion and cook until golden brown. Add chilli powder, ground cumin and fennel and fry for about 1 minute until aromatic.

- Stir in coconut milk and tamarind paste, then add tomato purée.

- Simmer sauce on low heat for 3 minutes until it reduces by about half.

- Lower fish into sauce and simmer for about 5 minutes until fish is opaque and flakes easily. Reduce gravy further to taste. Remove from heat. Serve curry garnished with curry leaves or fried onion.

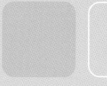

Japan & Korea
Feasting the Eyes

> "Like silver eels, the moonlight ripples shine:
> Look, I have caught one on my fishing line."
>
> *Chiyo-ni*

At the table, an artistically laid Japanese meal is set before the diner and it almost seems an insult to disturb the line, the form, texture and colour so painstakingly put together to emulate nature. A specially created winter dish may be a clear oyster *sashimi*, set in a creamy oyster shell astride a bed of lightly crushed ice with flecks of green seaweed crests. A soup to celebrate autumn could be a clear stock but would display ingredients to please the senses. The placement of each ingredient is essential to the whole composition. The diner is not only partaking of a delicate and exquisitely prepared meal, but is involved in the ritualistic appreciation of the environment.

The three basic elements in Japanese seafood are the *shoyu* (or soy sauce); the *dashi* stock made from *konbu* (giant kelp); and the dried bonito flakes *(katsuobushi)* which enrich the soups and stocks. The emphasis is on clean, sharp tastes, using dipping sauces to contrast with the subtle flavours of the sea.

Japanese cuisine was evolved by a people who had to practice austerity from early years. Land being scarce, the people learnt to appreciate whatever was available and fresh with each change of season. Partly because of Buddhist traditions that forbade any food that had received *phrana* or the breath of life, the chief sources of protein were fish and the soy bean in its various forms. Fortuitously, the warm currents that bathe the shores of insular Japan endow the waters with a wealth of marine life.

The Japanese eat more fish per head of population than any other people in the world, of varieties not normally consumed in other parts of Asia. Among some of the more unusual marine creatures consumed are the sea urchin and its roe, prized for the great flavour, and the deadly *fugi* or blowfish. Specially licensed restaurants remove the poison and serve slices of *fugi* as *sushi* or *sashimi*—all raw. Fish and shellfish are also made into fishballs or *used in* thick winter soups, light fresh salads, batters and delicate sauces. Sea vegetables like laver or seaweed and kelp are used as flavour enhancers and are a great source of iron.

Insistence on freshness is only one feature of the extreme care Japanese take when working with food. Intricate cuts and filleting methods that determine the best flavours being released are secrets imparted to apprentices by master chefs. Concern for texture, form and colour, and an eye for the presentation of food and garnishes, are as necessary as particular attention to the slicing of ingredients and vigilance in preserving the freshness of seafood and its flavours by not overcooking.

A Japanese meal is composed of many little snacks with sake or tea before the main meal of soup, meat or fish and rice, all placed together on the table. As a rule, when drinking, one eats only snacks. Chopsticks for rice (even at breakfast), soup bowls, plates and sauce dishes are provided for each diner. Soup bowls should be picked up with both hands and the contents sipped appreciatively. A *bento* box meal, set out in little containers with matching colours, textures and seasonal themes is a visual and culinary experience.

Newcomers to Japanese food, especially if they have been exposed to spicier Southeast Asian food, find the subtle soups and raw fish bland. Persistence in developing a palate that appreciates this, will bring a pleasant discovery—food tastes not raw at all, especially with dipping sauces.

Diners familiar with Japanese food may find some Korean dishes similar. Koreans, however, consider their cuisine midway between Chinese and Japanese food, with a heavy dependence on garlic, ginger, black pepper, sesame oil, soy sauces *(gan jang)*, bean paste *(dwen jang)* and hot chilli pastes *(go chu jang)*. The Korean 'hot pots' are full-bodied and gutsy compared to the subtle Japanese soups and seem calculated to warm the body so the cold can be kept out permanently. Koreans are fond of spicy and strong flavours, using *go chu jang* or chilli in meats, in soupy sauces as well as in *kim chee*, tasty and pungent vitamin-rich pickled cabbage and radish with garlic.

The year's supply of homemade sauces is made in the spring while in autumn, a festival celebrates the preparation of the winter *kim chee.* Some varieties of fish and shellfish—anchovies or oysters, for example—go into the *kim chee.* It is served with all meals, even at breakfast, with savoury rice gruel. Traditionally, the jars of pickle sat in the open under the raised houses where they matured until needed.

Despite a long tradition of eating beef, Korea remains a paradise for fish and shellfish. Fish is treated in much the same way as the Japanese treat their fish—raw or pickled. Fish for salads such as *O-jing Oh Hoe* and *for sashimi* such as *Kwang Oh Hoe*, are transported from the fishing ports and kept alive until the last minute, in keeping with the Korean tradition to savour the fresh and to spurn anything that is not.

Seafood and fish are sometimes combined surprisingly with meat, vegetable or poultry. Laver or *kim* (*nori* seaweed) is used as a relish. To treat *nori,* brush with sesame oil before toasting over an open flame and shredding into dishes as garnish. Dried salted fish is used as flavouring as well as a seasoning.

Food in Korea is served on a Korean dining table, at least a dozen dishes all together. Rice, soup, dried and fresh fish and drinks are all served on a large low table which is carried from the kitchen to the dining room—instant service for four to six persons.

Shirumono (Soups)

Soups are generally called *shirumono*, but can be further classified as clear soups *(suimono)* or the thicker home-style soups (sometimes called *miso* soups). Clear soups are either served as appetisers or halfway through a banquet, as a refresher or a palate cleanser.

A *suimono* is a clear soup made with fresh stock. Usually there are three ingredients added to the soup: a piece of fish; some sliced vegetables cut into decorative shapes; and a garnish to add fragrance to the dish. The garnish could be green seaweed or a sliver of citron or lemon rind, and is not eaten.

The *suimono* is traditionally served in lidded lacquer bowls which keep the soup hot and the flavours intact. Soups should be served piping hot, as flavours are lost when the liquid cools.

Miso soups are thick, hearty home-style soups commonly cooked in Japanese homes. *Miso* soup is made from stock and the fermented bean paste *(miso)* which is rich in protein.

A Japanese home-cooked meal consists of one soup and three side dishes, called *ichiju sansai*. Since soups are served hot, it is considered good form to slurp some air with the soup, making a gentle sound.

Sumashi-Jiru (Clear Soup with Fish)

Ingredients

Ling fillets	200 g, cut into 4–6 pieces
Salt	1/2 tsp
Ground pepper	1/2 tsp
Cornflour (cornstarch)	2 Tbsp
Watercress leaves	3–4 per serving
Lemon rind	from 1 lemon, cut into thin strips and soaked in cold water

Stock

Dashi (see pg 308)	1 litre
Salt	to taste
Light soy sauce	1 Tbsp

Method

- Season fish with salt and pepper. Pat dry and roll in cornflour. Dust off any excess cornflour and place fish in boiling water. Boil for 3 minutes until just cooked. Remove and keep fish fillets warm.

- Simmer *dashi*, taking care not to bring it to the boil. Add salt gradually and taste. Add soy sauce to taste. Keep soup on a simmer as *suimono* has to be served hot.

- Warm soup bowls in hot water, then discard water. Arrange a piece of fish and watercress in each bowl. Slowly pour in soup so fish pieces and watercress are not displaced.

- Add lemon curls, cover and serve immediately.

Suzuki No Suimono (Full-Bodied Fish Soup)

This is a thick winter soup made of sea bass. Serve it in an attractive lacquered bowl and garnish to make it traditional and Japanese.

Ingredients

Carrot	3-cm piece, cut into cubes
White radish (daikon)	2-cm piece, cut into cubes
Salt	1 tsp
Sea bass, white pomfret, perch, cod or threadfin fillets	250 g
Thin dashi (see pg 309)	1 litre
Lemon rind	from 1 lemon, cut into thin strips and soaked in cold water

Method

- Cook carrot and radish in boiling water with $1/2$ tsp salt until tender. Remove carrot and radish and bring water to the boil again.

- Rub remaining salt on sea bass and place in boiling water. Cook fish for 3–4 minutes until tender. Drain.

- Arrange cooked fish, carrot and radish into four bowls attractively. Heat dashi just to boiling point, then ladle into bowls carefully so as not to disturb the arrangement.

- Float a few strips of lemon rind on top and serve at once.

Iwashi No Suimono (Sardines in Soup)

Even though the Japanese do not eat much garlic and this dish is good without it, I have added a bit of garlic in this recipe to my preference.

Ingredients

Fresh sardines or small mackerel	500 g
Salt	$1^1/_2$ tsp
Sake or dry sherry	12 tsp
Ground pepper	to taste
Plain (all-purpose) flour	2 Tbsp
Thin dashi (see pg 309)	900 ml
Mirin	2 tsp
Garlic salt	a dash

Garnish

Spring onions (scallions)	4–6, cut into 5-cm lengths

Method

- Scale and gut fish. Slit open and discard backbone. Rub with $1/2$ tsp salt and rinse in salted water. Drain and blend (process) fish.

- Transfer fish to a bowl and add sake or sherry, $1/2$ tsp salt, pepper and flour. Mix well. Divide mixture evenly into 16 parts and shape into balls with wet palms.

- Boil thin dashi and add mirin. Bring to the boil again. Drop fish balls into soup and wait until they float. Continue to simmer.

- Meanwhile make several long cuts from one end of each spring onion length and place in cold water to form curls.

- Warm serving bowls and place 2 fish balls in each bowl. Ladle soup in, add a dash of garlic salt and garnish with spring onion curls.

Ika No Naruto Maki (Squid Rolled with Nori)

Maki refers to rolling the squid into a pinwheel pattern. This delicate pinwheel of green laver (*nori*) and white squid creates a pattern reminiscent of sea waves.

Ingredients

Squid	125 g, medium
Laver (*nori*) sheet	1
Spring onions (scallions) or garlic chives	5

Ginger Soy Sauce

Ginger	1 Tbsp, peeled and finely grated
Dark soy sauce	125 ml
Sake or Stone's ginger wine	2 tsp

Method

- Remove tentacles from squid. Cut open tube and lay squid flat on a cutting board, smooth side up. Score the surface with thin lengthwise cuts to tenderise squid. Do not cut too deep.

- Turn squid over and cut a piece of laver to fit the shape of squid. Lightly toast laver by holding it over a flame for 1 minute, then place laver over squid.

- Bunch spring onions or garlic chives together and place on laver.

- Hold squid firmly and roll up. Press down hard and keep joint or seam beneath.

- Hold squid roll firmly and cut slices 2-cm apart.

- Mix ingredients for ginger soy sauce and serve in a separate bowl with squid roll.

- Alternatively, serve the Korean way with a chilli-vinegar sauce. The Korean equivalent of this dish is called *O-jing Oh Hoe*. Mix together 2 Tbsp vinegar, 2 Tbsp chilli sauce and 2 cloves of pounded garlic and serve with squid roll.

Sashimi (Sliced Raw Fish)

Sashimi or sliced raw fish is the highlight of a Japanese chef's art and creative talent. The chef is able with slices of fish, crab, squid and prawn (shrimp) to create a selection of exquisitely arranged *sashimi*.

Sashimi is served early in the banquet so that guests can taste the fresh flavours of the fish before other conflicting tastes are introduced. It is important to use the freshest of fish for *sashimi*. In Japan, fish lovers and *sashimi* enthusiasts only use fish in season for *sashimi*, so winter means oyster or tuna *sashimi*; spring means sea bream; summer signifies freshwater carp and perch; and in autumn, clams and mackerel would be the ideal choice. Japanese advocate the use of fresh fish whatever the quality against the best quality frozen, as 'frozen fish negates the spirit of Japanese cuisine'.

For the best *sashimi*, start with a sharp knife and tweezers. The bones should be removed with tweezers and the fish should be sliced with care, while the freshest dipping sauces should be used to complete the arrangement. To serve, arrange the slices of fish on a bed of juniper leaves.

The garnish could be lemon or mint. A tiny knob of *wasabe* or horseradish should be placed near the slices. Arrangements are limited only by the imagination of the chef.

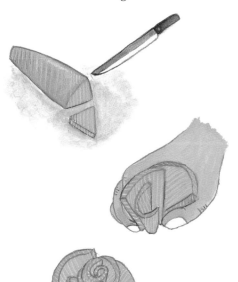

Filleting Technique

- There are 3–4 different ways of slicing fish for *sashimi*. The simplest one is the thick slice *(hira zukuri)* technique where slices are cut and laid one on top of the other and arranged on a plate with garnishes.

- The thin slice *(uzu zukuri)* technique is when firm fish is cut into paper-thin slices, then arranged as flowers or petals.

- The cube cut *(haku zukuri)* technique is when soft fish is cut into cubes.

Condiments for Sashimi

- *Daikon* (radish): cut around the circumference with a sharp knife until a long sheet unwinds. Fold the sheet and cut into thin threads.

- *Wasabe* (horseradish): this can be bought as a paste or powder or can be freshly scraped by grating the *wasabe* root on a fine grater.

- *Sanbizu Sauce*: either buy the commercial variety or make your own (see pg 311) well in advance of being used.

- *Ponzu* Sauce: (see pg 310).

Sashimi Flower

Whenever *sashimi* is mentioned, one imagines raw fish, squid or prawns (shrimps) exquisitely decorated into flowers or folded as petals and leaves. For this strikingly simple dish, all the talent needed is the ability to fold and tuck as in *origami*. The Koreans serve a similar assortment of raw fish and once the fish is chosen, the meat is sliced for *modum hoe* and the bones and head made into a hot spicy soup served with the meal.

Ingredients

Fresh perch, squid or
tuna fillet — 300 g, about 3-cm thick

Method

- Cut a long triangular piece of fish or squid using a sharp knife. Cut thin slices in triangular shapes at a 45° angle with a sharp knife. The way fish fillets are cut can affect their flavour. When *sashimi* fillets are cut paper thin, the taste is different to thickly cut slices.

- Arrange some slices, apex at the bottom, in a flower shape, like a cylinder. Fold slices around the cylinder until there are sufficient slices. Bend the slices back to resemble the petals of a rose. Place the 'rose' *sashimi* on a plate decorated with some real rose leaves.

- You may arrange the sashimi on a plate of shredded *daikon* with fish, squid and prawn (shrimp) *sashimi*.

The Sauces

- The sauces used are different for different cuts. With thin fillet slices, a tangy citrus and soy sauce dip is used, such as *Ponzu* Sauce (see pg 310).

Sakana No Mushi Mono (Steamed Fish Casserole)

A very delicate tasting fish casserole that allows the true flavours to emerge. For this casserole, make sure only the freshest fish is used. If you prefer a spicier dish, use pomfret and brush some *teriyaki* sauce on the fillets before placing the fish in the casserole.

Ingredients

Perch or pomfret fillets	200 g, cut into 3-cm slices
Salt	1/2 tsp
Japanese seaweed *(konbu)*	6-cm length
Soft bean curd *(tofu)*	50 g, cut into quarters
Dried bean curd skin *(yuba)*	1 sheet, 8 x 10 cm, soaked for 10 minutes and chopped
Shiitake or dried Chinese mushrooms	5–6
Watercress, snowpea shoots or carrot	50 g
Sake	2 Tbsp
Ponzu sauce (see pg 310)	

Garnish

Lemon	1 thin slice

Method

- Salt fish slices lightly and arrange on a plate with skin facing upwards.

- Wipe Japanese seaweed with a damp towel and place on base of casserole dish. This seaweed is not eaten but gives flavour to the food and is removed before serving.

- Place soft bean curd quarters and chopped bean curd skin in casserole dish. Place fish on top.

- Arrange mushrooms and watercress decoratively over fish.

- Pour *sake* carefully over all ingredients and place uncovered casserole dish in a steamer. Cover steamer and steam for 10 minutes. Wipe steamer lid regularly during steaming so condensation does not affect flavours. Alternatively, use a microwave safe casserole dish, cover with plastic wrap and cook in the microwave oven for 2 minutes on MEDIUM and then 3 minutes on HIGH.

- Remove casserole dish and arrange all the ingredients except seaweed on a serving dish. Brush fish with *ponzu* sauce and serve garnished with a slice of lemon.

Yakimono

Yakimono is the Japanese method of grilling foods. This is a very versatile method of food preparation and is particularly effective with fish and prawns (shrimps). The Japanese use a special smokeless charcoal grill *(hibachi)*, but any gas grill will do. In keeping with Japanese tradition, fish grilled in this way is skewered to look as though it is still alive and leaping out of the water. Salt-grilled sweet fish is absolutely delicious. As the salt is grilling, it becomes charred and imparts wonderful flavour to the fish.

Fish is often marinated before grilling, both to tenderise the flesh and to season it, mostly with *sake*, soy sauce and *mirin*. The fish should not be marinated for longer than 30 minutes. In the case of fatty fish like mackerel, salt is used to draw moisture and oil out of the fish.

The secret of producing authentic *yakimono* is to stop cooking as soon as the outside is crisp while the inside is just slightly cooked, moist and tender. There are several skewering techniques to be studied and mastered for success with this style of cooking. Either bamboo or stainless steel skewers should be used and only one side is skewered while the other presents a clean profile.

Stitch skewering

One-tuck skewering

Some Techniques of Skewering

- Long: with 2 pieces of fish and 2 skewers.

- One-tuck: one long fillet, rolled at one end and skewered.

- Two-tuck: both ends are rolled and skewered.

- Stitch: tender flesh like squid shrinks while cooked, so it is skewered (as with running stitches) before cooking.

- Rolled prawns: cut prawns and insert skewers so that heads and tails meet on the skewer.

Buri No Teriyaki (Yellowtail Teriyaki)

The Japanese often use *sake* to kill the fishy smell of seafood. Yellowtail is particularly tasty when grilled using this recipe, but any other fish can be used. For a Korean flavour, add chilli paste to the marinade.

Ingredients

Light soy sauce	7 Tbsp
Mirin	4 Tbsp
Sake	1/2 tsp
Chilli paste (*go chu jang*)	1/2 tsp, optional
Small yellowtail fillets	500 g, sliced crosswise into 6-cm pieces
Salt	1 tsp
Cooking oil	1 Tbsp
Boiling water	

Garnish

Vinegar	250 ml
Sugar	1 Tbsp
Chinese turnip or cucumber	200 g, sliced

Method

- Prepare garnish. Mix vinegar and sugar in a bowl and soak Chinese turnip or cucumber for 3 hours. Remove pickled vegetables and squeeze out excess vinegar. Set aside.

- Mix 4 Tbsp light soy sauce, 1 Tbsp mirin, *sake* and chilli paste to make marinade. Place fish in and marinate for at least 1 hour.

- In a saucepan, cook remaining soy sauce, *mirin* and salt for 3–5 minutes on medium heat, stirring until it thickens. Alternatively, place in a microwave-safe bowl and cook for 1 minute on HIGH. To thicken further, cook for another 1 minute on HIGH.

- Heat oil in a heavy-bottomed frying pan (skillet) over high heat. Add fish, skin side down, and move pieces around so that the skin does not stick to pan.

- Turn fish fillets over once and cook for about 2 minutes. Fish should look barely cooked. Place on an upturned rack.

- Pour boiling water quickly over fish to wash off oil.

- Gently coat fillets with thickened sauce and place fillets on serving plates.

- Thicken remaining sauce further and spoon some next to fish.

- Garnish each plate with a slice of pickled turnip or cucumber to serve.

Kogane Yaki (Grilled Sea Bass Coated with Egg Yolks)

Kogane means golden and the fillets coated with eggs look like golden parcels. This treatment gives the fish a smoky flavour and makes it tender.

Ingredients

Egg yolks	3
Mirin	1 tsp
Light soy sauce	$^1/_2$ tsp
Salt	$^1/_2$ tsp
Ground pepper	to taste
Sea bass, perch or white pomfret fillets	300 g, cut into 5-cm pieces
Teriyaki sauce	

Garnish

Radish *(daikon)*	1, cut decoratively and soaked in cold water

Method

- Skewer fillets so that one side is neat.

- Combine egg yolks with *mirin*, light soy sauce, salt and pepper.

- Grill fish for 2 minutes, then coat both sides egg yolk mixture. Grill and coat fish pieces with egg yolk mixture again until it forms a thick paste. Continue to grill for 3–5 minutes or until fish is cooked.

- Garnish with radish curls and serve with *teriyaki* sauce.

Ika Kenchin Yaki (Grilled Stuffed Squid)

Stuffed squid, sliced into rings, is colourful and ingenious.

Ingredients

Miso	1 Tbsp
Sake	3 Tbsp
Sugar	1 tsp
Mirin	2 Tbsp
Squid	500 g, about 6
Vegetable oil	1 tsp
Eggs	3, lightly beaten
Salt	½ tsp
Thin asparagus tips or French beans	3, boiled for 3 minutes then thinly sliced into strips
Carrot	1, medium, thinly sliced into strips

Garnish
Bamboo shoots

Method

- Prepare topping. Combine *miso, sake,* sugar and *mirin.* Refrigerate.

- Clean and wash squid, remove skin, head and tentacles. Wash tubes well and remove quill and glutinous material inside tube. Make a tiny slit on the pointed end of tube so it will not burst on grilling.

- Coat a flat frying pan (skillet) with oil and pour in beaten eggs. Tilt pan to cook egg until set. Sprinkle with salt, then cut into strips.

- Stuff squid carefully with vegetables and egg strips. Fill tightly and close tubes with toothpicks. Brush with topping.

- Skewer the tops of tubes so the stuffed areas of squid are not pierced. Grill on high heat for 3–4 minutes, turning squid as each side grills. Watch that tubes do not burst and check that heat is not too intense.

- When cooked, cut into slices and arrange on a plate of bamboo shoots cut into thin strips. Serve hot with a thin soy and ginger sauce.

Ayu No Shio (Salt-Grilled Fish)

This is a basic technique for grilling fish the Japanese way. There are three important rules: the skin should be crisp; the flesh should not be overcooked; and the fish should be served hot.

If the fish is skillfully skewered and grilled, it can be presented sitting upright as though it has just leapt out of the water onto the plate. The salt-grilling of fins and tail is largely cosmetic, to make the fins stand out. The Korean version, called *Saeng-son gui*, has a soy and hot chilli garlic sauce brushed over the fish before it is grilled.

Ingredients

Whiting or smaller fish	350 g, scaled, gutted and cleaned, head and tail intact
Sake or *mirin*	1 Tbsp
Ginger juice	1 Tbsp
Light soy sauce	1 Tbsp
Lemons	1, sliced
Salt	1 Tbsp
Green apple or *choko*	1, grated
Radish (*daikon*)	1, large or 2 medium carrots, grated
Cooking oil	1 Tbsp, optional

Sauce

Light soy sauce	2 Tbsp
Ginger	1/2 Tbsp, shredded
Lemon juice	1 Tbsp

Garnish

Pickled ginger slices
Juniper leaves

For Korean recipe

Dark soy sauce	1 tsp
Chilli garlic sauce	1 Tbsp

Method

- Decide which is the better side of the fish and skewer from the other side to create a look of movement and curves. Do not push skewer through to the other side of fish.

- Brush *sake* or *mirin*, ginger juice and light soy sauce over fish. Place some lemon slices into fish stomach cavity. Brush 1/2 tsp salt onto whole fish and more on tail and fins. This salting will ensure that the fins will not burn but will stand out realistically. For the Korean version, brush dark soy sauce and chilli garlic sauce over fish.

- Prepare serving dish. Arrange grated *choko* or green apple and *daikon* or carrot to look like waves on a serving dish.

- Make sauce. Mix light soy sauce, shredded ginger and lemon juice together and set aside.

- Grill fish over high heat on skewered side, until fish is golden brown. Turn over and grill the other side until fish starts to brown. Watch carefully so fish does not burn.

- Alternatively, remove fish eyes and use bamboo skewers to skewer fish. Preheat a browning dish in the microwave oven for 6 minutes on HIGH. Pour in cooking oil and place fish in dish. Cook uncovered for 2 minutes on HIGH for each side. Shield tail if it shows signs of cooking too fast. Fish cooked in the microwave will not be crisp but will have a lovely flavour. Remove and decorate hollowed eye sockets with carrot circles and peas.

- Serve on prepared bed of grated *choko* and *daikon* or carrot, accompanied with sauce. Garnish with ginger slices and juniper leaves.

Ebi No Kushiyaki (Salt on Skewer-Grilled Prawns)

Ebi no kushiyaki or salt-grilled prawns (shrimps) can be as simple or as elaborate as you like. Clams done the same way in Korea are called *Daehap gui*. They are sprinkled with black pepper, sesame seeds and finely chopped green onions. The Koreans grill foods the same way as the Japanese, but add a hot chilli paste to the marinade.

Ingredients

Fresh green king prawns (shrimps)	10, about 500 g
Sake	1¹/₂ tsp
Sea salt	1 tsp
Light soy sauce	3 Tbsp

Garnish

Sliced ginger	
Lemon	1, sliced

Method

- Cut legs, whiskers and pointed snouts off prawns, leaving shells, heads and tails intact. Carefully devein prawns.

- Skewer prawns laterally, inserting skewers at the heads and threading through to the tails. Prawns should be made to look alive. Twist them when skewering to give the effect of movement.

- Baste prawns with *sake* and leave in *sake* marinade for 10 minutes. Brush with salt.

- Grill prawns for about 2 minutes on one side, then 1 minute on the other side. Do not over-grill.

- Arrange prawns with skewers still on or with skewers removed on a plate with sliced ginger and lemon.

- Serve with light soy sauce as a dip.

Grirudo Shii Fuudo (Steam-Grilled Seafood)

Another form of grilling, called steam-grilling, evolved in Japan with the use of earthenware dishes called *horaku*. These were filled with marinated fish, the rims sealed with clay and then buried in hot coals to cook the fish. This is similar to Chinese beggar's chicken. Today the use of foil has taken the place of the claypot, but the technique is still the same, as foil keeps the heat inside and the food cooks in its own moist heat. Seafood packed with all sorts of mushrooms and vegetables lends itself to this type of steam-grilling.

Ingredients

Sake	2 Tbsp
Light soy sauce	2 Tbsp
Salted whiting or other white fish fillets	400 g, each cut into 3–4 pieces
Prawns (shrimps)	300 g, medium, deveined, with heads and tails intact
Shiitake mushrooms or large champignons	10
Rock salt	to taste, dry-roasted
Juniper leaves	5, 7 or 9
Gingko nuts or chestnuts	4–5, dry-roasted
Aluminium foil	1 sheet, 20 x 40 cm

Garnish

Ponzu sauce (see pg 310)	
Lemons	2, cut into wedges

Method

- Combine *sake* and light soy sauce, and brush on fish and prawns.

- Place fish, prawns and mushrooms on foil sheet. Enclose food tightly with foil.

- Grill foil parcel over very high heat, turning over after 6–10 minutes. Grill for 3 minutes on other side.

- Open parcel up and keep warm. The seafood and mushrooms will be tender and moist.

- Sprinkle rock salt on a serving dish. Arrange fish, prawns and mushrooms on top and garnish with juniper leaves and gingko nuts or chestnuts. Serve with *Ponzu* sauce and lemon wedges.

Mushimono (Steaming)

Steaming has been a prized method of releasing delicate flavours and aromas for centuries in Asia. Seafood responds well to the steaming method as the flesh is tender and the moist flavours are not lost through this method. Food may be steamed in individual portions with vegetables, or as a large main serving for the whole table.

It is important also to remember that steam can be controlled, varying from the slow, even heat produced by gentle steam, to a rolling boil which produces a bubbling steam.

Chawan Mushi (Egg Savoury Custard)

This warm, smooth and delicate dish is one of the few Japanese dishes eaten with a spoon. If cooking this in a microwave, steam on LOW and allow to stand for a few minutes before serving or the custard will look leathery. The Japanese call this 'old skin'.

Ingredients

Dried Chinese mushrooms	4, large, soaked to soften
Dashi	350 ml
Salt	$^1/_2$ tsp
Mirin	1 Tbsp
Light soy sauce	$^3/_4$ Tbsp
Eggs	4, gently beaten
Prawns (shrimps)	8, large, shelled and deveined

Garnish

Watercress	1 bunch

Method

- Squeeze excess water from mushrooms, wipe dry and cut each in half.
- Mix *dashi*, salt, *mirin* and soy sauce gently into eggs with chopsticks.
- Prepare 4 serving cups and divide prawns and mushrooms equally into each cup.
- Pour egg mixture on top and cover cups with foil.
- Place bowls in a steamer and steam for 15–16 minutes or until egg is set.
- Alternatively, place cups in the microwave oven and cover partly with plastic wrap. Cook for 3 minutes on LOW, then rotate cups and cook for 3 minutes more if necessary.
- Garnish with watercress and serve hot. *Chawan Mushi* is a very delicate custard, considered to be more of a soup than a firm custard. As such, it is eaten with spoons rather than chopsticks.

Nimono (Simmering)

Nimono is an important part of a Japanese meal and there are many types of simmered foods. Some are salt-simmered, others are dipped in cornflour and beaten egg and then simmered in *dashi, sake, mirin* and light soy sauce. A special dish with a drop lid that fits inside the rim is used for *nimono*.

There are two steps to *nimono*: firstly, certain ingredients are parboiled in water to draw out excess moisture; secondly, all ingredients are simmered to draw out the flavours and complete the cooking. The food is sliced diagonally and a thick-bottomed pan is used.

Sunomono or Aemono (Salads)

Salads are normally served as tiny side portions at the start of a meal, but could also be served at the end of a meal, just before the rice. There are two types of salad: vinegar salads *(sunomono)* and dressed salads *(aemono)*.

The Japanese are very creative in their salads. They enjoy contrasting flavours, pickling fruit such as kiwi fruit or strawberries with rice vinegar to go with seafood like clams or oysters, and also contrasting textures and colours. The word *aemono* means composed and the ingredient that links all these ingredients is the dressing.

Saba No Miso Ini (Fish in Miso)

Ingredients

Mackerel fillets	4 pieces, about 300 g
Salt	1 Tbsp
Boiling water	
Water	125 ml
Kelp (konbu)	10-cm piece
Ginger	2-cm knob, peeled
Miso sauce	1 Tbsp
Dark miso	5 Tbsp
Mirin	4 Tbsp
Sake	2 Tbsp

Method

- Pat cleaned fillets dry with absorbent paper. Sprinkle with salt and leave to stand for 15 minutes.

- Pour boiling water into a simmering pot, plunge fillets in and cook for about 5 minutes until white, then remove.

- Pour water into a saucepan and put kelp in. Bring to the boil. Take off heat and remove kelp.

- Grate or pound ginger and squeeze out juice. Reserve pulp and put ginger juice into water in pan.

- Place fillets in a simmering pot or heavy-based frying pan (skillet). Pour kelp and ginger liquid over fillets. Cover and simmer on low heat for 2–3 minutes.

- In another pan, combine miso sauce, dark miso, mirin and sake. Cook over medium heat for 2 minutes. Add sauce to simmering fish and cook for 4 minutes until sauce is thickened and reduced.

- Garnish with ginger pulp and serve warm in the pan. Allow guests to help themselves.

Orenji To Ika No Sarada

(Squid Salad with Orange Segments)

Orange segments are refreshing when combined with squid and sesame seeds. This salad complements a *Tempura* meal (see pg 236) as the colours blend and the textures contrast most effectively.

Ingredients

Squid tubes	125 g
Light soy sauce	2 Tbsp
Orange segments	4
Lemon or lime juice	2 tsp
Sesame seeds	25 g, dry-roasted
Laver *(nori)* sheets	1, shredded

Method

- Wash and clean squid tubes. Cut open and flatten. Brush with $1^1/_2$ Tbsp soy sauce and grill under an open grill or barbecue until squid turns brown. Shred into pieces.

- Carefully peel outer membrane off orange segments and discard.

- Toss shredded squid with orange slices. Sprinkle with lemon juice and remaining soy sauce. Toss lightly and chill.

- Divide salad into 4 bowls and serve garnished with toasted sesame seeds and shredded laver sheet.

Ho Ta Te No Miso Ae (Scallops Marinated in Miso Sauce)

Miso is a rich and full-bodied sauce which goes well with scallops. Try to mix the sauce in a *suribachi* or with mortar and pestle.

Ingredients

Scallops or clams	8, large
Spring onions (scallions)	4, cut into 3-cm lengths

Sauce

Miso	3 Tbsp
Mirin	3 Tbsp
Sugar	1 Tbsp
Rice vinegar	1 Tbsp
English mustard	1/4 tsp
Thick *dashi* stock	3 Tbsp

Garnish

Pickled ginger	2-cm slice, thinly cut or 2–3 Tbsp
Peanuts (groundnuts)	

Method

- Scrub scallops or clams and remove "beards" from shells. Place clams in a basin of lightly salted water in a dark place and cover. Allow them to leach dirt out for 3–4 hours. Wash well.

- If using scallops, place in a bowl and steam over boiling water for 5 minutes or cook in the microwave oven for 3 minutes on HIGH or until shells open. Remove scallop flesh from shells and reserve any liquid. Scrub shells then replace flesh and pour reserved liquid back into shells.

- Mix sauce by blending sauce ingredients together.

- Place 2 shells on a plate and put some spring onions in each shell. Spoon sauce over and sprinkle slivers of ginger or peanuts on top. Serve chilled.

Kani Sarada No Omuretsu (Crab Omelette Salad)

The Japanese cook omelettes in special rectangular omelette pans. In this dish, the bamboo rolling mat used to make *sushi* is helpful.

Ingredients

Cucumber	1/4, cut in half lengthwise, seeded and thinly sliced
Cooking oil	125 ml
Eggs	4, beaten with a pinch of salt
Crabsticks	3 or 150 g crabmeat
Grated ginger or radish (*daikon*)	3 Tbsp
Rice vinegar or egg white	

Method

- Soak cucumber slices in salted water for 30 minutes. Squeeze out water and pat dry with absorbent paper.

- Heat a non-stick rectangular pan with a little oil. Pour some egg in and tilt the pan around to create a thin omelette sheet. If a round omelette pan is used, trim omelettes into rectangular shapes after cooking. Continue until all the eggs are cooked.

- Lay one egg omelette at a time on a *sushi* bamboo mat. Arrange crabstick or crabmeat, cucumber and a strip of ginger or *daikon* on top of egg. Roll egg up firmly, using the mat to help. Seal with egg white or rice vinegar.

- Chill, then slice into circular servings like *sushi*. Place 2–3 omelette rounds in bowls. Serve with rice vinegar, soy sauce or *ponzu* sauce.

Kuraga To Kyuri No Sunomono
(Cucumber and Jellyfish Salad)

Ingredients

Salted jellyfish or dried *wakame* seaweed	25 g
Rice wine vinegar	5 Tbsp
Light soy sauce	4 Tbsp
Sesame oil	1 Tbsp
Sugar	1 Tbsp
Cucumber	1, thinly sliced and seeded
Salt	1/2 tsp

Method

- If using jellyfish, soak in water for 30 minutes and wash off salt. If using seaweed, soak in warm water for 30 minutes until it expands. Then wash in cold water, wipe dry and cut into small pieces.

- Prepare dressing. Combine vinegar, soy sauce, sesame oil and sugar. Stir well and heat gently. Leave to cool.

- Sprinkle cucumber slices with salt and leave for 20 minutes. Squeeze to get excess fluid out, then mix with jellyfish or seaweed. Add vinegar dressing and toss gently.

- Serve cold. The Japanese always arrange their food decoratively. For this salad, you may pick out some cucumber slices and arrange them nicely before serving.

Agemono & Tempura (Deep-Frying)

The Japanese methods of steaming and simmering did not include deep-frying or the method known as *agemono*. This was a European technique adapted by the Japanese who later refined it for their use. Deep-frying was most probably introduced in Nagasaki around 1540 when the ancient city was influenced by a community of missionaries and traders from Portugal who used to eat heavily battered fish on feast days or *Quattor Tempora* days of the Roman Catholic calendar. The Japanese adopted it, refined the batter to a light crispy skin and extended the range of foods from seafood to all types of vegetables.

The crucial factor in *tempura* is the batter. This should be so light and subtle that it could pass for a skin. *Tempura* frying has almost become an art form in Japan. The oil temperature is also crucial in *tempura* and all *agemono*. To check whether the oil is hot enough, hold the end of a bamboo skewer in the oil. If the oil around it starts to bubble, the oil is hot enough to deep-fry anything. The oil should be kept at a constant temperature to cook foods evenly.

Deep-fried food is normally served on top of folded napkins in individual dishes, on beds of shredded vegetables or other decorative garnishes.

Ebi To Nori No Agemono (Prawns Rolled in Nori)

This is not a typical Japanese dish, but it is indicative of the food trends in evidence today. I first tasted this in a Japanese restaurant in Hong Kong. Now I serve it with my favourite *Ponzu* sauce.

Ingredients

King prawns (shrimps)	8, large, shelled and deveined, heads removed and tails intact
Salt	
Laver *(nori)* sheets	8
Egg white	1, lightly beaten
Vegetable oil	450 ml
Ponzu sauce (see pg 310)	

Method

- Make slits across the middle of each prawn body so they will not curl when rolled. Wash in cold water, then salt lightly. Drain on absorbent paper for 5 minutes. Pat dry.

- Lay laver sheets flat on the work surface. Place a prawn on each sheet. Roll firmly and brush edge of laver sheet with egg white to seal.

- Pour oil into a heavy-based pan or wok until about 2-cm deep. Heat oil and test if it is ready by inserting a bamboo skewer in. When the oil around it starts bubbling, the oil is ready.

- Deep-fry rolls, 2 at a time, for about 3 minutes, rotating them to fry evenly. You may need to take them out earlier if the oil is very hot.

- Drain rolls on absorbent paper and keep warm. Serve hot with *ponzu* sauce.

Tempura (Japanese Deep-Frying)

In order to produce a thin film of batter that produces fine crispy pastry, use very fresh ingredients, keep the oil at a constant temperature and use iced water and batter that is barely mixed and remains lumpy with bits of dry flour suspended in the liquid. A pair of chopsticks should be used to stir the batter to arrive at such a consistency. The light pastry is only possible because the batter sticks to the food properly. Ideally, *tempura* should be made just before serving and should be eaten hot.

Ingredients

Prawns (shrimps)	8, large, shelled and deveined, with tails intact
Scallops	6
Chrysanthemum or local spinach leaves	1–2
Onions	2, large, peeled and thickly sliced into rings
Carrot	1, peeled and sliced diagonally
Plain (all-purpose) flour	125 g
Egg yolks	2
Cold water	250 ml
Cooking oil	500 ml

Dipping Sauce

Thick *dashi*	250 ml
Light soy sauce	3 Tbsp
Mirin	2 Tbsp

Garnish

Radish (*daikon*)	1
Red capsicum (bell pepper)	1, cored and thinly cut in strips
Ginger	5-cm knob, peeled and grated

Method

- Make deep cuts under prawn bodies to prevent them from curling when cooked.

- Arrange prawns, scallops, chrysanthemum or spinach leaves, onions and carrot on a tray. Dust with 1 Tbsp flour.

- Put egg yolks and cold water in a bowl. Mix lightly with chopsticks. Add remaining flour and mix lightly, but do not beat. Allow batter to remain lumpy with bits of dry flour floating in the mixture.

- Prepare dipping sauce. Mix ingredients together in a small bowl. Set aside.

- Make a few holes in the centre of radish and plug with red capsicum strips. Grate radish and pepper together to achieve a colourful and flavoured relish. Set aside.

- Fill a wok with oil and heat to 170°C. Test heat by inserting a wooden skewer into hot oil. If bubbles appear, the oil has reached the correct temperature.

- Dip some prawns, scallops, chrysanthemum or spinach leaves, onions and carrot in batter and place in hot oil. Deep-fry for 2–3 minutes until golden, turning all the time. Take out and drain on absorbent paper.

- Serve crisp and hot with bowls of dipping sauce, grated radish and capsicum and grated ginger.

Chiri Nabe (Red Sea Bream Cooked in a Pot)

The technique of cooking in a hotpot or *nabe* with a dash of *chiri* (chilli) in the sauce is Korean. *Nabemono* is the method of one-pot cookery often done at the table and eaten with a sauce. It is best made with a flavoursome fish stock, but if you are in a hurry, use prepared *dashi* stock.

Ingredients

Fish heads and bones	750 g
Shiitake or straw mushrooms	10, soaked for 10–15 minutes and squeezed dry
Soft bean curd (tofu)	1 piece, cut into 3-cm cubes
Leeks	2 stalks, cut diagonally into 3-cm pieces
Spinach	3 stalks, cut into 3-cm sections
Chinese cabbage	2 leaves
Red bream fillets	400 g, cut into 6-cm pieces
Salt	to taste

Sauce

Radish (daikon)	5-cm, grated
Lemon juice	4 Tbsp
Light soy sauce	50 ml
Red chilli	1, seeded and thinly cut into strips

Method

- Make fish stock by boiling bones and fish heads in 1 litre water. Strain.

- Arrange mushrooms, bean curd, leeks, spinach and Chinese cabbage on a tray.

- Mix the ingredients for the sauce together. Set aside.

- Stir another 450 ml water into the strained fish stock. Add fish pieces and bring to the boil. Skim off scum.

- Add some mushrooms, bean curd and cabbage. Cook quickly and add leeks, spinach and salt to taste. Allow guests to ladle soup, fish and vegetables into their individual bowls. Dip into sauce before eating.

Kanisu (Cucumber Crab)

The Japanese have adapted their tastes to Western foods very cleverly. The biting and pungent flavours of *wasabe* are today tempered by mixing it in an equal quantity of Japanese mayonnaise.

Ingredients

Crabmeat	300 g, fresh or canned
Salt	1 tsp
Water	450 ml
Cucumber	1, skinned and thinly sliced
Grated ginger	3 Tbsp

Salad Dressing A

Rice wine	3 Tbsp
Dashi (see pg 308)	3 Tbsp
Light soy sauce	2 tsp
Salt	a pinch

Salad Dressing B

Mayonnaise	1 Tbsp
Wasabe	1 Tbsp

Method

- If using fresh crabs, obtain crabmeat by steaming crabs for about 10 minutes until flesh is white. Cool and remove meat. If using canned crabmeat, squeeze liquid from crabmeat.

- Dissolve salt in water and soak cucumber slices for 20 minutes. Strain and squeeze dry using absorbent paper.

- Choose the salad dressing you prefer and combine the ingredients.

- Divide crabmeat and cucumber into 4 portions and place in 4 decorative dishes. Smear each portion with some ginger and pour salad dressing on top. Chill and serve cold.

Sushi

With its classic lines and clean astringent flavours, *sushi* has travelled all over the world as an exciting ambassador of Japanese food. It stands as an example of the impeccable finesse with which the Japanese have prepared, served and influenced modern food in the Western world.

Sushi originated as a result of an ancient process that sought to preserve an exotic carp or tuna. The fish was salted and allowed to mature on a vinegar-rice bed which was then discarded. Later on, the vinegar-rice was gradually included with the eating of the fish and *sushi* as we know it came into being.

The most important things to remember about *sushi* are that the seafood should be absolutely fresh and the vinegar-rice should be cooked in hot water first so that it imparts a glaze to the cooked grain. It should then be quickly cooled by fanning and by tossing with flat rice paddles rather like small table tennis bats. This makes the rice easy to handle. With the correct glutinous texture, grains will adhere to each other and to seafood.

In between bites of *sushi*, fresh or pickled ginger slices are served to refresh the palate. A serving normally consists of two 'fingers' of sushi which are picked up and eaten with the fingers. *Sushi* is lifted up, turned over and the seafood side dipped into the sauce as dipping the rice into sauces would loosen the grains and crumble them.

Many types of *sushi* are made for the Japanese market. The hand-shaped *sushi*, called *nigiri zushi*, originated in Tokyo. The well-known *maki zushi* or rolled *sushi* has come to us, rolled in laver or *nori* sheets, thus the name *norimaki zushi*. Another rolled omelette *zushi* or *fukusa zushi* is wrapped decoratively with a band of green *nori* ribbon in the centre.

No matter what the type, when a plateful of decorative *sushi* is laid out, it is always well-received. *Sushi* remains my favourite Japanese food, always evocative of exquisite taste and style.

Sushi Rice

Sushi rice varies with the seasons: in summer or in the tropics, a little more vinegar is needed. If you do not have kelp *(konbu)*, you can cook the rice without it.

Ingredients

Japanese rice	250 g
Kelp *(konbu)*	5-cm piece, optional
Water	750 ml
Rice vinegar	4 Tbsp
Sugar	4 Tbsp
Salt	2$\frac{1}{2}$ Tbsp

Method

- Wash the rice in several changes of water until it rinses clear.

- If using kelp, wipe with a damp cloth and make cuts in areas to release flavour.

- In a pan, boil water, add rice and place kelp on top. Cover and cook on medium heat. When water is boiling, remove kelp. Turn down heat and partly cover pan until all the water is absorbed.

- Cover pan fully and turn off heat. Allow rice to cook in steam. Small holes will form on the surface of the rice. These are called 'rice eyes'. They indicate that the rice is cooked.

- Place vinegar, sugar and salt in a small pan. Heat slowly to dissolve sugar and salt. Remove from heat. Cool by placing pan in a basin of cold water.

- Turn cooked rice into a wide basin. Spread rice out and toss with a flat spoon until it cools. Try not to break up rice grains. The rice needs to be cooled quickly to acquire a sheen on the grain.

- Spoon vinegar mixture onto rice and mix well. Cover rice with a damp cloth until it is needed.

Maki Zushi (Rolled Sushi)

Maki zushi is the generic name for rolled *sushi*, called *Kim Pab* in Korea. *Nori zushi* is the most common, and the size or thickness of the roll depends on ingredients used in the filling. This usually consists of mushroom or omelette.

The *nori* (or laver) seaweed is cultivated in Japan on fixed frames set in shallow water. The seaweed is then collected and dried in thin sheets, which are cut into standard lengths and sold, 10 sheets per package. *Nori* should be placed in airtight containers to keep it crisp. There are two sides: the shiny, smoother side should be on the outside; the rough textured back (the inside) is where the ingredients are laid before rolling. Before use, it should be 'toasted' by holding the glossy side to the flame, to make it crisp and to heighten flavours.

Wasabe is used with *norimaki zushi* when tuna and cucumber are part of the filling.

Ingredients

Sushi rice	500 g
Fresh seafood (white fish, raw tuna or prawns (shrimps))	125 g
Dashi	450 ml
Sugar	2 Tbsp
Light soy sauce	1 Tbsp
Laver (*nori*) sheets	4
Wasabe	
Vinegar	50 ml

Method

- Prepare *sushi* rice (see pg 241). If using prawns, shell and devein. Quickly cook prawns or fish in mixture of *dashi*, sugar and light soy sauce, or use them raw.

- Just before rolling *sushi*, toast laver. Pass shiny side over high flame. Laver will change from brown to dark green. Toasting laver increases the flavour and makes it crisp.

- Place laver sheet shiny side down on *sushi* bamboo mat. Wet hands with vinegar to keep rice from sticking. (This is called hand vinegar.) Spread 175 g rice on laver sheet with fingertips. Cover up to three quarters of laver sheet. Do not overfill sheet with rice or it will not roll well.

- Using your finger, line *wasabe* along centre of rice. Space strips of fish evenly in a thin line along *wasabe*.

- To roll, hold ingredients firmly in line with fingertips and thumbs, pushing up and turning mat. The edge of the mat closest to you will be facing the other end of mat. Press-roll inside mat firmly and continue to roll, leaving mat aside. Try to get the filling in the very centre of the roll. You will be able to achieve this with practice.

- Unroll mat and give laver roll a turn so that roll sits on the edge of laver sheet. Press down to seal edge.

- Place roll on a cutting board. Wet knife with some vinegar and cut from the centre. Cut firmly down. Wipe knife with a wet towel, then cut more, working towards ends.

Nigiri Zushi (Sushi Appetiser)

When well made, *nigiri zushi* makes a dainty hors d'oeuvre. Practice makes perfect.

Ingredients

Sushi rice	250 g
Squid tubes	150 g, cut into 0.5 x 6 x 3 cm pieces or prawns (shrimps), shelled and deveined
Rice vinegar	2 tsp, mixed with 6 Tbsp water
Sea bream, tuna or ling fillets	300 g, cut into 0.5 x 6 x 3 cm pieces
Wasabe	2 tsp
Salt	1 tsp

Method

- Prepare *sushi* rice (see pg 241).

- If using prawns, skewer with toothpicks to straighten. Cook for 1 minute in salted water or microwave for 2 minutes on MEDIUM. Cool and remove skewers.

- Use vinegar-water mixture to moisten palms before and while working as rice will stick to hands. Spoon 1 1/2 Tbsp rice onto your right palm and, using fingers, press gently but firmly into an oval.

- With your left hand, pick up a piece of fish or seafood. Brush *wasabe* lengthwise on underside and along oval rice wad, with a finger of the right hand.

- Press seafood onto wad of rice, still holding seafood with your left hand. Press together firmly with 2 fingers of your right hand so that seafood sticks to rice with *wasabe* sandwiched in the middle.

- Place completed *sushi* with seafood facing upwards on a plate. Decorate with garnishes of parsley, *kinome* sprigs, slivers of carrot and cucumber. Cones of *nori* filled with seafood are popular in *sushi* bars. To make these, cut *nori* into squares. Starting at one end, roll into a cone and fill with seafood and rice.

San-Suhn-Jo-Rim (Salted Fish)

Koreans use a great deal of fish and shellfish in their diet, although meat is also used in large quantities. Here I include a salted fish eaten with rice and *kim chee* which is very spicy and tasty.

Ingredients

Mackerel fillets	500 g, skinned cut into 5 x 5 x 2-cm pieces
Light soy sauce	3 Tbsp
Sugar	1 Tbsp
Ground pepper	1/2 tsp
Candied ginger	1 Tbsp, chopped
Garlic	2 cloves, peeled and chopped
Spring onion (scallion)	1, chopped
Chilli paste (*go chu jang*)	1 tsp
Salt	to taste

Method

- Place fish in a non-aluminium saucepan. Add soy sauce, 3 Tbsp water, sugar and pepper, then ginger, garlic, spring onion and chilli paste. Mix well.

- Cook on slow heat for about 8 minutes until fish is tender and becomes opaque in colour. Test for salt. Serve hot or cold with rice.

China, Hong Kong, Taiwan & Macau

Have You Eaten Rice?

> "Out in the garden in the moonlight, our servant is scraping a golden carp with so much vigour that the scales fly in every direction—perhaps they go as high as heaven. Those beautiful stars up there might be the scales of our fish."
>
> *Unknown, BEFORE THE REPAST*

Few cuisines are as well known or as published as that of the Chinese. There are some 20,000 cookbooks that deal with the subject and an infinite variety of recipes from the many regions in China. It is said that even if one cooked a different recipe each day, it would take 20 years to exhaust the list. The culture is food-oriented to the extent that when two people meet, the traditional greeting is 'Have you eaten rice?' Food is a means of communication, not only with the living, but with deceased ancestors, through ancestral altars.

The Chinese have from ancient times been skilled cooks of seafood. Their knowledge and involvement with seafood has not merely been culinary. The Chinese carp has been the subject of many beautiful legends, the most romantic being its similarity to the dragon. This is because of its fiery golden colours and its tenacity and strength in swimming upstream. The Chinese and Japanese regard it as a divine fish symbolic of strength.

As symbols go, the character for fish, 'yu' is a homonym for another, 'yue' meaning prosperity and abundance. The character for happiness is traditionally symbolised by twin carps. It is therefore customary to present a brace of fish to the family of the bride at an impending wedding. As fish symbols abound in Chinese folklore and legends, it forms part of the lunar new year menu, along with fatt choy, a dish that includes black mossy seaweed, another homonym, in Cantonese, for luck and prosperity.

Chinese cuisine has been refined over the centuries to produce as many cooking styles as there are villages in China today. It spans the cold northern deserts to the tropical south between the mountains of Yunnan to the coast and all that lies in between. Although the long coastline has been productive, China has had its share of drought, famine and flood. The primary produce in each region still determines what is eaten each day. Firewood was scarce, thus the curved bottom cast-iron wok was developed to stir-fry, stew and steam with minimum fuel.

Food styles follow the natural agricultural divisions in China. The best known are the southern or Cantonese school, the northern Beijing school, the eastern or Shanghai school and the Sichuan in the west. Food from China's peripheral areas (Mongolia, Tibet, Xinqiang, etc.), however, have colourful pasts and many exotic recipes.

There is a Chinese saying—that one should be born in Suzhou, eat in Guangzhou, dress in Hangzhou, and die in Liuzhou—this rings very true. Guangzhou, in the province of Guangdong (Canton) boasts of long coastlines and people who, over the years, have developed a camaraderie with the sea. Cantonese food relies on ingredients and light delicate sauces to retain natural flavours. This cuisine was introduced to the world, along with the art of high temperature stir-frying, to produce the particular aroma and heat called 'wok hey'. Cantonese seafood stir-fried with fermented bean curd, garlic, oyster sauce and soy sauce are some of the best the country has to offer. They are a prosperous people and dishes can be extravagant and flamboyant—witness their shark's fin, lobster and sea cucumber dishes.

Food from the north around Beijing is elegant and imperial in its concept. However, the northern cold dictated that oils like sesame be used in cooking, with vinegar and salt (to cut the oil), garlic, leek and *hoisin*, to cook into hearty soups, and tasty dumplings. All 'waterways' and therefore many food styles, led to the Forbidden City. The best dishes, freshest herbs and choicest ingredients in all of China met in the north, encapsulating food from many regions. Today, access to the sea in the gulf of Chihli provides fresh seafood and carp are plentiful in the Yellow River.

Distance from the sea has not made Sichuan fishless, but it has made Sichuan unique. Inland and freshwater ponds provide a rich supply of fish and prawns (shrimps) which are cooked into hot, spicy, robust and tongue-scorching dishes. The spices have definite links to India through routes that Buddhist monks and travellers, among them Fa Hsien, travelled from 2 A.D. The red chilli, the chilli-pickled Sichuan vegetable and the red peppercorn called *fagara* are perfectly at home in the land that calls itself the red basin because of its deep maroon soil. Food is aromatic, hot and gutsy to excite palates and to revitalise dried squid, dried prawns and scallop. Shark's fin stews are thick and flavoursome, and tender fish lips contrast in texture to sizzling rice crusts and tangy sauces.

The great Yangtze Delta pans open into a large river basin in the Shanghai region. This proximity to the coast not only yields a remarkable variety of fish and seafood but also reflects a culinary influence from successions of European settlers and business communities. The famous drunken prawns (shrimps), hairy crab and shellfish smoked in tea leaves are among spectacular dishes that come from this region.

A Chinese meal is a joyous, noisy community affair, hence the round table and revolving centre which allows easy access to food. An honoured guest is seated closest to the host who ensures that the guest is never neglected. Traditionally a banquet is served in courses; chopsticks are provided for individuals, and main dishes and soups are spooned into bowls. Steaming tea or brandy aids digestion, and dinner is concluded with a filling bowl of rice and a light, fruit pancake or sweet mousse to ensure that guests are replete.

Hei Bai Yu Pian (Sliced Fish Pieces in Wine)

This delicately flavoured dish is one of my favourites as the texture of the soft fish contrasts pleasantly with the crunchy black cloud-ear fungus, leaving a pleasant, musky after-taste.

Ingredients

Sea bream or sea bass fillets	400 g, cut into 5-cm pieces
Cloud-ear fungus or dried Chinese mushrooms	50 g, soaked in warm water to soften
Cooking oil	125 ml
Sugar	1 tsp
Ginger wine	2 Tbsp
Fish or chicken stock	50 ml
Dark soy sauce	1 Tbsp
Light soy sauce	1 Tbsp
Cornflour (cornstarch)	1 Tbsp, mixed with 2 Tbsp water
Salt	to taste
Ground white pepper	to taste
Sesame oil	a few drops

Marinade

Salt	a pinch
Ground black pepper	1 tsp
Cornflour (cornstarch)	2 tsp
Egg	$^1/_2$

Garnish

Coriander (cilantro) leaves

Method

- Combine marinade ingredients and sprinkle over fillets. Set aside in a cool place.

- Drain softened fungus or mushrooms and slice. If using mushrooms, discard stalks.

- Heat oil in a wok and fry a few pieces of fish at a time. Remove them when they are half-cooked and place in shallow bowl to keep warm.

- Drain off all except 2 Tbsp oil and reheat. Add in sugar and ginger wine and cook until bubbling. Lower heat and add fish slices.

- Add stock, dark and light soy sauce and stir. Add in cornflour mixture and stir gently to thicken.

- Add salt and pepper to taste and a few drops of sesame oil. Remove fish pieces from heat and place on a dish.

- Continue to add fungus or mushrooms into wok and cook for 1 minute. Pour over fish and garnish with chopped coriander leaves. Serve hot.

Cui Ching Hung Yu (Crispy Aromatic Fish)

The carp, a native of the fresh waters of Central Asia, has been domesticated by the Chinese since the 10th century. The dark grey-brown species *(Cyprinus carpio)* is the tasty, high-protein carp served at tables.

Ingredients

Whole carp or grouper	600–700 g, scaled, gutted and cleaned
Dried Chinese mushrooms	25 g, soaked in warm water to soften
Green capsicum (bell pepper)	25 g, cored and cut into thin strips
Peas	25 g
Ginger	2-cm knob, peeled and finely chopped
Garlic	2 cloves, peeled and minced
Onions	2, peeled and finely sliced
Water chestnuts	25 g, finely chopped
Cooking oil	750 ml

Seasoning

Eggs	2, beaten
Salt	1 tsp
Rice wine	1 Tbsp
Ground white pepper	$1/2$ tsp
Cornflour (cornstarch)	1 Tbsp

Sauce

Tomato sauce	3 Tbsp
Sugar	2 Tbsp
White rice wine	4 Tbsp
Chicken stock or soup	50 ml
Sesame oil	$1/2$ tsp
Cornflour (cornstarch)	1 Tbsp

Garnish

Lettuce	5 leaves, shredded

Method

- Cut fillets from fish carefully and score with criss-cross lines. Leave head and central spine intact.
- Drain softened mushrooms, discard stalks and slice finely.
- Blanch mushrooms, capsicum and peas in boiling water for 30 seconds, then drain on absorbent paper.
- Prepare seasoning. Combine eggs, salt, rice wine and pepper. Brush mixture on fillets and coat with cornflour.
- Put ingredients for sauce in a pan and heat. Stir well to mix cornflour. Add ginger, garlic and onions and bring to the boil.
- Add water chestnuts and mushrooms, capsicum and peas. Cook for 1 minute. Keep warm until fish is ready.
- Heat oil in a wok until it becomes hazy. Plunge in fish head and central spine for about 4 minutes until golden. Drain on absorbent paper.
- Reheat oil and fry each fillet for about 4 minutes until crisp and golden.
- Spread lettuce on a serving plate and place fish head and spine on top. Assemble fish fillets on spine and pour sauce over. Serve hot.

Variation

- You may also use smaller fish such as whiting, trout or snapper. Use two fishes and follow the same basic recipe.

Si Chuan Ching Cheng Lei Yu

(Steamed Sichuan Carp)

In this recipe, freshwater carp is cooked after being smeared with roasted rice flour, which gives it an unusual texture.

Ingredients

Sea bream, carp or snapper	600 g, scaled, gutted and cleaned
Salt	1 tsp
Rice flour	1 1/2 Tbsp
Ground Sichuan pepper	1 tsp
Light soy sauce	2 Tbsp
Belly pork	125 g, finely sliced
Dried Chinese mushrooms	5–6, soaked in warm water to soften, stalks discarded and sliced
Ginger	6-cm knob, peeled and shredded
Garlic	2 cloves, peeled and pounded
Sweet soy vinegar	1 Tbsp
Cooking oil	1 Tbsp
Red chillies	4–5, seeded and shredded
Pickled Chinese plums	3–4
Coriander (cilantro)	3 sprigs, sliced
Spring onions (scallions)	4, sliced

Garnish

Onions	2, peeled, sliced and crisp-fried

Method

- Rub the outside and inside of fish with salt.

- Combine rice flour with ground Sichuan pepper and fry in a dry wok for 3 minutes on high heat to heighten the flavour. Alternatively, cook in the microwave oven for 1 minute on HIGH.

- Mix light soy sauce with roasted rice flour and Sichuan pepper mixture, pork, mushrooms, ginger, garlic, sweet soy vinegar, oil, chillies and Chinese plums. Stir in 2 Tbsp water to form a paste so that it will spread well on fish.

- Place fish on a steaming plate with a slight rim. Brush paste over fish and stuff remaining paste into stomach cavity. Stuff some coriander and spring onion into stomach as well.

- Steam for 25 minutes. If using a larger fish, steam a further 5 minutes.

- Remove from heat. Garnish fish with remaining coriander and spring onions and serve with fried onions.

Tien Sien Hong Shao Yu (Red Cooked Spicy Fish)

This cleverly made caramelised sauce is a true testament to the art of the Chinese chef. If the sauce is cooked on a simmer and allowed to thicken, its dark reddish colour could transform the dish into a spicy and crunchy masterpiece.

Ingredients

Whole sea bass, river shad, threadfin or snapper	1 kg, scaled, gutted and cleaned
Mustard greens	2–3 stalks
Vinegar	450 ml
Peanut or vegetable oil	450 ml
Sugar	2 Tbsp
Ginger	2-cm knob, peeled and finely chopped
Garlic	1 clove
Dark soy sauce	1 Tbsp
Chinese wine (shao hsing)	2 Tbsp
Spring onion (scallion)	1, shredded
Salt	to taste
Ground white pepper	to taste

Garnish

Spring onion (scallion)	1, shredded
Onions	2, peeled, sliced and crisp-fried

Method

- Score fish on both sides.

- Soak mustard greens in vinegar for 1 hour, then slice. Save vinegar in a bottle for reuse.

- Heat oil in a wok until it becomes hazy. Lower in fish and fry for 5–6 minutes until golden on both sides. Drain on absorbent paper.

- Remove all but 1 Tbsp oil from the wok. Add sugar and cook until it caramelises into a dark, thick syrup.

- Add ginger and garlic, dark soy sauce, wine, spring onion and 1 Tbsp vinegar. Cook on low heat until it thickens and is reduced to half its volume.

- Add pickled mustard greens and cook for 1 minute on high heat. Add salt and pepper to taste.

- Lower fish into wok and simmer for 1 minute, ladling sauce over fish continuously.

- Slide fish onto a dish and pour sauce over it. Garnish with spring onions and fried onions.

Ke Chia Bai Yu Chiu (Hakka Fish Balls)

The Hakka, or guests from the north, settled in Hong Kong years ago and brought with them many interesting recipes. This one for fish balls can easily be made, but if you are short of time, buy ready-made fish balls and proceed with the cooking method.

Ingredients

Snake ling, mackerel or perch fillets	350 g
Salt	1 Tbsp
Cornflour (cornstarch)	1 tsp
Ginger	2-cm knob, peeled
Spring onions (scallions)	3
Chinese wine (*shao hsing*)	2 Tbsp
Egg	1

Preparation

- Wash fish and towel dry. Remove flesh by gently scraping at flesh with an upended spoon held at right angles to the table. Collect meat from fish bones as well. Discard bones. Pound meat with the blunt edge of a Chinese cleaver or use a mortar and pestle or a blender. Mix 125 ml water and 2 tsp salt to use while making balls. Use a few drops in the mixture.

- Add remaining salt and cornflour and continue to pound with roughly chopped ginger and spring onions until smooth. Remove the thicker ginger and spring onion pieces, add Chinese wine and a few drops of salted water to the mixture and continue mixing well.

- Separate egg white and yolk. Add egg white and mix well until mixture is well amalgamated.

Cooking Method

- Bring a panful of water to the boil. Holding 2–3 Tbsp of fish paste in your left fist, squeeze paste out and scoop out a ball with a spoon held in your right hand.

- Drop each ball into the bowl of salty water, then into the boiling water. It will rise to the surface as it cooks. Remove fish balls with a slotted spoon and cool.

Serving Suggestion

- Fish balls can be used in a variety of ways: they can be frozen; the 'soup' can be utilised as stock; and the balls served with a fish sauce.

- The best way to eat fish balls is in a soup with shredded cabbage or with noodles, garnished with spring onion, onion crisps and preserved turnip.

Yu Zhi Mei Xiang Tang (Shark's Fin Soup)

Ingredients

Canned or fresh crabmeat	400 g
Chicken meat	300 g, steamed and shredded
Chinese wine (shao hsing)	5 Tbsp
Cornflour (cornstarch)	1 Tbsp
Frozen, canned or processed shark's fin	300 g, cleaned and soaked (see pg 302)
Ginger	2-cm knob, peeled and shredded
Spring onions (scallions)	2
Rich chicken stock	1.5–2 litres
Ginger juice	extracted from 5-cm knob ginger
Light soy sauce	2 Tbsp
Dried Chinese mushrooms	4, soaked in warm water to soften and sliced
Salt	to taste
Ground white pepper	to taste

Soup Thickener

Bean flour or cornflour (cornstarch)	2 Tbsp, mixed with 50 ml water
Egg	1, beaten
Sesame oil	1 tsp
Dark soy sauce	1 tsp
Ground white pepper	a dash

Garnish

Black sweet soy vinegar	4 Tbsp
Sweet, pickled chilli	2 Tbsp, sliced
Brandy	a dash, optional

Method

- If using fresh crabmeat, cook and shred. Marinate chicken meat and crabmeat in 1 Tbsp Chinese wine and cornflour.

- Place shark's fin in a pot with 750 ml–1 litre water, 2 Tbsp Chinese wine, ginger and whole spring onions. Bring to the boil then discard water. This is to refresh frozen, canned or processed fins.

- Boil chicken stock in a pan for 10–15 minutes until it reduces slightly. As it boils, add ginger juice, soy sauce and 2 Tbsp Chinese wine and stir.

- Add chicken shreds and simmer, stirring well. Add crabmeat and leave soup to boil gently. Reserve marinade.

- Add marinade liquid and sliced mushrooms. Add shark's fin, then simmer for 20 minutes. Add salt and pepper to taste.

- Combine ingredients for soup thickener and pour in a steady stream into simmering soup. Stir well.

- Serve hot with sweet soy vinegar and sweet pickled chilli in separate dishes as garnish. A dash of brandy added to soup improves the flavour.

Yu Zhi Dan (Shark's Fin Omelette)

It is always a source of surprise that a little bit of gelatinous fibre (as shark's fins really are) can produce such exquisite flavours. But, of course, many wonderful ingredients go into it to produce this wonderful omelette.

Ingredients

Canned or processed shark's fin	350 g
Ginger	2-cm knob, peeled and shredded
Cooking oil	2 Tbsp
Garlic	3 cloves, peeled and chopped
Belly pork	50 g, finely minced
Eggs	4, beaten with $\frac{1}{2}$ tsp ground white pepper and 1 tsp salt
Bean sprouts	125 g, heads and tails removed
Spring onions (scallions)	2, finely sliced
Coriander (cilantro) leaves	25 g
Ground white pepper	to taste
Salt	to taste
Sesame oil	1 tsp

Garnish

Lettuce leaves	6, shredded

Method

- Simmer shark's fin in 750 ml water with shredded ginger to refresh it. Strain shark's fin and discard water and ginger.

- Heat oil in a wok until it becomes hazy. Sauté garlic until golden and add minced pork. Stir-fry until pork turns dark.

- Add shark's fin and continue to stir-fry.

- Increase heat and add eggs. Stir quickly to break up egg. Add bean sprouts and stir in spring onion and coriander leaves. Add pepper and salt to taste.

- Toss evenly and dot with sesame oil. Dish out onto a plate of shredded lettuce. Serve hot.

Ching Cheng Chen Pi Long Xia

(Lobster Steamed in Tangerine)

Ingredients

Lobster	1, large, about 750 g
Salt	1/2 tsp
Ground white pepper	1/2 tsp
Sesame oil	1 tsp

Stuffing

Garlic	3 cloves, peeled and chopped
Dried tangerine peel	25 g, soaked and finely shredded
Preserved sweet lemon skin	2 pieces, shredded
Light soy sauce	1 tsp
Sugar	1/4 tsp
Salt	to taste
Preserved soy beans	1 Tbsp, washed and mashed

Stock/Sauce

Chicken stock	2 Tbsp
Cornflour	3/4 tsp, mixed with 1 Tbsp cold water

Garnish

Spring onions (scallions)	12, sliced into thin rings
Onion	1, peeled, sliced and crisp-fried
Coriander (cilantro) leaves	1 handful
Chinese wine (shao hsing)	1 Tbsp

Method

- If using live lobster, clean and prepare (see pg 301). Clean then use a heavy knife to cut through entire tail length of lobster to expose flesh. Make a slit down centre of flesh with knife. Wipe lobster dry and rub salt and pepper around flesh.

- Combine all stuffing ingredients except soy beans in a bowl.

- Place lobster on a steaming platter and stuff soy beans inside. Spread combined stuffing over lobster.

- Steam lobster for 12 minutes until cooked. Remove from heat and keep fish warm.

- Collect liquid from steaming and reserve.

- Sprinkle lobster with sesame oil for additional flavour.

- Combine chicken stock and cornflour mixture and heat. Stir in reserved steaming liquid and simmer until sauce thickens. Pour sauce carefully over lobster.

- Sprinkle spring onions, fried onion, coriander leaves and wine on lobster. Serve hot.

Cui Yan Da Xia (Prawns Baked in Salt)

An interesting southern Chinese dish that is certainly finger-licking material. The subtle flavours of the sea are retained in this clever dish. Remove coat and tie and abandon formal eating to do this meal some justice.

Ingredients

King prawns	1 kg
Chinese wine (shao hsing)	2 Tbsp
Light soy sauce	1 Tbsp
Cornflour (cornstarch)	1 Tbsp
Sichuan pepper	1/2 tsp
Sesame oil	2 Tbsp
Coarse kitchen salt	500 g
Greaseproof paper	1 large piece

Dipping Sauce

Light soy sauce	1 Tbsp
Mustard or dark vinegar	1 Tbsp

Method

- Wash prawns, cut off legs and whiskers but leave heads intact.

- Mix Chinese wine, soy sauce, cornflour and Sichuan pepper in a bowl and leave prawns to marinate in it for 1 hour.

- Place prawns on greaseproof paper and dot with sesame oil. Wrap into one large parcel.

- Place salt in a wok or crockpot, cover and heat up gradually. When pot is very hot (about 160°C), make a dent in the salt and place parcel in. Cover with more salt and leave to bake for 25–30 minutes.

- Remove parcel from heat and open carefully without letting prawns come into contact with salt.

- Mix soy sauce and mustard or vinegar to form dipping sauce. Serve prawns hot with dipping sauce.

Microwave Method

- Place salt in a microwave-safe container and cook for 15 minutes on MEDIUM.

- Make a dent in the salt and place parcel in. Cover with more salt.

- Cook for 8 minutes on MEDIUM, then allow to stand in hot salt for 5 minutes. Remove parcel and serve as above.

Hung Yun Xiao Pao (Prawns in Green Paper Parcels)

I have served these parcels with great success as an entrée for a seafood dinner. They make interesting packets served individually but, more importantly, make your guests feel that they have been singled out for special favours.

Ingredients

Green or fresh prawns (shrimps)	500 g, medium, shelled, deveined, washed and chopped
Ginger wine	2 Tbsp
Minced pork	50 g
Bamboo shoots	25 g, shredded
Garlic	2 cloves, peeled and chopped
Sugar	1 tsp
Salt	to taste
Ground white pepper	to taste
Dark soy sauce	1 Tbsp
Egg white	from 1 egg
Cornflour (cornstarch)	1 Tbsp
Peanut oil	450 ml
Greaseproof paper	10 sheets (15 x 15-cm)

Garnish

Lettuce heart	1, shredded
Tomatoes	2, sliced

Method

- Place prawns in a bowl with ginger wine and minced pork. Mix well.

- Add in bamboo shoots, garlic, sugar, salt, pepper and dark soy sauce and mix well.

- Stir in egg white and cornflour to thicken and make it sticky.

- Divide mixture into 10 portions. Spoon 1 portion onto each sheet of greaseproof paper. Fold into an envelope and tuck ends in securely. Staple if necessary.

- Heat oil in a wok until it is very hot and smoking. The oil must be hot so that parcels will not absorb too much oil. Deep-fry 2–3 parcels at a time for 2–3 minutes.

- Carefully open parcels on plates before serving with lettuce and tomato slices.

Tien Zui Bei Fang Xia (Prawns from the North)

Ingredients

King prawns	500 g
Salt	1 Tbsp
Cooking oil	2 Tbsp
Garlic	3 cloves, peeled and diced
Spring onions (scallions)	3, sliced
Light soy sauce	1 Tbsp
Hoisin sauce	1 Tbsp
Chinese wine (*shao hsing*) or gin	2 Tbsp
Sugar	1 Tbsp
Sesame oil	a few drops

Garnish

Chinese cabbage

Method

- Clean prawns and cut off feelers and legs. Remove vein carefully with a skewer and leave head and shell intact.

- Rub prawns with salt and leave for 20 minutes. Rinse in icy water and dry with absorbent paper.

- Heat oil in a wok until it becomes hazy. Add garlic and stir. Add prawns and spring onions.

- When prawns turn pink, add soy sauce, *hoisin* sauce, wine and sugar. Cook until prawns dry up a little, then add sesame oil. Add salt to taste and remove from heat.

- Serve prawns on a bed of shredded cabbage.

Microwave Method

- Prepare ingredients as above. Preheat a microwave-safe browning dish for 6 minutes on HIGH until hot. Add oil and cook for 30 seconds. Add garlic then prawns and spring onions and stir. Cook for 2 minutes on MEDIUM.

- Add soy sauce, *hoisin* sauce, wine and sugar and stir. Cook for 2 minutes on HIGH. Add sesame oil and stir. Cook for 1 minute on MEDIUM. Remove and serve as above.

Ching Doe Hai Xien (Mixed Seafood with Nuts)

Part of the charm of eating seafood cooked with nuts is the contrast in colours, textures and flavours. It is also part of the balance of *yin* and *yang*, practised for centuries, that advocated that cool foods be balanced with warm and heat-creating foods. Asians call this 'cooling' and 'heaty' foods.

Ingredients

Squid tubes or scallops	125 g
Cooking oil	175 ml
Garlic	2 cloves, peeled and chopped
Cauliflower	125 g, sliced into bite-sized pieces
Chicken or prawn (shrimp) stock	50 ml
Prawns (shrimps)	300 g, medium, shelled, cleaned and deveined
Snow peas (mange-tout)	125 g, cut in half
Macademia or cashew nuts	125 g
Spring onions (scallions)	2, sliced into bite-sized pieces
Ginger	2-cm knob, shredded and juice extracted
Cornflour (cornstarch)	$1/2$ tsp, mixed with 3 Tbsp chicken stock
Ground white pepper	to taste
Salt	to taste

Marinade

Egg white	from 1 egg
Chicken stock	2 Tbsp
Cornflour (cornstarch)	1 Tbsp
Cooking oil	1 tsp
Salt	$1/2$ tsp
Sesame oil	a few drops

Method

- Cut each squid tube into 4 and score so they will cook well. Wash scallops if using.

- Prepare marinade. Mix $1/4$ of the egg white with the other marinade ingredients and allow seafood to sit in marinade for 1 hour in the refrigerator.

- Heat 2 Tbsp oil in a wok until it becomes hazy. Brown garlic until golden and add cauliflower. Cover and cook for 3 minutes with chicken or prawn stock until cauliflower is soft. Transfer to a bowl.

- In the same wok, heat remaining oil. Quick-fry prawns, squid or scallops and snow peas for 1 minute and remove.

- Leaving 1 Tbsp oil in wok, fry nuts until crisp. Re-introduce cauliflower and stock, seafood and snow peas back into wok with spring onions and shredded ginger and ginger juice. Add cornflour mixture to thicken. Heat through and toss well.

- Add pepper and salt to taste and transfer to a serving plate. Serve hot.

Hua Liang Xia (Glassy Prawns)

This is a tedious recipe to prepare, but the glassy effect created by cooking prawns (shrimps) in sugar is stunning. Allow an afternoon for preparation, but you may cook other items and do other chores in the meantime.

Ingredients

Fresh white prawns (shrimps)	500 g, shelled, cleaned and deveined
Baking soda	2 tsp
Sugar	1/2 tsp
Salt	to taste
Cornflour (cornstarch)	1 Tbsp
Chinese wine (shao hsing)	1 tsp

Garnish

Spring onions (scallions)	2, roughly chopped
Red chilli	1, seeded and chopped
Ginger	3-cm knob, peeled and sliced

Method

- Pat prawns dry.

- Combine baking soda and 250 ml water and put prawns in for 2 1/4 hours. Drain and rinse in two changes of cold water to remove soda flavour.

- Place prawns in cold water for 30 minutes and drain.

- Boil water and plunge prawns in for 1–2 minutes. Drain. Alternatively, cook prawns in the microwave oven for 1 minute on HIGH or until prawns turn pink.

- In a pan, combine sugar, salt, cornflour, wine and 2 Tbsp water. Stir and bring to a slow boil. Add prawns and stir until sauce thickens.

- Arrange some garnish in the centre of a plate and pile prawns around garnish. Pour thickened sauce over prawns and sprinkle with remaining garnish. Serve hot.

Fei Chui Xia (Drunken Prawns)

This famous recipe for drunken prawns (shrimps) will only appeal to the adventurous. I admit that although it was specially prepared for me, I was too upset by the whole procedure to truly savour and appreciate the flavours of this Bacchanalian fantasy. I shall describe the procedure to you and leave the rest to your sense of adventure as to whether you would like to cook the dish with live prawns or with the freshest raw green prawns instead. Be assured that the flavours will not be lost should you choose the latter.

Ingredients

Fresh prawns	500 g, medium
Chinese wine (*shao hsing*)	450 ml
Thick chicken stock	450 ml, warmed
Garlic	3 cloves, peeled and shredded
Ginger	3-cm knob, peeled and shredded
Light soy sauce	1 Tbsp
Spring onions (scallions)	2–3, roughly broken
Salt	to taste
Ground white pepper	to taste

Garnish

Brandy	50 ml
Light soy sauce	125 ml
Spring onions (scallions)	2, cut into thin strips
Garlic	4 cloves, peeled, sliced and crisp-fried

Method

- Place prawns in a casserole dish and pour in Chinese wine. (Live prawns will agitate and jump.) Allow prawns to soak for 10 minutes to absorb flavours, then carefully ignite wine with a match.

- Place casserole dish over a lightly burning wick or a food warmer.

- Add warmed chicken broth, garlic, ginger, soy sauce and spring onions. Season to taste with salt and pepper.

- Ladle prawns into individual serving bowls and drizzle in some brandy. Serve with soy sauce, spring onions and crispy fried garlic in separate saucers. The flavours are delicious and will improve with heating the wine and broth further.

Xuan Xiang Mei Xia (Shanghai Garlic Steamed Prawns)

This recipe encapsulates the sophisticated and subtle tastes of Shanghainese food.

Ingredients

Prawns (shrimps)	400 g, cleaned and deveined
Garlic	3 cloves, peeled, thinly sliced and crisp-fried
Chinese wine (*shao hsing*)	1 Tbsp
Cornflour (cornstarch)	1/2 tsp
Salt	1/2 tsp

Sauce

Light soy sauce	2 Tbsp
Dark soy sauce	1 tsp
Sugar	1/2 tsp
Water or chicken stock	50 ml

Garnish

Spring onions (scallions)	3, roughly broken
Garlic	4 cloves, peeled and thinly sliced

Method

- Butterfly prawns (see pg 297) and arrange on a heat-proof (flameproof) plate.

- Take half the fried garlic and mix with wine and cornflour. Pour mixture over prawns, pushing some into prawn tail shells.

- Sprinkle with salt and steam in a bamboo steamer for 10 minutes. Carefully remove plate from steamer and keep prawns warm.

- Heat light and dark soy sauce, sugar and water or stock until boiling. Ladle sauce over prawns.

- Garnish with broken up spring onions and sliced garlic.

Microwave Method

- Instead of a steamer, place prawns arranged in a pinwheel shape on a microwave-safe plate. Cover with plastic wrap and cook for 3 minutes on MEDIUM, then 1 minute on HIGH. Remove plastic wrap and cook for another 1 minute on HIGH. Serve hot with sauce as above.

Mei Xien Bai Dai (Jewels in a Fan—Scallops in Shells)

Ingredients

Fresh scallops with shell	10
Cooking oil	1 Tbsp
Ginger	3-cm knob, peeled and shredded
Garlic	3 cloves, peeled and chopped
Spring onions (scallions)	2, chopped
Dried Chinese mushrooms	125 g, soaked for 30 minutes, drained and halved
Snow peas (mange-tout)	125 g, sliced diagonally

Marinade

Chinese wine (*shao hsing*)	2 tsp
Cornflour (cornstarch)	1 tsp
Light soy sauce	1 Tbsp

Sauce

Sesame oil	1 Tbsp
Chinese wine (*shao hsing*) or gin	1 Tbsp
Salt	to taste
Ground white pepper	to taste
Bean flour or cornflour (cornstarch)	1 tsp

Garnish

Snow peas (mange-tout)	1–2, boiled whole

Method

- Soak scallops in water for a few minutes to remove any grit. Pat dry. Slide scallops from shells and retain shells for use later. Remove stomachs and corals (roe). Slice scallops in half lengthwise, holding knife parallel to the table.

- Combine marinade ingredients and allow scallops to sit in marinade for 30 minutes.

- Heat oil in a wok until it becomes hazy. Stir-fry scallops for 2 minutes, then remove from heat.

- In the same oil, sauté ginger, garlic and spring onions until fragrant. Add mushrooms and snow peas. Cook for 30 seconds and add combined sauce ingredients. Cook a further 1 minute until sauce thickens. Add scallops, stir to mix well and remove from heat.

- Replace scallops in shells and arrange on serving plate with other sautéed ingredients. Garnish with snow peas to serve.

Bai Zu Xiang Lian (Necklace of Pearls—Plain Steamed Scallops)

In Hong Kong, this dish is cooked with fresh scallops in the shell. If fresh scallops in shells are unavailable, buy them without the shell and cook them the same way.

Ingredients

Scallops	15
Ginger	2-cm knob, peeled and shredded
Garlic	2 cloves, peeled and chopped
Red chilli	1, seeded and chopped, optional
Salt	to taste
Ground white pepper	to taste

Marinade

Chinese wine (*shao hsing*)	2 Tbsp
Cornflour (cornstarch)	1 Tbsp
Sesame oil	2 Tbsp

Garnish

Coriander (cilantro) leaves	1 sprig, roughly broken

Method

- Clean scallops. If using scallops in shell, scrub off dirt from shells. Slide scallops off shells and retain shells for use later.

- Combine marinade ingredients.

- Place scallops in a heatproof (flameproof) dish and pour marinade over. Top with ginger, garlic, chilli, if using, and salt and pepper to taste.

- Place in a steamer and steam for 6–8 minutes. Remove from heat.

- Arrange 2 scallops in 1 shell on each plate for each guest. Top with steamed ginger, garlic and chilli and resulting juices. Garnish with coriander leaves and serve.

Si Chuan Xiang Mo Yu

(Spicy Sichuan Squid—A Cold Salad)

You may use fresh squid, although dried squid is often used in inland Sichuan. This dish is fresh and tangy, and rather Japanese in flavour.

Ingredients

Squid	500 g
Baking soda	1 Tbsp (if using dried squid)
Cucumbers	2, halved
Salt	1/2 tsp
Sichuan vegetable	25 g, soaked, drained and chopped
Sweet vinegar	2 Tbsp
Light soy sauce	1 Tbsp
Ginger juice	2 Tbsp
Garlic	1 clove, peeled and sliced
Spring onions (scallions)	2, chopped

Garnish

Cucumber	1/2, sliced
Sesame seeds	1 tsp, dry-roasted

Method

- Wash squid and peel off skin. If using dried squid, dissolve baking soda in some water and soak covered for 2–3 hours or until squid has softened. Drain and wash off soda.

- Cut squid along the length to open the body. Flatten on a cutting board with the inside facing up. Cut long strips, 3-cm wide and make diagonal cuts with a sharp knife. Do not cut too deep. Turn over and make criss-cross cuts so squid will curl when cooked.

- Rub cucumbers with salt and leave for at least 2 hours. Wash salt off and slice with diagonal cuts.

- Plunge squid pieces into a pan of boiling water. Take them out as they curl and drain.

- Place squid with cucumber and Sichuan vegetable in a bowl.

- Combine vinegar, soy sauce, ginger juice, garlic and spring onions and pour over squid and vegetables. Toss and refrigerate.

- Serve cold, garnished with cucumber slices and sesame seeds.

Tian Tang Niao Zui

(Bird Beaks from Heaven—Crab Claws in Prawn Paste)

Crab claws covered in a soft paste of delicately spiced prawns (shrimps) are elegant finger foods as they come with their own natural 'handles' or claws. These are great for cocktails or finger food parties.

Ingredients

Crab claws	10
Cooking oil	250 ml

Marinade

Spring onions (scallions)	2, sliced
Ginger	2-cm knob, shredded
Chinese wine (*shao hsing*)	1 Tbsp
Salt	1/2 tsp

Coating

Prawns (shrimps)	350 g, small, cleaned, shelled and deveined
Water chestnuts	25 g, peeled and chopped
Garlic	1 clove, peeled and chopped
Ground white pepper	to taste
Salt	to taste
Breadcrumbs	125 g
Egg white	from 1 egg, beaten

Method

- Crack and remove most of crab claw to expose meat. Retain pincers to act as handles.

- Combine ingredients for marinade in a heatproof (flameproof) bowl and leave crab claws to marinate for 1 hour.

- Place bowl in steamer and steam for 4 minutes or until crab claws are red. Alternatively, use a microwave-safe bowl and partly cover with plastic wrap. Cook in the microwave oven for 5 minutes on MEDIUM or until claws turn red and flesh is whitish.

- Use prawns to make a prawn farce (see pg 311). Mix in water chestnuts and garlic. Season with pepper and salt.

- Make a flat circle with 1 Tbsp farce. Use it to coat crab claw and press firmly until it adheres to claw. Dip each coated claw in breadcrumbs then in egg white, then once more in breadcrumbs.

- Heat oil until it becomes hazy. Deep-fry 3–4 claws at a time, removing as soon as they turn brown.

- Alternatively, omit breadcrumbs and bake claws under the grill for 10–12 minutes, turning as each side browns.

- Serve crab claws with a dipping sauce, such as a mixture of vinegar and soy sauce. This can be an entrée or part of a 'cold dish'.

Alternative Recipe

- Instead of crab claws, use butterflied and flattened prawns. Coat with a prawn and pork (3 parts prawn: 1 part pork) farce following the same recipe, ingredients and directions. The prawns will not need to be steamed beforehand. Use 25 g lard to help the paste to adhere. Grill as crab claws.

Jing Huang Mei Hao (Crispy Fried Oysters)

Oysters can be prepared in many ways and the people of Fujian have a particularly tasty way of cooking it.

Ingredients

Opened oysters	500 g
Salt	a pinch
Ginger juice	extracted from 2-cm knob
Cooking oil	750 ml

Batter

Plain (all-purpose) flour	125 g
Cornflour (cornstarch)	1½ Tbsp
Baking soda	1 tsp
Water	125 ml

Dip

Sichuan peppercorns	2 Tbsp, dry-roasted until slightly darkened
Salt	1 tsp

Method

- Clean opened oysters by gently soaking in water with a pinch of salt. Lift off oysters gently, as oysters are soft and very delicate, then drain. Cover oysters in ginger juice.

- Make a batter with flour, cornflour, baking soda and water. Mix well. Adjust with either more water or flour until batter is thick enough to coat oysters without dripping off.

- Prepare dip. Grind roasted Sichuan peppercorns to a powder and mix with salt. Set aside.

- Heat oil in a wok until it becomes hazy. The oil should be very hot or the batter may absorb too much oil.

- Dip oysters in batter and gently lower a few at a time into hot oil. Deep-fry for about 2 minutes until crisp and golden. Continue until all are done, removing with a wire ladle or slotted spoon. Drain.

- Serve with dip in a separate saucer.

Jiang Xu Xiang Peng Hao Hei

(Kiangsu Braised Oysters)

Ingredients

Shelled oysters	500 g
Cooking oil	2 Tbsp
Garlic	4 cloves, peeled and chopped
Ginger	3-cm knob, shredded
Ginger juice	extracted from 2-cm knob
Spring onions (scallions)	2, roughly broken
Chinese wine (shao hsing)	1 Tbsp
Straw mushrooms or enoki mushrooms	200 g, finely sliced
Red capsicum (bell pepper)	1, cored and thinly sliced
Cornflour (cornstarch) or bean flour	1/2 Tbsp, mixed with 1 Tbsp water
Sesame oil	a dash
Salt	to taste
Ground white pepper	to taste

Garnish

Coriander (cilantro) leaves

Method

- If using fresh oysters, prepare them (see pg 300) to get a shelled weight of 500 g.

- Heat oil in a pan. Add garlic and cook until golden and aromatic. Add ginger, ginger juice and spring onions and sauté for 1 minute. Add wine, mushrooms and capsicum, then oysters.

- Stir on high heat for 30 seconds, then add cornflour mixture. Lower heat and stir gently. Finally, add sesame oil and salt and pepper.

- Serve hot, garnished with coriander leaves.

Shi Zi Tou Yu ('Lion's Head' in Earthenware Pot)

Fish head is considered a delicacy in China. Only the wealthy could afford to eat it in the way it was meant to be served—with only the head—the rest of the body was discarded or given to the servants. Fish head casserole is particularly delicious, especially when it is slowly simmered in a stewpot with the lovely jellied flavours released. If you are using a clay pot, soak the pot in cold water for 1 hour before use.

Ingredients

Large snapper or jewfish head	1, about 500 g
Ground white pepper	1/2 tsp
Salt	1/2 tsp
Cornflour (cornstarch)	1 Tbsp
Light soy sauce	2 Tbsp
Chinese wine (shao hsing)	1 tsp
Dried Chinese mushrooms	50 g, soaked in warm water to soften, discard stalks
Bamboo shoots	25 g
Roast pork	125 g
Spring onions (scallions)	4
Cooking oil	2 Tbsp
Chinese cabbage	1, sliced
Chicken stock	250 ml
Sugar	1/2 tsp
Light soy sauce	2 Tbsp
Dark soy sauce	1/2 tsp
Soft bean curd	50 g, cut into cubes

Method

- Choose a fleshy fish head, clean and remove gills, fins and viscera. Scale and wash. Using a heavy mallet to thump the blunt edge of the knife, half head lengthwise. Coat fish head with pepper and salt, then cornflour.

- In a bowl, mix light soy sauce and Chinese wine and place fish in. Turn fish over after 2 hours.

- Slice mushrooms (optional), bamboo shoots, roast pork and spring onions into thin diagonal slices.

- Heat 1 Tbsp oil in a wok and fry fish head until golden, turning to cook evenly.

- Place stewpot over slow heat and pour in remaining oil. When oil is hot, sauté cabbage until soft. Add mushrooms, bamboo shoots, sliced pork and fish head.

- Add 50 ml stock, cover and cook on slow heat for 1 1/2 hours. Do not let the liquid in the stewpot dry up. Add more stock to keep liquid simmering.

- After 1 hour, add sugar, soy sauces, remaining stock, bean curd and spring onions. Cover and cook for a further 20 minutes. Add pepper and salt to taste. Serve hot.

Variation

- For even greater flavour, sauté ingredients in a frying pan (skillet) or wok before pouring into the stewpot. Pour in a dash of Chinese wine or sherry at the end.

Microwave Method

- Sauté ingredients, then pour into a casserole dish. Cook in the microwave oven for 10 minutes on MEDIUM, 20 minutes on LOW and 2 minutes on HIGH. Stir well at the end of each cycle and spoon sauce over fish head.

Chien Yiu Yu Xiang (Pearls in the Deep—Fried Squid Balls)

This is a Taiwanese dish. It is quite simple to prepare, especially if you have a food processor.

Ingredients

Squid	500 g
Lard	1 Tbsp
Cooking oil	250 ml

Dipping Sauce

Stone's ginger wine	50 ml
Chilli sauce	2 Tbsp

Garnish

Watercress

Method

- Clean squids. Remove head, tentacles, quills and ink sacs. Cut through tubes and peel off skin.

- Pound squid with a meat mallet or pulverise in a food processor. Add lard gradually to mix completely. Shape into balls with wet hands.

- Combine ginger wine and chilli sauce to make dipping sauce. Set aside.

- Heat oil in a wok and drop 4–5 squid balls into hot oil. Lower heat to medium and cook for about 3 minutes until squid balls float to the surface. If oil is too hot, the squid balls may become too tough. Drain and continue until all the squid balls are cooked.

- Arrange as part of a cold dish platter or as finger food. Garnish with fresh watercress and serve with dipping sauce.

Xiang Mo Yu (Crispy Squid)

Ingredients

Squid	500 g
Vegetable oil	250 ml
Cornflour (cornstarch)	75 g

Marinade

Spring onions (scallions)	2, finely chopped, juice extracted
Ginger	5-cm knob, pounded, juice extracted
Star anise	1, pounded
Stone's ginger wine	1/2 Tbsp
Salt	1/2 tsp

Dip

Ground Sichuan pepper	1 Tbsp
Salt	1 tsp

Method

- Clean squids. Remove ink sacs, quills, tentacles and discard. Slice tubes into 1-cm wide rings.

- Prepare marinade. Mix spring onions and juice, ginger and juice, star anise, ginger wine and salt. Leave squid to sit in marinade for 1 hour.

- Shake marinade off squid and roll in cornflour to coat lightly.

- Heat oil until it becomes hazy. Drop 3–4 squid rings into hot oil at a time. Keep moving rings around and cook for about 2–3 minutes until brown. Drain on absorbent paper and continue until squid rings are all cooked.

- Combine Sichuan pepper and salt and serve with squid rings.

Fu Yong Xia (Crab Omelette)

Ingredients

Crabmeat	400 g
Salt	to taste
Ground white pepper	to taste
Cooking oil	1 Tbsp
Spring onions (scallions)	4, white and green parts separated and chopped
Ginger	2-cm knob, peeled and chopped
Garlic	1 clove, peeled and chopped
Chinese wine *(shao hsing)*	1 Tbsp
Green capsicum (bell pepper)	1, small, cored and cut into cubes
Bean sprouts	75 g, heads and tails removed
Eggs	6, lightly beaten with 2 tsp light soy

sauce

Garlic chives	2, sliced
Fish sauce	1 tsp
Sesame oil	a few drops

Method

- Buy cleaned crabmeat or if using fresh crabs, steam crab and discard gristle. Remove meat in chunks. Dust crabmeat with salt and pepper.

- Heat oil in a wok and stir-fry white part of spring onions until soft. Add crabmeat, ginger and garlic and stir well.

- Add wine and cook until dry. Then add capsicum and bean sprouts. Toss lightly to mix well and turn heat down.

- Pour eggs around crabmeat. Stir carefully while eggs cook around crab, turning heat up and adjusting heat whenever necessary.

- Add some garlic chives and toss well. Sprinkle in fish sauce and sesame oil before removing from heat.

- Garnish with remaining chives and serve hot.

Ching Cheng Pang Xie (Steamed Crabs)

This recipe belongs to my friend, Steven Wong, who is a gourmet chef when he is not working at his professional career.

Ingredients

Mud or blue swimmer crabs	1 kg, about 2–3
Chinese wine (*shao hsing*) or cooking wine	3 Tbsp
Ginger	2-cm knob, peeled and shredded
Spring onions (scallions)	2, roughly broken
Salt	1 tsp

Dipping Sauce

Sweet vinegar	50 ml
Ginger	2-cm knob, peeled and shredded
Ground Sichuan pepper	$1/_2$ tsp

Method

- Clean and wash crabs (see pg 298). Carefully cut each body in half and break off legs and claws. Collect coral (roe). Place crabs and roe in a heatproof (flameproof) dish.

- Combine wine, ginger and spring onions. Pour over crabs. Add salt.

- Steam crabs for 12 minutes.

- Meanwhile, mix sauce ingredients together.

- Remove cooked crabs and coral from steamer and serve hot with dipping sauce.

Fragrant Steamed Pomfret from Macau

Macanese cuisine is unique to Macau. This distinctive cuisine has developed over several centuries and comprises the traditional ingredients of classic Portuguese cuisine, improvised with local ingredients. The Portuguese colonisers introduced fiery peppers and chillies, kidney beans, tomatoes, peanuts, sweet potatoes, tamarind, saffron, pineapples and mangoes to Macau. They also brought new spices such as cinnamon, nutmeg, cloves and pepper. To these, the Cantonese added their own vegetables like cabbage and ginger.

The pomfret is renowned for its sweet flavour. In Southeast Asia, two varieties of pomfret are very popular—black pomfret and white pomfret. The black pomfret is used in curries and the delicate white fleshed pomfret for steamed dishes. Oriental sole, threadfin or whiting are good substitutes if pomfret is not available.

Ingredients

Ginger	4 thin slices, 2 shredded and 2 quartered
Brandy	1 tsp
Pomfret	1, large, about 1.5 kg, cleaned and gutted
Cloud ear fungus	100 g, soaked to soften and thinly sliced
Dried Chinese mushrooms	3, soaked in warm water, drained and finely sliced
Spring onions (scallions)	2, cut into 5-cm lengths and shredded
Light soy sauce	1 Tbsp
Cornflour (cornstarch)	2 tsp
Cooking oil	1 Tbsp
Salt	to taste
Ground white pepper	to taste
Sesame oil	a few drops
Banana leaf	1, large

Garnish

Spring onion (scallion)	1, chopped
Coriander (cilantro) leaves	1 sprig, chopped

Method

- Place shredded ginger in brandy.

- Take fish and cut a slit close to central bone. Insert ginger shreds taking care not to detach flesh. Put 2 quarter slices of ginger in as well.

- Line a steamer tray with banana leaf. Place fish on banana leaf and place cloud ear fungus, mushrooms, remaining ginger and spring onions around fish.

- Mix soy sauce with cornflour and pour over fish.

- Heat cooking oil until very hot and sprinkle over fish. Season with salt and pepper, then cover and steam for about 15 minutes.

- Test to see if fish is cooked by piercing fish with a knife or fork. The fish is ready when the knife or fork cuts through effortlessly.

- Lift banana leaf with fish and other ingredients carefully onto a platter. Sprinkle over sesame oil and garnish with spring onions and coriander leaves. Serve hot.

Portuguese Codfish Balls

Ingredients

Salted cod fish	450 g
Potatoes	450 g
Olive oil	1 Tbsp
Onion	1, large, peeled and sliced
Garlic	3 cloves, peeled and sliced
Salt	to taste
Parsley	1 sprig, chopped
Eggs	3, separated, optional
Ground black pepper	1 Tbsp
Plain (all purpose) flour	100 g

Method

- Soak cod fish in water overnight, changing water twice to remove salt. Boil cod fish in water for 2 minutes and cool. Reserve water. Remove skin and bones from fish and shred as thinly as possible.

- In water used for boiling cod fish, cook potatoes. Then cool, peel and mash.

- Squeeze out any excess liquid from shredded cod fish and add to mashed potatoes.

- Heat olive oil in a pan and cook onion until transparent. Add garlic and cook for 1 minute. Take off heat and stir mixture into mashed potato.

- Add salt to taste. Then add parsley, egg yolks and pepper. Stir to combine.

- Whip egg whites until they form soft peaks and fold into potato mixture.

- Flour hands and make dumplings with potato mixture.

- Heat remaining olive oil in a pan until it is smoking. Drop 3–4 dumplings into hot oil and deep-fry until golden. Drain on absorbent paper and serve warm.

Har Loke (Spicy Cantonese Prawns)

This is a tasty dish of prawns (shrimps) in spicy ginger-garlic and salted soy bean sauce.

Ingredients

Prawns (shrimps)	500 g
Ginger	3-cm knob, shredded, and juice extracted
Chinese wine (shao hsing) or Stone's ginger wine	3 Tbsp
Chilli sauce	1 tsp
Hoisin sauce	2 Tbsp
Dark soy sauce or sweet soy vinegar	2 Tbsp
Salt	1/2 tsp
Sugar	1/2 tsp
Cornflour (cornstarch)	2 tsp, mixed with 1 Tbsp cold water
Cooking oil	2 Tbsp
Garlic	2 cloves, peeled and chopped
Preserved soy beans	1 1/2 Tbsp, washed and mashed
Spring onion (scallion)	1, roughly broken

Garnish

Red chillies	2, sliced
Red capsicum (bell pepper)	1, cored and sliced

Method

- Do not shell prawns but devein through the joint between the head and the body with a skewer. Cut off feelers and legs with scissors (optional).

- Marinade prawns in ginger juice and 1 Tbsp wine for 30 minutes. Reserve ginger shreds.

- In a bowl, mix chilli, hoisin and dark or sweet soy sauces with remaining wine, salt, sugar and cornflour mixture.

- Heat oil in a frying pan (skillet) until it becomes hazy. Sauté garlic, soy beans and ginger shreds. Add prawns and stir-fry for 3–4 minutes until prawns turn red.

- Add cornflour mixture to prawns and stir until sauce thickens. Add spring onion, stir and remove from heat.

- Garnish with chillies and capsicum. Serve hot.

Microwave Method

- Preheat a browning dish for 6 minutes on HIGH. Add oil and heat for 30 seconds on HIGH. Add garlic and soy beans, then ginger shreds. Add prawns and stir quickly into oil. Cook uncovered for 2 minutes on HIGH.

- Add mixed sauces, stirring well into prawns. Cook for 4 minutes on HIGH, uncovered. Stir and cook for another 2 minutes on HIGH until sauce thickens. Add spring onions and remove from heat.

- Garnish with chillies and capsicum. Serve hot.

Nai Xiang Bao Yu (Creamy Abalone)

To cook and eat fresh abalone is not such a daunting prospect. Its taste alone is worth it all. Abalone can be obtained fresh in the shell, frozen from Chinese grocery stores or canned. This is a delicate and festive dish.

Ingredients

Canned abalone	300 g
Cooking oil	1 Tbsp
Garlic	1 clove, peeled and chopped
Onion	1, peeled and chopped
Plain (all-purpose) flour	1 Tbsp
Abalone stock (from can)	250 ml
Lettuce or Chinese cabbage	200 g, shredded
Bean flour	2 Tbsp, mixed with 2 Tbsp water
Cream or milk	3 Tbsp
Salt	to taste
Ground white pepper	to taste

Garnish

Spring onions (scallions)	3, shredded

Method

- Slice abalone thinly to obtain fine broad pieces.

- Heat oil in a wok and sauté garlic and then onion. Add flour and sauté until lightly brown.

- Add stock and mix well. Increase heat slowly and bring to the boil. Lower heat and allow stock to simmer.

- Add lettuce or cabbage and abalone and stir for 1 minute. Add bean flour mixture and cream or milk to thicken sauce.

- When sauce thickens, mix well and remove from heat. It should not take too long. Add salt and pepper to taste.

- Serve garnished with spring onions.

Macau Grilled Prawns

For this recipe, use the long variety of red chillies which are not too hot unless you prefer a spicier dish.

Ingredients

Garlic	50 g, peeled and diced
Spring onions (scallions)	100 g, chopped
Red chillies	100 g, chopped
Light soy sauce	2 Tbsp
Tiger prawns (shrimps)	2 kg, shelled and deveined, with heads removed and tails intact
Salt	to taste
Freshly ground pepper	to taste
Olive oil or butter	

Method

- Combine garlic, spring onions, chillies and soy sauce. Place prawns in marinate. Sprinkle in salt and pepper.
- Drain prawns from marinade and brush with olive oil or butter.
- Place prawns on a grill or barbecue. When prawns turn red on one side, turn over to cook the other side.
- Serve with a light lettuce and cucumber salad.

Buying & Preparing Fish

> " Certainly to have a fresh fish and to cause it
> to become unfresh is a terrible act. "
>
> *Yuen Mai*

In recent years, the importance of fish in the diet has received a great deal of attention, and it has been hailed as a 'Miracle Food'. Fish is the least fattening and the healthiest of all animal proteins. It is a 'complete' animal protein as it contains all the eight essential amino acids and is rich in the minerals zinc, silenium, phosphorus, potassium and calcium; and in vitamins A, D and E. Fish is low in saturated fats and is rich in Omega 3 (polyunsaturated fatty acids). These fatty acids are more unsaturated and therefore superior to the fatty acids found in vegetables and margarines (Omega 6).

Omega 3 first attracted attention when two Danish doctors, Dyerberg and Bang, observed that the eskimos in Greenland lived on a fairly high fat diet but had low levels of cholesterol in their blood. Their arteries were fairly free of fatty deposits and heart disease was rare. When the eskimos changed their diets, however, they developed the same rate of heart disease and were not 'protected' any more. It was discovered that their protection in Greenland was a daily intake of around 500 g fish, a far greater intake than in most parts of the world. Further studies were carried out in the Netherlands and in Japan with similar results: in three totally different communities, the only linking factor was a high intake of fish and a low incidence of heart disease.

Fish survive the cold without freezing because they develop high levels of Omega 3 polyunsaturated fats that do not become solid. When polyunsaturated fats are refrigerated, they do not solidify (as compared to saturated animal fats). All fish have this polyunsaturated fat, but in colder waters the level is higher. The benefit to humans, then, is the effect this has on preventing the formation of blood clots. It also has the ability to stop red blood cells from clumping together, preventing the build-up of fatty deposits on artery walls, and also keeping the arteries soft and pliable.

All fish, shellfish and crustacea contain Omega 3: generally darker fleshed fish have a higher Omega 3 content than white fish. This prevents heart disease in three important ways. Studies have proved that it lowers the triglycerides or blood fat levels in the bloodstream, and the thinner blood allows the blood to move more freely. Most importantly, Omega 3 has also been found to work to reduce the level of cholesterol in the blood.

Many studies have confirmed the value of the beneficial effects of Omega 3. The name 'Omega 3' has to be differentiated from the polyunsaturated fatty acids (PUFA) found in vegetable oils (Omega 6), which is now thought to compete with Omega 3 for absorption into the system and hence to reduce the known beneficial effects of Omega 3. Thus not only does the total saturated fat intake need to be reduced, but the balance between the intake of Omega 3 and 6 needs to be altered by eating more fish rich in Omega 3. Of the extensive nutritional research that has been done recently, here is a brief summary of current advice. (The information comes from Rosemary Stanton, Consultant Nutritionist, and the New South Wales Fish Marketing Authority.)

- All fish and seafood are high in protein.
- All fish and seafood are low in saturated fat (of 27 varieties studied, the average fat content was 2%).
- All fish and seafood provide polyunsaturated fats, including the valuable Omega 3 fats.
- All fish and seafood are relatively low in kilojoules (of 27 varieties studied, the average K count was 415 calories per 100 g).
- All fish are low in cholesterol (the average cholesterol count for the 27 varieties was 61 mg/100 g; for crab it was 68 mg/100g and for cooked school prawns (shrimps) 190 mg/100 g).
- All fish and seafood are an excellent source of iodine, the mineral which modulates the thyroid gland.
- Oysters and mussels have very high levels of iron—higher than red meats (iron is essential for making red blood cells).

- Fish is an excellent source of niacin, a B group vitamin needed for healthy skin and releasing energy in the body.
- Seafood is a good source of vitamin B12, a vitamin sometimes lacking in a vegetarian diet.
- Seafood also supplies thiamin (vitamin B1) and other important B group vitamins.

FISH

Choosing Fish

As Asia spans about a quarter of the world and the species of fish and their subspecies are so great, it would be impossible to pinpoint specific seafood varieties for recipes and expect the cook to obtain identical species in the market. The cook depends on what the market offers each day. A sensible way to overcome this problem is to group fish according to certain categories such as by texture, colour, fish family and oil content of the fish. This will make the substitution of a similar type of fish possible in any recipe. (See also pages 320–325 for equivalent types of fish.)

Texture and Colour

Fish can be broadly divided by texture into a few basic types. When a fish fillet is examined, the fish muscle can be seen as having short fibres (unlike meat) separated by large sheets of connective tissue running the whole length of the fish. If the fish is fresh, then the muscle blocks are held firmly by the connective tissue. When cooked, it is converted to gelatin and the fish 'flakes' or breaks up.

There are fine, delicately textured fish, such as the sea wrasse in Hong Kong, medium textured fish, such as mullet, which have smaller flakes, and coarse, firm fish such as shark and tuna. If the muscle blocks are large, then the cooked fish will break up into large coarse flakes but if the muscle blocks are close together, the flakes will be fine, with a delicate texture.

Fish should never be overcooked: the gelatinous connective sheets could dry up and the flesh could turn dry and hard.

The Oil Content

Fish can also be classified according to the colour of the flesh. Some fish are dark fleshed and oily, while others are light pink or white in colour and moist or dry in texture.

The oil content of a fish must be established if the fish is to be grilled or baked. To try and grill a moist or dry fish could be disastrous unless a sauce is used as a basting liquid.

The oil content in a fish is sometimes distributed all over the fish but in other cases it is possible to identify the main fat deposit underneath the skin, sometimes seen in a darker strip along the length of the fillet. However, there are some fish specially chosen for fish head curries or stews, which have a large proportion of fat deposited close to the head (or near the tail). To be able to identify these characteristics in fish helps the cook decide on the best fish to use in any recipe.

OILY	MOIST		DRY
Anchovy	Barramundi	Red Mullet	Grouper
Bonito	Black Pomfret	Rock Cod	Leather Jacket
Crab roe	Carp	Sea Perch	Octopus
Herring	Cod	Shad (Hilsa)	Pearl Perch
Kingfish	Crab	Silver Bream	Salmon
Mackerel	Gemfish	Spanish	Scallop
Mullet	Goat Fish	Mackerel	Shark
Pilchard	Jewfish	Snapper	White Pomfret
Sardine	Mackerel	Threadfin	Whiting
Sprat	Oyster	(Kurau)	
Tuna	Prawn (Shrimp)	Trevally	

Buying Fish

Asian cooking depends on having the freshest of ingredients. It cannot be overemphasised that freshness is essential. Although fish and shellfish cooked Asian-style may utilise many sauces, it must be remembered that these sauces are added to enhance the fresh flavours, not to mask them.

To get the best from your fish, shop early at a good fish and seafood market, and deal with a regular fishmonger.

Fresh fish should have the following characteristics:
- Fish should be bright, glossy and have a sheen.
- The eyes should be bright and bulging—not sunken.
- The eyes of some deep-sea fish could sometimes look bloodshot from being brought rapidly up to the surface from the deep. These fish are quite safe to eat, unless the eyes look dull.
- The flesh should be firm and spring back when touched and the stomach should be firm, not flabby nor distended.
- Fish should smell of the sea. It should not smell unpleasant.
- The gills should be red, not brown.
- Scales should be firm, not loose.

When buying cutlets, steaks and fillets, they should:
- look 'pearly' and lustrous—smooth and firm around the edges—and have the same firm characteristics of whole fish, with skins firmly attached.

Preparing Fish

You can do two things. Have the fishmonger dress (scale), clean and fillet fresh fish for you, or do it yourself. If you do it yourself you will be able to identify with the spirit of Asian cooking.

The first step is to maintain freshness. All fish should be gutted and have their gills removed as quickly as possible. The key to cleaning a fish that is to be served whole is to do the utmost to preserve its shape, texture and condition.

There are several ways of doing this.

Scaling Fish

This is done best with a dull knife or a special serrated fish scaler.
- Place the fish on a few newspaper sheets. Grasp the tail with one hand then scrape off the scales working round the body. Wash the fish in running water. Scrape skin, especially alongside gills and around the head to remove any remaining scales and slime. Wash, then blot dry with paper.
- The fishmongers in Asia use a palm-held wooden comb with tiny nails embedded in it for easy scaling.
- Flat fish like flounder or sole need to be scaled only on the upper side.

Gutting Small Fish

Open the gill and mouth. Insert the tip of the knife and cut through the bone below the jaw. Insert two chopsticks or a fork beyond the gills **(1)**; turn the chopsticks or pierce the viscera with the fork, wind round fork once (like lifting spaghetti) and pull gently **(2)**.

Gutting Large Fish

Holding the head flat on a firm cutting board, insert a sharp knife just below the gills and cut a long slit down to the stomach cavity. If the knife has a sharp tipped end, this will work much better. Carefully remove innards and wash the cavity with cold running water.

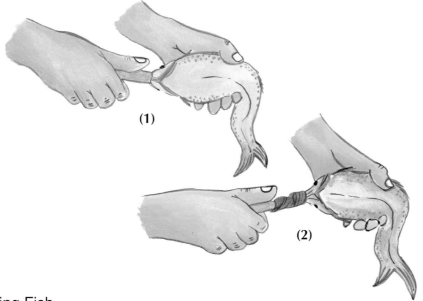

Filleting Fish

The shape of a fish determines the way it should be gutted and filleted. There are two general fish types: round fish **(3)** and flat fish **(4)**. Starting with a fresh fish and a sharp knife makes filleting easier.

For a round fish, hold fish down firmly. Run the knife along the innards to cut the blood pockets. Rinse in cold water. Remove the head by making an incision below the pectoral fin **(5)**. Cut down to the spine with a cleaver, then hit the cleaver with the ball of the palm.

Cut lightly along the belly **(6)** and slide the blade along the backbone and over the ribs **(7)**. Turn the fish over and make an incision from tail upwards, cutting above the bones to release fillets **(8)**. This is called 'three-piece cutting' or *sonmai oroshi* cutting.

For flat fish, you cut four fillets, two on either side of the bone. Place the fish on a cutting board, make deep cuts behind the gills, remove the head with the tip of a knife, scrape scales and remove the viscera and rinse well.

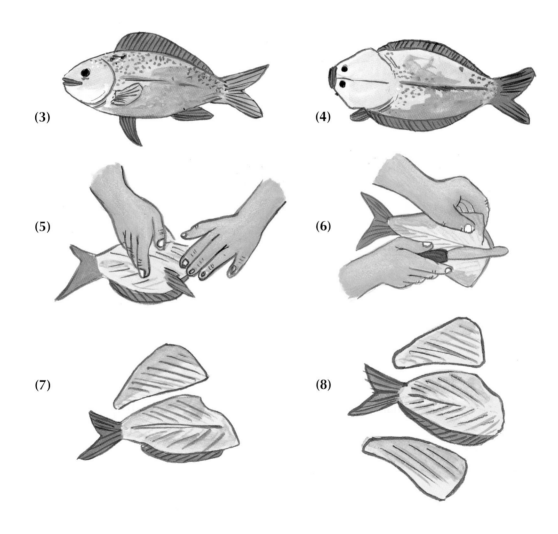

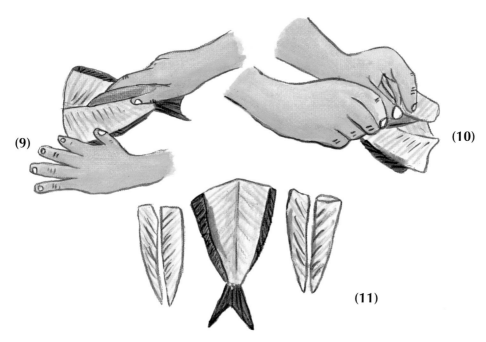

(9)　　　　　　　　　　(10)

(11)

Make an incision down the fish spine to the tail **(9)**. Cut along one side close to tail and remove fillet **(10)**. Turn over, repeat on other side. This method allows for four narrow fillets to be cut from one fish **(11)**. This is referred to as 'five-piece cutting'.

To Skin Fillets

Use a flat broad knife. Insert it between skin and flesh and cut through. Try to get a grip on some skin with your left hand and pull skin while moving your knife forward with your right hand held almost parallel to the board. The fillet should come out in one piece.

Cutting Fish into Steaks or Cutlets

These cuts of large fish are popular for Indian curries. Scale, gill and gut the fish and remove fins. Break through the bone with a wide-bladed knife and hammer down on handle. Or use a small saw and cut into 2.5-cm slices at an angle across the body, starting from the tail. Separate into cutlets **(12)**. Use the head and tail for fish stock or curry.

(12)

Skinning Fish

Some fish need to be skinned. This is best done by your fishmonger but if you need to skin a leather jacket or hardtail *(kembong)*, make a cut along the tail and get a grip on the skin. Pull as hard as you can with pliers in the direction of the head. The skin will come off easily if the fish is fresh.

To Score a Fish

Scoring allows the flavours of other ingredients to penetrate the fish. It ensures more even cooking and increases the area of crisp crust in fried fish. To score, lay the fish on a cutting board, slice gently into the flesh up to 1 cm to open one or more slashes in its side. Turn it over and do the same on the other side.

Freezing Fish

Deep-sea fish undergo a chilling process while still at sea, as fishermen try to keep their catch fresh and in mint condition. Once the fish reaches the fishmonger, it is allowed to defrost and can be regarded as fresh. It may be unwise to re-freeze such fish, as quality and texture will be lost. Rubbing fish with some turmeric and salt before freezing helps preserve its freshness.

To Cut Fish for *Sashimi*

Some fish, such as kingfish or tuna, can have what is called a milky condition, caused by parasites. Buy only firm, brightly coloured meat.

- Tuna is sold filleted in lengths of *sashimi* thickness. Purchase what you need, then slice into 2-cm thick pieces.
- For salmon, shape fillet into triangles, and cut into thin slices for rosette.
- For sea bass, fillet, then remove bones with tweezers. Skin by cutting fillet in half, holding the skin and pulling the knife forward. Slice fillets in diagonal slices like Chinese vegetable slices about 1-cm thick or even thinner.
- Cut carp into paper-thin slices, moving knife towards yourself, remove and arrange like a rosette, while holding pieces in one hand.
- Score across squid to tenderise the flesh.

PRAWNS (SHRIMPS)

The types of prawn available in the market are too numerous to mention, but the main ones are the white banana prawn, the green tiger prawn, the school prawn and the giant spiny clawed prawn with one long walking leg. The flesh of this freshwater prawn is sweet, moist and delicious. Prawns are sea-trawled and cultured in freshwater ponds. In fact, today the freshwater prawn industry has become a major financial concern in most Southeast Asian countries and earns a great proportion of export dollars.

Preparing Prawns

For all Asian recipes, prawns and shellfish are purchased raw and 'green', not cooked, since re-cooking cooked prawns makes them tough and bland in flavour. They should be purchased fresh, with the heads firmly attached to the bodies. There should be a translucent sheen to the shells which will fade to a dullness as the prawn loses freshness. Another clear indication of the freshness of a prawn is to check the elasticity in the flesh and the viscera (intestines).

Prawns should be cleaned thoroughly in cold running water, but not allowed to soak in water for any length of time. The feelers and legs should be cut off. The shell, head and tail should only remain if the recipe calls for it. Otherwise the sharp end of the snout should be clipped off and the rest of the head retained. The term 'shelling' means taking off the shell of the prawn. Washing a shelled prawn with salt water removes some of the 'fishy' smell.

To Devein Prawns

There are three methods, all used by Asian cooks.
* Insert a toothpick between the prawn head and body. This technique is used if the recipe calls for prawns with heads and tails left on.
* Cut through the shell on the back and remove the vein (13). This technique is used if juices need to penetrate the prawn, especially in Chinese and Indian recipes.
* Remove the head and shell, then devein. The vein will come out easily (14). It can be reached by gently moving the pinkish prawn roe, locating the vein and pulling it out gently with the fingers. The pinkish prawn roe is situated right next to this area and should not be disturbed, especially if the recipe calls for steaming the prawns, as roes make a good sauce, adding to the rich flavours.

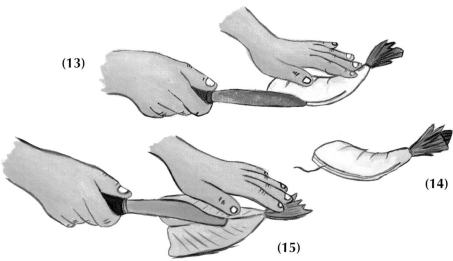

(13)

(14)

(15)

Special Effects

To butterfly prawns, shell and take off the heads, but keep the tails intact. Place prawns on a clean dry chopping board. Using a sharp knife, cut the length of the prawn from the head two-thirds of the way down to the back. Gently flatten the prawn with the ball of the palm, pressing down from the back to flatten it **(15)**. For a more elaborate butterfly effect, snip the underside of the tail and flatten that as well.

To create pinwheels, butterfly as above but do not flatten. Make a slit halfway up the prawn. Pull the tail through the slit so it gives the effect of a prawn doing cartwheels.

For *tempura*, prawns are slightly flattened and scored on the underside so that they will not curl when being fried.

To skewer a prawn for barbecuing or for *yakitori*, insert skewers from tail to top or skewer three or four prawns across the bodies, keeping them together.

To Freeze Prawns

Prawns are best frozen after deveining. Place the prawns in a plastic container (such as an ice cream container), cover with water and seal until it freezes into an ice block. This can be kept successfully for up to two months.

If you intend to use prawns within the fortnight, freeze in a plastic bag, well flattened so that air is not trapped in it. Place this on the floor of your freezer compartment and freeze until solid. Then you can place it on top of anything else in the freezer.

Once prawns and shellfish are defrosted and thawed they should never be refrozen.

CRABS

The most common Asian crabs are the serrated mangrove crabs, the blue swimmers with white and blue claws and the mask crabs which have imprints of masks on their shells. The Shanghai hairy crab is a species found in China. The king crab has a rich flavour absorbed from its diet of coconuts. It is horseshoe-shaped, with a spike at the back.

Crabs should be purchased alive. Choose crabs which feel firm and solid as these have the most meat. Females are preferred as they contain delicious roe. To tell the difference between male and female, check the abdomen piece (like an apron over the underside). Females have rounded bell-shaped aprons and males have tapering abdomens.

To Kill a Crab

If the crab is purchased with its claws tied up, then it is an easy matter to either plunge the whole crab in a pot of boiling water for a few seconds or to place it in the freezer for 30 minutes, where the cold will kill it. After it is frozen, it can easily be cleaned and prepared. This freezing technique has been recommended as the safest method of killing crabs, while the Chinese technique of inserting a chopstick (or an ice pick) into the brain is the quickest and the most painless method.

Cleaning a Crab

The crab should then be washed and its shell scrubbed clean and the abdomen discarded, especially the feathery gills. The claws should be twisted away from the body **(16)** and cracked open before cooking so that sauces can penetrate the meat. The body should then be opened by prying the underside from the shell, spongy gills and inedible parts discarded, and the remaining pieces cut up, or the meat picked out, depending on the recipe.

(16)

Freezing Crabs

Crabs freeze well. Clean, then pack into plastic bags and keep frozen. While frozen crab is good, the quality cannot be matched by cooking live, fresh crab.

LOBSTER

True lobster is not found in Southeast Asian waters, but the slipper lobster and spiny lobster are plentiful and freshly available in most Southeast Asian markets.

To kill lobster, follow instructions as for the killing of crab. Once this is done, use a heavy knife and cut through its entire tail length to expose the meat underneath, and separate the shell.

If serving lobster in the shell, turn lobster over, twist off short legs and, with sharp scissors, snip around the outer edge of the thin plastic-like shell. Lift up the shell to expose tail meat. Scoop it out with a knife. This is the meaty or tasty 'tail' part of lobster that is cooked.

SQUID

These have tubular bodies with tentacles at one end. The body is covered with a red-purple skin which can be peeled off after washing **(17)**. The clear bone or quill should be discarded before preparing for the table **(18)**. (The cuttlefish has a thick cuttlebone unlike the soft quill in the squid.) The eyes should be cut away and the ink sacs removed under running water. The hard beak should be 'popped' out and discarded and the thick roe inside the tubes removed **(19)**.

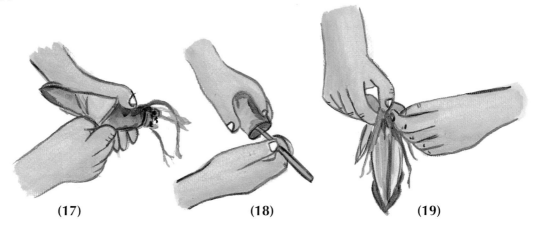

(17)　　　　　**(18)**　　　　　**(19)**

Scoring squid is done for two purposes, aesthetic and practical (as with all Asian cooking). To score, cut the tube open, turn it inside out and lay it flat on the chopping block. Using a sharp knife, slice a short way into the flesh. Make cuts in the flesh so that they are parallel to one another. Turn squid over and make another series of parallel cuts at right angles to the first set of lines, creating a diamond pattern. When squid is plunged into boiling water, they curl and look like small pine cones. Cutting is also done to tenderise the squid.

Squid can be stored in plastic bags or plastic containers in the refrigerator for one day, but need to be cooked the next day at the latest. Once cleaned, squid freeze well and keep for a month at least in the freezer.

BIVALVES

Oysters are available in most Asian markets, as are all the bivalves mentioned below, but the horn shell and cockle are the most popular varieties. It should be noted, however that with increasing pollution of river estuaries and deltas, the danger of eating these bivalves raw has increased. All bivalves should be bought live, which means they should be tightly closed. In a heated or warm market, some bivalves may open. If they close when touched, they are alive and fresh.

All bivalves can be freed of mud and dirt by placing them in a bucket of lightly salted water which is then placed in a cool, dark spot for a few hours. They will leach sand and purify themselves. However, if you do not have the time to do this, wash in several changes of water and scrub the shells with a clean brush.

OYSTERS

Popular for their subtle flavour, these can be eaten raw or cooked. Small oysters are fried or made into omelettes. In countries where oysters are not bred in clean prepared beds, it is good practice to clean them using the methods described above.

To clean and open oysters, soak them to leach sand and dirt, then rinse in water. Using a towel, hold the oyster in the left hand and pry open the shell with a sharp knife (20), or cut the muscle between the shells. This will release the shell and it will open. Take out the oyster carefully (21), reserving the liquid for cooking or stock. Ready-opened oysters can be purchased in brine.

Clean before cooking by rinsing in lightly salted water.

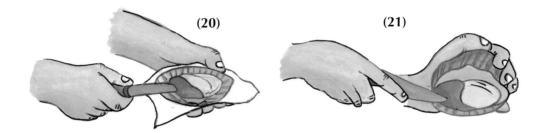

(20)　　　　　　(21)

MUSSELS

Choose mussels with dark brown shells which are green or blue at the edges. Treat as oysters, pulling at 'beard' before scrubbing shells. Pippies and mussels, cooked with shells, are popular.

SCALLOPS

These are fan-shaped shells and can be cooked with or without shells. The edible portion is the soft and pearly disc with a coral ovary. The dark intestine should be removed. The flavour of scallops comes from the fresh juices surrounding the meat, so they should never be soaked for long in water.

COCKLES

Cockles are smaller than scallops, often about 1–2 cm in size when shelled. Because of the blood inside the shell, they are known as blood shell or ark shell cockles. Cockles should be cleaned well, then plunged into boiling water and when open, scooped out of the shell.

ABALONE

The abalone is a mollusc that grips the rocky shores with its muscular foot. When prized away from the rock, the muscular foot (which is the part eaten) is tensed and this makes the meat tough.

To prepare fresh abalone for eating, follow these steps. You need a short, strong-bladed knife.

- Cut around the edge of the shell and scoop out the foot. As it is handled, it traumatises and contracts automatically, becoming tough.
- Brush and clean off the dark skin from the underside of the foot. You may need to scrub well.
- Trim the frilly edges off (this is the digestive tract).
- Slice the abalone across its breadth into thin slices, then beat with a meat mallet to soften the meat. It should be only lightly cooked.
- If abalone does become tough through overcooking, it should be cooked further (with more liquid) when it will eventually tenderise into a delicious texture.

SEA CUCUMBER

The Chinese believe that shark's fin, abalone and sea cucumber are all excellent tonic foods, so these are prized among cooks.

Dried sea cucumber can be obtained from Chinese grocers. Because of its spongy consistency, the sea cucumber bloats to four or five times its size after soaking in water. It is possible to purchase ready-prepared sea cucumber today so that soaking and cleaning may be eliminated.

SHARK'S FIN

The preparation of shark's fin is tedious and messy if it is purchased from a Chinese grocer in its unprocessed form. It needs soaking in many changes of water, boiling and cleaning. It is thankfully available in its cleaned and dried form in plastic boxes or packets. It can be soaked in water for 20 minutes or so, drained and then used in soups.

There are many qualities of shark's fin, some are available in cans or frozen ready-prepared, and the most expensive is often the best quality. A good grocer can always advise you.

Preparing the Ingredients

Ingredient	Substitute	How to Prepare
Coconut: to buy a fresh coconut, pick it up and shake it. If it feels heavy and has a lot of 'water', it is fresh. The eyes should be firm but not hollow.	Substitute with canned coconut milk, powdered coconut milk, yoghurt or cow's milk. If canned coconut milk is used, it can be refrigerated for a short time and the cream that rises to the top used for curries and gravies.	Break coconut in half with the back of a cleaver and remove flesh by 'shredding', using a scrapper or put flesh in a blender. Desiccated coconut can be soaked in warm water then blended to produce coconut milk. Combine a cup of warm water with one cup dried, flaked or desiccated coconut to extract a cup of coconut milk.
Coconut cream: the thick cream that rises to the top when coconut milk is refrigerated.	Thick yoghurt cream, powdered milk, cream or coffeemate, powdered soy substitute.	When coconut flakes (scraped coconut) are mixed with very little water and squeezed or kneaded, the liquid produced is called coconut cream. After this first squeezing, more water can be added to the grated coconut and a thinner milk, called 'second' or 'third' milk, can be obtained. If coconut milk is left to stand, the cream rises to the top and can be skimmed for use.
Coconut water: the liquid contained in the centre of the coconut. This is not the coconut cream or milk.	Sugar syrup and a dash of lemon juice.	Cut open coconut to reveal water inside, the clean and sweet liquid used to cook fish Cambodian style.
Buko: the soft flesh of the young coconut.	No substitute.	Cut open a young green coconut. The flesh is soft, white and tender, and can be scooped out with a spoon and used as required in the recipe.
Rice washings	A thin starch or cornflour (cornstarch) solution.	Wash rice in a bowl. Rub grains hard against each other until a milky liquid forms. This is the starchy liquid used to thicken curries and fish soups.
Prawn (shrimp) paste	Use dried prawns as closest tasting substitute. Mix dried prawns and fish paste.	Should be dry-roasted over a naked flame or heated for 1 minute in the microwave oven to heighten the flavour. Then crumble into sauce or gravy.
Spices		To dry-roast, place in a pan or wok without any oil and stir until slightly roasted and aromatic. This can also be done in the microwave oven, about 2 minutes on HIGH.
Tamarind	Lime or lemon juice.	Place tamarind and some water in a bowl, stir with fork or fingers to work into a paste. Strain off dregs and use.

Asian Sauces & Techniques

Thai Curry Pastes

Red curry pastes may be obtained from supermarkets or oriental spice shops, in bottles or cans, in dried and powdered form. The homemade version, however, is always fresh, more aromatic and tasty.

Try a stone mortar and pestle for blending; the pestle crushes thick fibres in herbs and releases the oils. Blending in a liquidiser or a food processor merely cuts the fibres and breaks up the herbs. The pounding process, when the oils are pressed and released, makes a more aromatic curry.

Krung Gaeng Ped (Red Curry Paste)

Ingredients

Ingredient	Amount
Pure ground chilli powder	1 Tbsp or 8–10 small red dried chillies
Red shallots	3, peeled
Galangal *(kha)*	6-cm knob, peeled
Lemon grass *(ta-khrai)*	3-cm length
Coriander roots (phak chee)	3-cm length
Coriander seeds (phak chee)	1 Tbsp, ground
Cumin *(yee-ra)*	1 tsp
Salt	
Lime rind	from 1/4 lime
Peppercorns	1 tsp
Kaffir lime leaves (bai makrut)	1/2 tsp
Garlic	2 cloves, peeled
Prawn (shrimp) paste (kapee)	1 tsp
Cooking oil	4 Tbsp

Method

- Pound chilli powder or chillies, shallots and galangal with lemon grass and coriander roots with mortar and pestle.

- Combine with rest of ingredients except oil and grind (process) into a paste.

- Add oil.

Krung Gaeng Khiaw Wan (Green Curry Paste)

This is the hottest of Thai curries as it is made from green chilli. The unripe chilli is strongest when green and sweetens to a milder, richer flavour as it reddens and ripens.

Ingredients

Galangal (kha)	6-cm knob, peeled
Ginger	2-cm knob, peeled
Lemon grass (ta-khrai)	3 stalks
Garlic	3 cloves, peeled
Cumin seeds (yee-ra)	1 tsp
Black peppercorns	10
Cloves	5
Nutmeg	1/2
Coriander (phak chee) roots	3-cm length
Red shallots	5
Lime rind	from 1/4 lime
Green chillies	8, seeded, if you want it mild
Salt	1 tsp
Vegetable oil	4 Tbsp

Method

- Pound galangal, ginger, lemon grass and garlic.
- Blend cumin seeds and peppercorns in a coffee grinder. Combine with pounded ingredients and add remaining ingredients. Grind or blend with oil.

Fish Curry Powder (Make in small quantities)

Ingredients

Coriander (phak chee) seeds	2 Tbsp
Cumin seeds (yee-ra)	1 Tbsp
Rice grains	1/4 tsp
Fenugreek seeds	1/2 tsp
Black peppercorns	1/2 tsp
Chilli powder	1 heaped tsp
Ground turmeric	1/2 tsp

Method

- Dry-roast coriander, cumin and rice grains for about 3 minutes until aromatic. Add fenugreek and dry-roast for a few seconds more, being careful not to leave it too long as it will turn bitter.
- Grind (process) roasted ingredients and peppercorns, then add chilli powder and ground turmeric to the mix.
- This is sufficient to make a curry with 600 g fish.

Sambal Belacan (Prawn Paste and Chilli Sauce)

Ingredients

Shrimp paste *(belacan)*	2-cm square, dry-roasted
Red shallots	2, peeled
Fresh red chillies	4—5
Lime juice	extracted from ½ lime
Lime rind	
Salt	to taste

Method

- Pound roasted prawn paste with shallots and chillies, leaving chillies in large pieces.
- Mix in lime juice and rind.
- Add salt to taste.

Nam Prik Paad (Chilli Jam)

Ingredients

Garlic	8 cloves, peeled
Red shallots	10, peeled
Dried prawns (shrimps)	125 g
Dried chillies	12, large
Vegetable oil	2 Tbsp
Tamarind paste *(ma khaam)*	1 Tbsp
Palm sugar	2 Tbsp
Fish sauce *(nam pla)*	1 Tbsp

Method

- Grill or bake garlic, shallots and prawns until darkish brown and aromatic. Pound each ingredient separately until fine. Set aside.
- Fry chillies in 1 Tbsp hot oil for a few seconds. Pound until fine.
- Mix tamarind paste with 2 Tbsp water.
- Heat remaining oil and stir-fry pounded ingredients until aromatic. Add palm sugar, fish sauce and tamarind. Cook until sauce is thick.

Chicken or Fish Stock (Chinese, Malaysian, Thai Style)

Ingredients

Chicken or fish bones and heads	1 kg
Spring onions (scallions)	125 g
Black peppercorns	6
Celery	125 g
Garlic	5–6 cloves, peeled

Method

- Boil 2 litres water. Add in all ingredients.

- When soup boils, turn to a low simmer. If water reduces, add 250 ml water. After 1½ hours, increase heat and boil for 10 minutes. Remove and strain off dregs.

- Cool stock if refrigerating or freezing. Frozen stock keeps well. To defrost slightly, place 250 ml frozen stock in a microwave for 6 minutes on LOW.

Thickener (For Chinese and Singaporean Food)

Ingredients

Stock or water	50 ml
Chinese wine *(shao hsing)* or Stone's ginger wine	1 Tbsp
Cornflour (cornstarch)	1 Tbsp, mixed with 2 Tbsp water

Method

- Heat stock and add wine when bubbling.

- Add cornflour mixture to stock and stir until sauce thickens. Add seasoning as specified in recipe.

Dashi (Japanese Stock)

The characteristic flavour of Japanese food depends on *dashi* accented with soy sauce or *sake*. The two main seasonings for *dashi* are *konbu* (seaweed, the best quality from Hokkaido) and freshly shaved bonito flakes. Very good quality prepared *dashi* stock is marketed in little brown bottles.

Ichiban Dashi (Thin Dashi Stock)

Ingredients

Kelp (konbu)	25 g
Water	1 litre
Dried bonito flakes (katsuo bushi)	25 g

Method

- Add kelp to saucepan of water and bring to a slow boil. Remove kelp just before water boils and reserve it to make a thicker stock.
- Add bonito flakes. Bring water to full boil and immediately remove from heat.
- Allow flakes to settle, then strain them off through muslin. Dashi should be clear. Flakes can be reused for thicker stock.

Niban Dashi (Thick Dashi Stock)

This stock is used for simmered dishes, seasoned stock and miso soups, where a stronger flavour is required.

Ingredients

Kelp (konbu)	25 g (or reserved from ichiban dashi)
Dried bonito flakes	25 g (or reserved from ichiban dashi) + 15 g extra
Water	1 litre

Method

- Add (reserved) kelp and bonito flakes to water and heat to just boiling point. Lower heat and simmer for 15–20 minutes until stock is reduced to one-third of original quantity.
- Add extra dried bonito flakes and immediately remove saucepan from heat.
- Allow flakes to settle (about 1 minute) and then strain stock through muslin. You could use a strainer but the stock will not be clear.

Ponzu Sauce

Ingredients

Lemon juice	250 ml
Rice vinegar	125 ml
Dark soy sauce	250 ml
Light soy sauce *(tamare)*	2 Tbsp
Wine *(mirin)*	3 Tbsp
Dried bonito flakes	15 g
Kelp *(konbu)*	3-cm piece

Method

- Mix all ingredients together and let stand for 24 hours.
- Strain through muslin into a jar and allow to mature for 3 months. This sauce keeps for at least one year.

To Smoke a Fish, Thai Style

Smoked fish is commonly served in northern Thailand with a hot and sour sauce. Small stalls lining coastal areas have interesting methods of smoking fish. The simplest is an ordinary grill suspended above coals in a shoebox-type burner. The grill above this box has a lid that fits over it so that the smoke is contained and the fish is gradually smoked.

Ingredients

Kingfish or sea perch	500–600 g
Sauce	
Red chillies	10, chopped
Tamarind paste *(ma khaam)*	1 Tbsp, mixed with 2 Tbsp water, strained
Garlic juice	1 Tbsp
Lime juice	2 Tbsp
Sugar	1 tsp
Salt	½ tsp

Method

- Scale, gut and clean fish, removing gills as well. Dry with absorbent paper.
- Begin smoking by heating charcoal. Traditionally, coconut husks were used.
- Place fish on grill, cover and smoke, turning fish every 5 minutes for 30 minutes, or until fish is golden brown.
- Mix all sauce ingredients together. Set aside.
- To test if fish is done, pierce with a sharp knife. If there is any liquid, the fish needs 5–10 minutes more smoking. Once done, serve smoked fish on a dish with sauce.

Sanbizu Sauce

Ingredients

Rice wine	125 ml
Dashi	60 ml
Light soy sauce	to taste

Method

- In a saucepan, bring rice wine, *dashi* and light soy sauce to the boil, stirring well once the sauce has come to the boil.

- Remove from heat and cool. Place in tiny bowls to make individual dipping sauce bowls.

To Make Up a Prawn (Shrimp) Farce

A prawn farce is a blended mixture of prawn meat, made by chopping prawns into a 'farce' with cornflour (cornstarch) and some fat to bind it together. In Hong Kong, pork fat is used, with a light seasoning of salt, pepper, wine, sesame oil or spring onions (scallions). This is a popular method of dressing or stuffing seafood and is used throughout Asia.

To make a farce, rub a tablespoon of cornflour on to the shelled and deveined prawns, then wash them under cold running water, drain and wipe gently with absorbent paper. Pound the prawns into a paste, either using the blunt edge of a cleaver or using a pestle and mortar. As prawns are pounded, they become pasty. Gather pounded prawns up with the edge of a knife, then pile up and pound some more, adding fat.

The mixture should be mixed well with the fingers, lifted and dropped forcefully back into the bowl, then mixed up again. This firms the paste. This is repeated 4–5 times until it becomes a sticky, well amalgamated farce which can be used to spread over other meat or bread, or used as stuffing.

Canadian Rule for Cooking Fish

Calculate 10 minutes cooking time for every 2.5-cm thickness of fish (at the thickest part of the fish). This rule applies to all fish, regardless of variety, and refers to barbecuing or baking. Lay fish on its side, measure at the thickest part and cook to perfection.

Amchur
Dried mango powder in Indian tandoori mixes and curry pastes.

Assam gelugor
Dried sections of tamarind fruit in Malay and Straits Chinese cooking.

Aubergine
Available round or long, deep to light purple, or light green to white. Also known as eggplant or brinjal. Pea aubergines are of Thai origin and are small like cherry tomatoes.

Bamboo shoot
Sold in cans, braised in water. Fresh variety from wet markets require prolonged boiling.

Banana stem
Tender stem from the top of the tree used in Burmese and Indian cooking.

Basil (Sweet basil)
Herb for seasoning red meats and fish.

Bean curd
Cream-coloured jelly from liquid extracted from soy beans and set with gypsum.

Bean curd cubes (preserved)
Soft bean curd preserved in brine and wine with chillies for a red, strong-flavoured seasoning.

Bean curd, dried
Firm 'cake' produced by compressing soft bean curd to extract liquid.

Bean curd, fried
Cubes of soft bean curd deep-fried until surface is brown and crusty and the inside almost dry.

Bean curd skins, dried
Thick, pale translucent dried soybean sheets.

Bean flour (thickener)
Mung bean flour. Used to thicken sweets and sauces. Substitute: cornflour.

Bean pastes (Taucheo)
Made from soy beans and other ingredients. Differs in flavour. Available canned, in jars or by weight at specialist stores. Hot bean paste is made from soy beans with chilllies and oil, very hot and slightly salty. Sweet bean paste is made from fermented soy beans, flour, sugar and spices. Substitute: Hoisin sauce.

Beans or paste, salted soy
Preserved, dark brown soy beans, or the salty paste from these beans, ground.

Belacan
Paste made from prawns and salt, allowed to ferment then mashed. Sold in slabs or flat cakes. No real substitute, closest being heiko or petis.

Besan flour
Chickpea flour. Roast chickpeas and grind. Available commercially.

Brinjal (See Aubergine)

Buko (PHIL)
Flesh of young coconut.

Cabbage, Chinese
Two varieties: Chinese white cabbage (pak choy), and flowering whole cabbage (choy sum). Substitute: Tientsin cabbage.

Cabbage, salted
Chinese white cabbage pickled in salt and partially dried.

Candlenut (Buah keras)
A hard nut used to thicken curries. Substitutes: almonds or macadamia.

Capsicum (Bell pepper)
Sweet, large green, red or yellow peppers. Do not confuse with chilli peppers.

Cardamom
Many varieties, slightly different in flavour. Used in Indian and Sri Lankan food.

Chillies
More than 100 varieties. Varies in flavour, shape, colour and intensity of heat. Green when young and red when ripe. Green chillies are sharper in flavour than red.

Chilli, bird's eye
Small, fiery hot chillies, called bird's eye as birds are attracted to them.

Chilli, dried
Shrivelled-looking, dark red chillies. Soak in hot water before blending.

Chilli jam
Prepared Thai chilli paste, called nam prik paad.

Chilli sauce
Many varieties available commercially. Sambal oelek is the Indonesian variety.

Chives, garlic
(Or chive shoots.) Used as garnish. Delicate but pungent in flavour. Another variety is yellow chives. Similar to garlic chives, but yellow rather than green.

Cinnamon
Spiral bits of bark from the cinnamon tree. Adds flavour and tang to curries, drinks and desserts.

Cloves
Dried buds of a tree native to the Moluccas. An essential sweet spice, a good clove will ooze a glistening oil when the stalk is pressed.

Coconut, cream
Sold in cans, UHT packs or frozen. May be used to make coconut milk, to individual instructions.

Coconut, desiccated
Dried grated coconut, easily reconstituted by soaking in water.

Coconut, grated fresh
Grated coconut flesh. May require dry-roasting in some recipes.

Coconut, milk
Extracted from grated coconut kernel, or from desiccated coconut.

Cocum
A dried sour fruit used mainly in fish dishes. Substitute: *Assam nipis*.

Coriander
These seeds are a main ingredient in curry powder. Ripe seeds are strongly aromatic, sweet and pleasant, but the leaves can be rather pungent. Also known as Chinese parsley.

Cumin
Aromatic seed, essential in curry powder. Resembles caraway but has a different flavour. Black cumin is peppery, one of five spices called *panch phora*.

Curry leaves
Used in India, Malaysia and Sri Lanka. Added fresh with onions and sautéed at the start of curry-making.

Cus cus
Small white seeds in used in *kurmah* (white curry). Soak in milk or water before use.

Daikon (JAP)
White mild-flavoured radish. Pickled for use with Japanese food.

Dashi (JAP)
Clear stock from seaweed and dried bonito. Essential soup starter or part of a dipping sauce. Instant *dashi* is available.

Daun salam (MAL)
Java laurel leaf. Mint-like herb. Substitute: Curry leaves.

Dhal
General term for varieties of lentils or split peas.

Dried fish
Many varieties. Dried anchovy *(ikan bilis kering, dilis)* and dried threadfin *(ikan kurau kering)* are most popular. To clean dried anchovy, remove head and stomach, wash and dry well before frying. A smaller specimen is called whitebait.

Dried prawn (shrimp) and chilli powder
Available packed. To make, blend 2 Tbsp dried prawns with 1 Tbsp chilli powder. Dry-roast for 3–4 minutes. Cool to store.

Drumsticks
Olive-green, segmented vegetable. Scrape skin off to reveal lighter green flesh. Cut at joints and halve lengthwise. Chew cooked flesh and discard fibre.

Eggplant (See Aubergine)

Fennel (Sweet Cumin)
Used in Southeast Asian cooking. Roasting heightens flavour. Powder used rather than paste.

Fenugreek
Small, angular, bitter brown seeds. Used sparingly, it imparts a unique flavour to Indian curries.

Fish sauce
Bottled flavouring sauce made by steeping fish in brine. Thai, Vietnamese and other varieties are just as effective.

Five-spice powder
Reddish spice powder mix of star anise, fennel, cinnamon, cloves and Sichuan pepper.

Fungus, black (cloud-ear)
Wrinkled 'ear'-shaped dark brown fungus. Bland tasting, crunchy texture.

Gabi leaves
Used in Burmese and Filipino cooking. Substitute: yam leaves.

Galangal, greater
Delicate flavoured yellow root with pink fibrous knobs, called Siamese ginger or galangal root.

Galangal, lesser
Native to China, known as aromatic ginger. The root is dried and should be pulverised before use. Lesser galangal root is pickled in Thailand to give *krachai*.

Garam masala
Powdered spice mixture used in Indian cooking. Store small quantities in an airtight bottle. A good mixture has:
  2 Tbsp coriander seeds
  1 Tbsp cumin
  1 tsp cardamoms
  1 tsp black pepper
  $\frac{1}{2}$ tsp cloves
  $\frac{1}{2}$ tsp nutmeg
Peel cardamoms to extract seeds. Roast on high heat for 4 minutes, stirring once. Grind or mill finely.

Jackfruit, seed
Large fruit with leathery skin and segmented yellow interior. Roasted seeds are cooked in curries. Substitute: cashewnuts.

Kaffir lime & leaves
Citrus fruit with bumpy dark green rind and concentrated aromatic oils. Leaves and zest are used in cooking. Substitute: grated lime rind, citrus leaves.

Kailan
Kale or Chinese broccoli is a leafy emerald green vegetable with firm stems.

Kalamansi
Small, soft lime, grown extensively in Southeast Asia and used especially in the Philippines.

Kangkong (MAL)
Water convolvulus or water spinach. Green and leafy with a hollow stem. The Thai variety has dark green leaves and red stalks; the Chinese one is thicker, larger and lighter green. Tender tops are eaten raw or cooked.

Katsuobushi
Bonito flakes used in Japanese stocks, also known as Maldive fish.

Kemangi
Variety of basil used in Malaysia.

Lemon grass
Common herb in Southeast Asia. Has long grass-like leaves. Stem and leaves are fibrous and end near the root in a bulbous base, the most fragrant part normally used in cooking. It has a lemony scent and imparts a delicious flavour to food cooked in chilli or curry. Reconstitute dried roots with water.

Lemon, sweet preserved
Lemons preserved in sugar are found in Chinese shops.

Lemon zest
Grated peel combined with oil from peel.

Lentils (See Dhal)

Limes
Small and round, with thin dark green skin. Aromatic in cooking. Do not confuse with kaffir lime.

Long Beans
Also known as snake beans or yard-long beans.

Maldive fish
Hard pieces of dried wood-like fish. See *Katsuobushi*.

Mint leaves
Several varieties are used. The most common in fish dishes is Vietnamese mint (Polygonum, *daun kesum*).

Mushroom, black, dried
Greyish black and fragrant when cooked. Best if thick and firm, pale cream on underside. Soak about 30 minutes to soften and remove stem before use.

Mushroom, button
Champignons, usually sold canned.

Mushroom, *Enoki*
These are tiny, whitish-yellow and have long stems and minute round caps. Mild, pleasant flavour and aroma and crisp texture.

Mushroom, straw
Sold fresh or canned. Very delicately flavoured, this mushroom is contained within a sheath.

Mustard seed, black
Two varieties. Black and yellow. Black mustard seeds are smaller and more pungent than yellow ones.

Mustard seeds
Ground, this gives a yellow paste, a spice in cooking and pickling.

***Nam pla* (THAI)**
Also *Nuoc mam* (VIET). (See Fish sauce)

Nam prik pao
Thai green curry paste.

Noodles, Laksa
White rice noodles. Can be substituted with spaghetti.

Noodles, Rice sticks (*Beehoon*)
Thin rice flour noodles. They expand when deep-fried to become light and crisp. Also known as rice vermicelli.

Noodles, *Udon*
Japanese noodles made with wheat flour.

Noodles, Wheat
Also known as Shanghai noodles. Can be made with egg (yellowish) or without (whitish) and in different thicknesses.

***Nori* (Laver sheets)**
Crisp seaweed sheets, sweet and seaweedy in flavour. They are rolled around *sushi* or vinegared rice. Toast lightly to render it pliant for rolling around *sushi*.

Nutmeg
Mostly used to flavour sweets and cakes but also used in garam *masala*.

Nuts, Gingko
Kernel of the maidenhair tree fruit. Buy canned in specialty food shops. Fresh nuts should be cracked with a knife or nutcracker and the hard outer case removed, then the nuts placed in hot water to remove the thin brownish inner skin.

Oil, Ghee
Clarified butter. Important in Indian cooking. It imparts a distinctive flavour.

Oil, Mustard
Pressed from black mustard seeds. Used in Bengali cooking.

Oil, Peanut
Widely used in Malaysia.

Oil, Sesame
Pressed from sesame seeds, this aromatic oil is used as a seasoning, a flavouring agent and an ingredient in sauces. Gingelly is the Indian version.

Onions
Most common are the large brown/purple (Bombay or Spanish) or yellow/white varieties.

Onions, Pickled
Small white onions pickled in vinegar on brine.

Onions, Red shallots
The smaller red onion most commonly used in Asia.

Onions, Spring (Scallions)
Of the onion family. Resembles a small leek. Has long deep green stalks and a bulbous white base.

Pastes, *Miso*
Fermented soy bean paste. Made by boiling soy beans, mashing them, adding rice, wheat and barley then fermenting the mixture. Used as a salad dressing, pickling medium or condiment.

Pastes, Prawn *(Haeko)*
Similar to *belacan* but milder. Available in jars from Chinese grocers. Use in small quantities. See also *Belacan*.

Pastes, Prawn *(Patis, Bagoong)*
This is a thick and greyish liquid paste. Similar to *belacan* and prawn *haeko*.

Pastes, *Taucheo*
Salted soy bean paste. Made from fermented soy beans. Used as a seasoning.

Pastes, Tomato purée
Sold in bottles and cans. Useful for thickening curries; used widely in North India.

Pawpaw (Papaya)
The ripe fruit is eaten fresh. The unripe fruit is used as a meat tenderiser and to impart its flavour.

Pepper, Bell (See Capsicum)

Pepper, Paprika
Canned or bottled as pimiento or dried and powdered for paprika. Bright red. Widely used in Asia for the colour it lends to curries.

Pepper, Sichuan (Fagara)
Also known as brown peppercorns. Of little resemblance to black peppercorns. Has a pungent, slightly anise flavour and aroma. Roast lightly before use. An ingredient of five-spice powder.

Plums, pickled Chinese
May be purchased bottled in specialty shops. These are small dark plums that impart a sweet-sour flavour to fish.

Rice flour
Finely ground flour from polished white rice. Gives a particular texture to certain pastries.

Rice, glutinous
A type of rice with flatter, more rounded grains. Sticky when cooked.

Rice paper
Very fine paper made from a paste of rice flour and water, similar to spring roll sheets. Used in Vietnamese food.

Rice, *Sushi*
Japanese method of serving raw fish, on rice flavoured with vinegar, salt, sugar and horseradish (or wrapped in seaweed) as opposed to *sashimi* which is raw fish by itself.

Rice, Thai sticky
Another type of rice. A good accompaniment to Thai curries.

Rice water
Water from washing rice, used to thicken soups.

Saffron
Threadlike bright orange crocus stigma. Saffron has a strongly sweet, pungent smell. Usually soaked in warm water or milk and the coloured liquid added to food for colour and flavour. Do not confuse with turmeric or artificial saffron which has the colour but not the fragrance.

Sauce, Fish (See Fish sauce)

Sauce, *Miso*
Thick soy paste.

Sauce, Oyster
Viscous, dark brown sauce produced from oysters and soy sauce. Used as a flavouring and/or colouring agent and as a condiment.

Sauce, Plum
Sweet thick sauce made from Chinese sour plums and seasoning. A condiment and flavouring agent.

Sauce, Sambal oelek
Combination of chillies and salt, used in cooking or as an accompaniment.

Sauce, Soy (dark and light)
Sauce extracted from soy beans fermented with salt. Contains caramel as a colouring.

Sauce, Sweet
Dark soy vinegar. Thick with strong sweet flavour.

Sauce, Sweet (Hoisin)
Seasoning sauce produced from red beans, soy beans, sugar and spices. Sweet, spicy and tangy in flavour. Sold bottled or canned.

Sauce, Teriyaki
Teriyaki refers to the technique of grilling foods while basting with soy sauce and mirin. Commercial Teriyaki sauce is a combination of the two.

Sauce, Worcestershire
Spicy, dark brown sauce of English origin. Known as Usutaa sauce in Japan.

Sausage, Chinese
Known in Cantonese as lup cheong. Made with pork, including fat, and is highly spiced which helps to preserve it.

Screwpine leaves
For flavouring or colouring food. Crushed or boiled to release flavour and colour.

Seaweed, Kelp (Konbu)
Dark greenish-brown. An important agent in flavouring dashi. The white mould that lightly dusts its surface contributes to the sweetish flavour. Do not wash away.

Seaweed, Laver, Nori
The most common and useful seaweed that the Japanese consume. Used as a sushi-wrap and garnish.

Seaweed, Wakame
Called 'lobe-leaf' in English. Sold dry, this seaweed has a dusty brown colour. When soaked, it turns green and is often used as a salad garnish.

Skin, Spring roll
Very fine skin made from a paste of rice flour.

Skin, Wonton
Dough mde from wheat flour.

Sour starfruit (Belimbing)
Sour species of starfruit. Small, with a sharp flavour.

Star anise
Eight-pointed spice. One of the main ingredients of five-spice powder.

Stock (See recipes on pages 308–309)

Sugar, Palm
Dark caramelised sugar obtained from the sap of the coconut palm. Sold in round, cylindrical cakes. Keeps indefinitely if dry. Easily reconstituted into syrup in if chopped up and boiled in a little water.

Sichuan vegetables
Made from salted turnips, radish or Tientsin cabbage. Preserved in brine with chilli.

Tamarind
Sour, pulpy fruit of a large tree, shaped like a bean. The leathery pod has dark seeds covered with the flesh.

Tempe (MAL)
Fermented soybean cake. Used in Indonesian and Malay cooking.

Turmeric
Yellow rhizome of ginger family, one of the main ingredients in curry cooking.

Wasabe
A pungent paste made from the powdered wasabe root. Substitute: horseradish.

Wine, Chinese glutinous
Chinese rice wine made from glutinous rice.

Wine, Mirin
Sweet cooking sake. Used in glazes and dipping sauces.

Wine, Sake
Used as an ingredient in marinades. Substitutes: brandy or dry sherry.

Wines, Shao hsing
Fine yellow rice wine from Shao hsing, China.

Star anise

Sugar cane

Greater galangal

Palm sugar

Lesser galangal

Red and green
chillies

Assam gelugor

Lemon grass

Bird's eye
chillies

Yam bean

Torch ginger
flower

Sugar-snap peas

Drumsticks

Spring onions
(Scallions)

Snow peas

Long beans

Yam stalk

Wing beans

Garlic chives

Sour Starfruit
(Belimbing)

Starfruit

Pawpaw (papaya)

Aubergine
(Eggplant/brinjal)

Pea aubergines
(Eggplants/brinjals)

Capsicum
(Bell pepper)

Lady's fingers

Cherry tomatoes

Limes

Daun kaduk

Coriander
(Cilantro/Chinese parsley)

Curry leaves

Kaffir lime leaves

Vietnamese mint
(Polygonum leaves/
Daun kesum)

Flowering chives

Mint leaves

Thai sweet basil

Turmeric leaf

319

Abalone
Haliotis asinina
Single shelled mollusc. Fleshy foot is eaten. Canned form available only in Southeast Asia. Ormer is another name for abalone.
Substitute: none

Anchovies
Stolephorus heterolobus
Small oily fish, up to 15 cm. Dried and salted in Malaysia, Singapore, Indonesia and the Philippines.
Substitutes: Sprats, Whitebait, Herring

Balmain Bugs
Ibacus spp.
Small shellfish, only 30% body weight edible. Known as shovel-nosed lobster.
Substitute: any shellfish.

Bass, Sea (Yellow Grouper)
Epinephelus awoara
Adults are brilliant yellow with yellow spots. Lean, tender and dry flesh.
Substitutes: Black Sea Bass, Brown Coral Cod, Yellow Marble Honeycomb, Grouper, Cod (Bacahlau), Atlantic Cod, Atlantic Pollock, Cusk

Bombay Duck (Bummalow)
Harpodon nehereus
Up to 40 cm. Pale, almost translucent colour. Soft flesh and hard needle-like teeth. Eaten fresh or dried.
Substitutes: Dried: any small dried fish can be substituted, though taste will be different. Fresh: Garfish (temperate or tropical water)

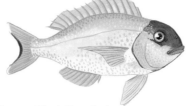

Bream, Black Sea, Red
Mylio berda
Dark grey, silver or olive colour. Moist white fine-textured flesh, sweet flavour.
Substitutes: Threadfin, Snapper, American Sea Bream, Porgy, Scup, Tilapia (freshwater)

Carp, Freshwater Common
Cyprinus carpio

Carp, Freshwater Chinese Grass
Ctenopharyngodon idellus
Moderately compressed body, colour and size vary. Tasty and high in protein.
Substitutes: *Freshwater:* Freshwater Perch, Walleye (Pike), Northern Pike, Yellow Perch, Murry Cod. *Seawater:* Mullet, Red Mullet, Snapper, American Sea Bream, Porgy, Scup, Jewfish, Cod (Bacahlau), Atlantic Cod, Atlantic Pollock, Cusk

Catfish
Arius thalassinus (sea)
Tachysurus thalassinus (sea)
Clarias batrachus (fresh)
Whiskers, delicate flesh, oily elongated body. Avoid touching poisonous glands on fins.
Substitutes: Mullet, Eel

Clam, Razor
Solen grandis
Fan-shaped ridges.
Substitutes: Cockles, other clams

Cobia (Blackfish)
Rachycentron canadum
Up to 1 m. Silver black stripes along flank.
Substitutes: Spanish mackerel, other types of mackerel

Cockles (Blood Clam and Arkshell)
Anadara granosa
Brownish to white shells, 7 cm.
Substitutes: All types of shellfish

Cod, Atlantic Polar
Gadoid spp. (Gadoid)
World's most valuable food fish. White, flaky and firm meat, lean. Eaten dried, salted or flaked in Southeast Asia.
Substitutes: Cod (Bacahlau), Murray, Ling, Giant Sea Perch, Walleye (Pike), Northern Pike, Yellow Perch, Rockfish, Coral Cod, Hake, Haddock, Atlantic Pollock, Cusk

Fish for Fish—How to Substitute

Cod, Blue Eyed
Hyperglyche antartica
Firm white flesh.
Substitutes: Other cods, including Cod (Bacahlau), Atlantic Cod, Atlantic Pollock, Cusk

Cod, Coral (Australian)
Cephalopholis miniatus
Firm white flesh
Substitutes: Other cods, including Cod (Bacahlau), Atlantic Cod, Atlantic Pollock, Cusk, Sea Perch, Rockfish, Bream, Walleye (Pike), Northern Pike, Yellow Perch

Crab, Mud
Scylla serrata
Red, brown, black and red pincers. Most important edible crab in Southeast Asia, more flesh than other crabs. Roe tasty.
Substitutes: Other crabs, lobster

Crayfish
see Lobster, Rock

Cuttlefish
Sepia pharaonis
25–30 cm. Interior shell distinguishes it from squid, also broader.
Substitute: Squid

Croaker, Spotted, Yellow
Johnius diacanthus
75 cm. Dark blotches on back, spots on upper body. Firm dark flesh, moist, mild-tasting. Also called Drum.
Substitute: Jewfish, Sea Trout, Californian Corbina

Dory, Silver (King)
Glaucosoma hebraicu
White with fine to medium texture, mirror-like scales. Fairly dry flesh.
Substitutes: Snapper, John Dory, Pearl Perch, Orange Ruffy, Bream, American Sea Bream, Porgy, Scup

Crab, Blue Swimmer
Portunus pelagicus
White and blue claws. Can be eaten without shell.
Substitutes: Other crabs, lobster

Crab, Hairy
Sesarma meinerti
Small blackish legs, hairy
Substitutes: Other crabs, lobster

Dory, John
Zeus faber
Fine white or green/grey colour. Succulent, fairly dry flesh. Smooth skin.
Substitutes: Perch, Walleye (Pike), Northern Pike, Yellow Perch, Bream, Ling, Snapper, American Sea Bream, Porgy, Scup

Flounder (Big Mouth)
Psettodes erumei
20–40 cm. Brown colour, both eyes on same side. Delicate, very tasty white flesh.
Substitute: Sole, Petral Sole, Pacific Halibut

Gemfish (Silver Kingfish)
Rexea solandri
60–90 cm. Creamy pink, moist flesh, firm with large flakes. High fat content. Usually sold in fillets or cutlets. Keeps shape well.
Substitutes: Mullet, Mackerel, Jewfish, Grouper, Barracuda, Red Emperor

Herring, Wolf
Chirocentrus dorab
30–50 cm. Blue-green back, silvery sides.
Bony, tasty flesh.
Substitutes: Pilchard, Sardine, Ikan Parang.
Also known as Snake Ling

Hilsa, Ilisha, Helsa
(Shad, River Shad, Five-spot Herring)
Clupea kanagurta
35 cm. Good flavour, firm fish with flakes
and small bones, moderately oily. Roe is
popular. Both seawater and freshwater.
Substitutes: Anchovies, Herring, Sardine,
Pilchard, Sprat

Jellyfish, Brown, Silver
Rhopilema esculenta
15 cm. Sold dried. Tender, crunchy and
elastic when softened in water.
Substitute: Sea Cucumber

Jewfish, Brown, Silver
Sciaena dussumieri
Firm dry pink flesh, mild flavour.
Substitutes: Mulloway, Croaker, Sea Trout,
Californian Corbina

Kingfish (Wahoo)
Acanthocybium solandri
2 m max. Dark slate blue back, light silver-
grey belly. Pink to dark flesh lightens when
cooked. Soft dry texture and mild flavour.
Substitutes: Mackerel, Swordfish, Trevally,
Tuna

Krill
Palae mon sp., Acetes sp., Euphausia spp.
Tiny pale small prawns, no larger than 5 cm.
Substitutes: Small prawns, known in Malaysia
as *Gerago*

Ling
Gerypterus blacodes
Deepwater Australian fish. Dense texture,
sweet white flesh.
Substitutes: Cod, including Cod (Bacahlau),
Atlantic Cod, Atlantic Pollock, Cusk, Giant
Sea Perch, Rockfish

**Lobster, Freshwater (Spiny Clawed or
Giant Freshwater Prawn)**
Macrobracium rosenbergii
30 cm long. Second walking leg is long, ends
with spiny pincer. Blue varieties more tender
than grey.
Substitutes: Prawns, Crayfish, Tiger Prawns

Lobster, Rock or Spiny
Panulirus sp.
30 cm long, attractive and colourful when
alive. Sweet tender white flesh.
Substitutes: any other shellfish, crayfish

Lobster, Slipper
Thenus orientalis
Yellow underside.
Substitute: Crab

Mackerel, short-bodied
Rastrelliger brachysoma
20 cm long. Oily fish with high fat content.
Dark, medium flaked fish. Salted and dried
in Thailand, Cambodia and Philippines.
Substitutes: Chubb, Sardines, Kembong,
Herring

Mackerel, Spanish, Spotted
Scomberomorus ghuttatus
50 cm long. Dark back, silvery sides, 3 rows
circular spots. Flesh firm, dry and flavoursome, no obtrusive bones.
Substitutes: Other Mackerels, Mullet,
Herring, Kingfish, Scad

Mackerel, Spanish, Striped
Scomberomorus commersoni
NOTE: There are many other species of
mackerel available in temperate and tropical
waters. 80 cm–1 m long, dark blue or green-
grey back, vertical grey stripes on sides. Flesh
similar to Spanish, Spotted
Substitutes: Other Mackerels, Mullet, Herring

Milk fish
Chanos chanos
Greenish-grey back, silvery sides. Fine-
textured, sweet, moist, tender flesh. Smaller
fish prized in the Philippines.
Substitutes: Snapper, Herring, Sardine,
Mullet, also known as Bangus, American Sea
Bream, Porgy, Scup

Mullet, Grey, Green Back Grey
Liza subvirides
25 cm long. Rose or greenish back, dark stripes along scales. Oily firm pink flesh with distinct flavour, few bones.
Substitutes: King Fish, Herring, Mackerel, Pilchard, Tuna, Mullet (red), Goatfish, Blackspot

Mussels
Perna viridis, Perna canaliculus
Up to 20 cm, usually 8–10 cm. Green shell turns yellow if exposed to sun. Eat cooked or raw.
Substitute: Cockles

Oyster
Crassostrea gigas, Crassostrea cucullata
The Asian variety is smaller than temperate oysters, up to 10 cm in size with black exterior.
Substitutes: Temperate or tropical oysters, other shellfish

Perch, Pearl
Glaucoosoma hebraicum
Up to 1 m. Tender delicate tasting white flesh with medium flake.
Substitutes: Threadfin, Grouper, Whiting, White Pomfret, Monkfish, Orange Roughy

Perch, Sea, Silver, Giant (Barramundi)
Lates calcarifer
1 m long. Golden brown above, silvery below with brown fins and small eyes. Served dried. Fish mau (air bladder) prized.
Substitutes: Threadfin, Grouper, Whiting, White Pomfret, Golden Perch, Orange Roughy

Pike, Sea
Sphyraena sp., Sphyreana jello
50 cm–1 m. Dark brown above, white below with vertical bars. Soft textured white and dark flesh.
Substitutes: Sea Perch, Rockfish, Pearl Perch, Whiting, all species of Dory, Bream, Mullet and Threadfin, Freshwater Cod, Burbot, Skipjack, Snook, Cod (Bacahlau), Atlantic Cod, Atlantic Pollock, Cusk

Pilchards
see Herring, Sardine

Pomfret, Black
Formio niger
10–20 cm. Brownish grey with blue, darker fins.
Substitutes: Any perch, White Pomfret, John or Silver Dory, any firm fish

Pomfret, White, Silver
Pampus argenteus
20–30 cm. Silver grey to white with tiny black dots. No pelvic fins. Soft dry flesh easily separated from bone.
Substitutes: Whiting, Threadfin, Grouper, Pearl Perch, Butterfish, Brill

Prawn (Shrimp)
Penaeus sp.
Banana White 25 cm: 7–8 adults to 1 kg
Giant Tiger up to 30 cm: 5–6 adults to 1 kg.
Beak has teeth above and below.
Green Tiger 10 cm. Indian White 20 cm: 8–9 adults to 1 kg. Moist flesh. King: 10 adults to 1 kg.
Substitutes: Any other prawn or spiny lobster. Prawns can be used in most recipes regardless of size or type—Dublin Bay Prawns, Scampi, Langoustines.

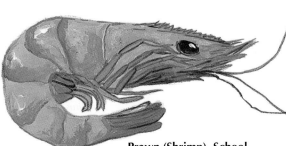

Prawn (Shrimp), School
Metapenaeus sp.
Small, 15–20 adults to 1 kg. Often used dried in Asian recipes.
Substitute: Any other prawn, scampi

Red Emperor (Government Bream)
Lutjanus sebae
A big fish usually found 5–10 kg. Dark pink deepening to red with three darker lines across the body. Prized for its tender, sweet flesh and red colour. Used in Asian dinner parties. Normally steamed or baked.
Substitute: Snapper

Sardine
Sardinella aurita
About 15 cm. Makes excellent eating, though small.
Substitutes: Pilchards, Shad, 5-Spot Herring, Hilsa

Scallop
Amusium pleuronectes
Up to 15 cm. Light brown fan-shaped shell. White round meat with red coral at end.
Substitutes: Oysters, Mussels

Sea Cucumber (White Sea Slug)
Holothuria sp.
Up to 40 cm. White with plain white underside, cucumber-shaped. Available in cleaned and dried form.
Substitutes: Inferior Black Sea Cucumber

Sea Wrasse
Choerodon schoonleini
Up to 80 cm. Tender flesh.
Substitutes: Pomfret, Butterfly Fish, Goat Fish or any reef fish

Seer
see Kingfish

Shad
see Hilsa

Shark
Scoliodon sp.
50–60 cm. Grey-brown to buff with yellow and white tint. Fine grey brown flesh.
Substitutes: Sting-ray, Eagle-ray, Baby Shark

Shrimp
see Prawn, Krill

Snake Ling
see Wolf Herring

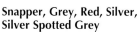

Snapper, Grey, Red, Silver, Silver Spotted Grey
Lutjanus sp.
40–80 cm. Grey or pink. Moist white flesh with medium flake and distinctive flavour.
Large species can be dry.
Substitutes: Barramundi, Silver Dory, Red Emperor, American Sea Bream, Porgy, Scup

Sole, Oriental
Euryglossa orientalis
Up to 25 cm. Grey or brown spotted back. Fine white soft moist flesh with delicate flavour.
Substitutes: Black or White Pomfret, small Threadfin, Ikan lidah, Flounder, NZ Sole Turbot, Megrim, Whiff, Sailfluke, Plaice, Petral Sole, Pacific Halibut

Sprats
see Anchovies

Squid
Loligo edulis
Up to 20 cm. Soft internal quill, good delicate flesh ideal for stuffing. Tentacles edible.
Substitute: Cuttlefish

Sting-Ray (Eagle-Ray)
Dasyatis uarnak or Aetobatis narinari
Triangular shape up to 30 cm. Only wings are sold. Moist and delicate flavour, large flakes.
Substitutes: Shark, Leather Jacket, Tailorfish, Baby Shark, Chubb, Mackerel, Skate

Fish for Fish—How to Substitute

Tailorfish
Eleutheronema tetradactylon, Polinemus indicus
Silver, 20–40 cm length.
Substitutes: Any Reef Cod, Rock Cods, Bream, Cod *(Bacahlau)*, Atlantic Cod, Atlantic Pollock, Cusk

Threadfin, tassel fish
Eleutheronema tetradactylon, tridactylon
Silvery grey above, creamy below, fish highly prized.
Substitutes: White Pomfret, Ling, Silver Dory, *(Kurau)*

Trevally, Hardtail, Yellow Stripe
Family Carangidae
40 cm. Iridescent with blue back.
Substitutes: Cod, Bream, American Sea Bream, Porgy, Scup, Snapper, Warhou, Silver Warhou, Swordfish, Cod *(Bacahlau)*, Atlantic Cod, Atlantic Pollock, Cusk

Trout, Brown, Coral, Ocean, Rainbow
Salmon sp.
Medium flake and moisture, delicate and delicious pink flesh. Brown Trout is large. Rainbow Trout is up to 1 kg.
Substitutes: Bream, American Sea Bream, Porgy, Scup, Dhu fish, Sea Perch, Rockfish, Snapper

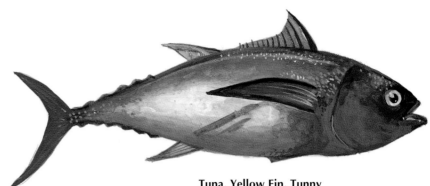

Tuna, Blue Fin
Thunnus maccoyii (Southern)
Kishonella tonggol (Northern)
Pinkish red firm texture which suits sashimi.
Substitutes: Any other Tuna, Mackerel, Mullet, Sardine, Kingfish

Tuna, Skipjack
Katsuwonus pelamis
Dark flesh, high fat content. Dried fish popular in Sri Lanka. Also known as Bonito or Maldive fish.
Substitute: any other Tuna.

Tuna, Yellow Fin, Tunny
Thunnus albacares
Tropical water fish.
Substitutes: Any other Tuna, Kingfish, Mackerel

Whitebait
see Anchovies

Whiting, Indian, Sand, Silver, Trumpeter
Sillago sihama
Up to 30 cm. Light grey or olive above, silverbelow. Sweet delicate flavour, fine soft white flesh, moist and bony.
Substitutes: Bream, Coral Trout, Flounder, Leather Jacket

Yabbies
Cherax destructor
Small crustacea, larger than prawns. Good eating, though little flesh.
Substitutes: other crustacea, Balmain Bugs, Crayfish

Weights & Measures

Quantities for this book are given in Metric and American (spoon and cup) measures. Standard spoon and cup measurements used are: 1 teaspoon = 5 ml, 1 tablespoon = 15 ml, 1 cup = 250 ml. All measures are level unless otherwise stated.

LIQUID AND VOLUME MEASURES

Metric	Imperial	American
5 ml	$^1/_6$ fl oz	1 teaspoon
10 ml	$^1/_3$ fl oz	1 dessertspoon
15 ml	$^1/_2$ fl oz	1 tablespoon
60 ml	2 fl oz	$^1/_4$ cup (4 tablespoons)
85 ml	$2^1/_2$ fl oz	$^1/_3$ cup
90 ml	3 fl oz	$^3/_8$ cup (6 tablespoons)
125 ml	4 fl oz	$^1/_2$ cup
180 ml	6 fl oz	$^3/_4$ cup
250 ml	8 fl oz	1 cup
300 ml	10 fl oz ($^1/_2$ pint)	$1^1/_4$ cups
375 ml	12 fl oz	$1^1/_2$ cups
435 ml	14 fl oz	$1^3/_4$ cups
500 ml	16 fl oz	2 cups
625 ml	20 fl oz (1 pint)	$2^1/_2$ cups
750 ml	24 fl oz ($1^1/_5$ pints)	3 cups
1 litre	32 fl oz ($1^3/_5$ pints)	4 cups
1.25 litres	40 fl oz (2 pints)	5 cups
1.5 litres	48 fl oz ($2^2/_5$ pints)	6 cups
2.5 litres	80 fl oz (4 pints)	10 cups

DRY MEASURES

Metric	Imperial
30 grams	1 ounce
45 grams	$1^1/_2$ ounces
55 grams	2 ounces
70 grams	$2^1/_2$ ounces
85 grams	3 ounces
100 grams	$3^1/_2$ ounces
110 grams	4 ounces
125 grams	$4^1/_2$ ounces
140 grams	5 ounces
280 grams	10 ounces
450 grams	16 ounces (1 pound)
500 grams	1 pound, $1^1/_2$ ounces
700 grams	$1^1/_2$ pounds
800 grams	$1^3/_4$ pounds
1 kilogram	2 pounds, 3 ounces
1.5 kilograms	3 pounds, $4^1/_2$ ounces
2 kilograms	4 pounds, 6 ounces

LENGTH

Metric	Imperial
0.5 cm	$^1/_4$ inch
1 cm	$^1/_2$ inch
1.5 cm	$^3/_4$ inch
2.5 cm	1 inch

OVEN TEMPERATURE

	°C	°F	Gas Regulo
Very slow	120	250	1
Slow	150	300	2
Moderately slow	160	325	3
Moderate	180	350	4
Moderately hot	190/200	370/400	5/6
Hot	210/220	410/440	6/7
Very hot	230	450	8
Super hot	250/290	475/550	9/10

ABBREVIATION

tsp	teaspoon
Tbsp	tablespoon
g	gram
kg	kilogram
ml	millilitre

Acknowledgements

There is a great deal of work that needs to be done before any production of this size and nature can be launched. It was possible only with the help, advice and encouragement of many people.

My first thank you goes to my late husband, Selva, whose initial research work on freshwater fish in Batu Berendam, Melaka, and love for fish and seafood fired my initial enthusiasm. Thanks also to all his colleagues and our friends all over Asia and Australia, without whose help I would never have got anywhere.

I would like to thank V. Selvarajah, formerly of the Malaysian Fisheries Division, who not only advised and gave me access to copious material and FAO charts but who also pointed me in the right direction with names and fisheries contacts in Asia; and Eric Alfred, formerly of the Maritime Museum, Sentosa Island, Singapore whose advice, help and sense of humour kept the subject totally in perspective.

The Fish Marketing Authority, New South Wales, particularly Annette Forrest and Bettina Jenkins, for their advice, loan of charts and materials, and to their consultant nutritionist, Rosemary Stanton, whose information on Omega 3 has been one of my main motives for progressing with this book.

My thanks also go to the following:

In Thailand: Bob Halliday of the Bangkok Post, and Chalie Amatyakul, ex-chef of the Oriental Hotel Cooking School. **In Hong Kong:** Steven Wong of the Kong Kong Tourist Promotion Board; Teresa Tang of the Home Management Centre; and the Kuok family, especially Siew Choong and Chye Kuok for opening doors for me. **In the Philippines:** Soraya Kassim of the Australian Embassy; Nora Daza; Millie Reyes; and Dr J. Camoens of the Asian Development Bank. **In India:** Deepak Pawar of ICRISAT, Hyderabad; Vimala Raman; the staff of the Catering College in Taratolla, Calcutta; my generous hosts, the Ramanathans, in Madras; Dr and Mrs Vas; Mr Reddy and the chefs of the Savira Hotel; and Sally George. **In Malaysia and Singapore:** Vimala and Mahalingam; Michelle and Giram Sandhu; and Annie Lee for their concern, help and support. Annie, Yvette Lee and Radha Jeyaram whose recipes are featured here. **In Australia:** Geoff Croft for his initial sketches, my computer whiz Anand Selvarajah; Dr Rajah Selvarajah for the glossary work; and my friends whose friendship I sorely tested. Thanks go especially to Radha Jeyaram, Eri Totsuka, Shirley Grafton-Williams, Mohd Kassim; and finally Anushiya Selva Rajah for testing the recipes and for patiently picking up the pieces, both mental and physical.

seafood
sensation